Ian McEwan

MANCHESTER
1824

Manchester University Press

Contemporary British Novelists

Series editors:
Daniel Lea

already published

J. G. Ballard   Andrzej Gąsiorek
Pat Barker   John Brannigan
Jim Crace   Philip Tew
Graham Swift   Daniel Lea
Irvine Welsh   Aaron Kelly
Jeanette Winterson   Susana Onega

Ian McEwan

Dominic Head

Manchester University Press

Manchester and New York

distributed exclusively in the USA by Palgrave

Published by Manchester University Press
Oxford Road, Manchester M13 9NR, UK
and Room 400, 175 Fifth Avenue, New York, NY 10010, USA
www.manchesteruniversitypress.co.uk

Distributed exclusively in the USA by
Palgrave, 175 Fifth Avenue, New York,
NY 10010, USA

Distributed exclusively in Canada by
UBC Press, University of British Columbia, 2029 West Mall,
Vancouver, BC, Canada V6T 1Z2

British Library Cataloguing-in-Publication Data
A catalogue record for this book is available from the British Library

Library of Congress Cataloging-in-Publication Data applied for

ISBN   978 0 7190 6656 6 *hardback*
ISBN   978 0 7190 6657 3 *paperback*

First published 2007

16 15 14 13 12 11 10 09 08 07   10 9 8 7 6 5 4 3 2 1

Typeset
by Florence Production Ltd, Stoodleigh, Devon
Printed in Great Britain
by CPI, Bath

To Mum
Loving, kind, generous and inspiring
Peggy Jane Head
27 May 1933–7 July 2006

Contents

Series editor's foreword   *page* ix
List of abbreviations   xi
1   Introduction   1
2   Shock-lit: the short stories and *The Cement Garden*   30
3   Dreams of captivity: *The Comfort of Strangers*   52
4   Towards the 'implicate order': *The Child in Time*   70
5   Unravelling the binaries: *The Innocent* and *Black Dogs*   91
6   'A mess of our own unmaking': *Enduring Love*   120
7   *Amsterdam*: McEwan's 'spoiler'   144
8   'The wild and inward journey of writing': *Atonement*   156
9   'Accidents of character and circumstance': *Saturday*   177
10 Conclusion: McEwan and the 'third culture'   200
    Select bibliography   209
    Index   217

Series editor's foreword

Contemporary British Novelists offers readers critical introductions to some of the most exciting and challenging writing of recent years. Through detailed analysis of their work, volumes in the series present lucid interpretations of authors who have sought to capture the sensibilities of the late twentieth and twenty-first centuries. Informed, but not dominated, by critical theory, *Contemporary British Novelists* explores the influence of diverse traditions, histories and cultures on prose fiction, and situates key figures within their relevant social, political, artistic and historical contexts.

The title of the series is deliberately provocative, recognising each of the three defining elements as contentious identifications of a cultural framework that must be continuously remade and renamed. The contemporary British novel defies easy categorisation and rather than offering bland guarantees as to the current trajectories of literary production, volumes in this series contest the very terms that are employed to unify them. How does one conceptualise, isolate and define the mutability of the contemporary? What legitimacy can be claimed for a singular Britishness given the multivocality implicit in the redefinition of national identities? Can the novel form adequately represent reading communities increasingly dependent upon digitalised communication? These polemical considerations are the theoretical backbone of the series, and attest to the difficulties of formulating a coherent analytical approach to the discontinuities and incoherencies of the present.

Contemporary British Novelists does not seek to appropriate its subjects for prescriptive formal or generic categories; rather it aims to explore the ways in which aesthetics are reproduced, refined and repositioned through recent prose writing. If the overarching architecture of the contemporary always eludes description, then the grandest ambition of this series must be to plot at least some of its dimensions.

Daniel Lea

List of abbreviations

The following abbreviations are used for references to these editions of McEwan's work. (Date of first publication given where a later edition is used.)

Am   *Amsterdam* (London: Jonathan Cape, 1998)

At   *Atonement* (London: Jonathan Cape, 2001)

BD   *Black Dogs* (1992; London: Picador, 1993)

CG   *The Cement Garden* (1978; London: Picador, 1980)

CS   *The Comfort of Strangers* (1981; London: Vintage, 1997)

CT   *The Child in Time* (London: Jonathan Cape, 1987)

D   *The Daydreamer* (1994; London: Red Fox, 1995)

EL   *Enduring Love* (London: Jonathan Cape, 1997)

FL   *First Love, Last Rites* (1975; London: Picador, 1976)

I   *The Innocent* (1990; London: Picador, 1990)

IBS   *In Between the Sheets* (1978; London: Vintage, 1997)

IG   *The Imitation Game* (1981; London: Picador, 1982)

MA   *A Move Abroad: 'Or Shall We Die?' and 'The Ploughman's Lunch'* (London: Picador, 1989)

RB   *Rose Blanche* (1985; London: Red Fox, 2004)

S   *Saturday* (London: Jonathan Cape, 2005)

1

Introduction

Writing about contemporary literature is a hazardous business for a variety of reasons, most of which stem from the speculative nature of this branch of criticism. Without the benefit of hindsight, the critic is drawn to make judgements about the worth of a writer, and to posit ideas about his/her place in literary history. Both elements of this critical process are vulnerable: judgements are often made in the absence of consensus; and the related business of tentatively articulating an emergent literary history might construct, for posterity, an anachronistic understanding of literature's importance.

In the case of Ian McEwan, his current standing, as one of the most significant British writers since the 1970s, seems secure. More problematic is the related claim I would wish to advance: that he is possibly the most significant of a number of writers (including Martin Amis, Kazuo Ishiguro and Graham Swift) who have resuscitated the link between morality and the novel for a whole generation, in ways that befit the historical pressures of their time. Implicit in such a claim is the assumption that the novel is a significant form of cultural expression – by which I mean a special vehicle for an oblique form of social and cultural work – that is worthy of detailed study and public appreciation. This is the assumption that may ultimately prove vulnerable: social change and technological developments make the survival of the novel as the primary form of literary expression impossible to predict with certainty. Given the persisting human hunger for narrative, however, and that the novel preserves certain narrative principles that film (the chief rival in the narrative stakes) is not so dependent upon, my hunch is that McEwan will continue to be studied in fifty years, as a latter day Joseph Conrad, perhaps.[1]

McEwan is one of those rare writers whose works have received both popular and critical acclaim. His novels grace the bestseller lists, and he is well regarded by critics, both as a stylist and as a serious thinker about the function and capacities of narrative fiction. It is that bridge between notionally different readerships, the ability to make the serious popular, and the popular serious, that indicates McEwan's importance, as a writer who has helped reinvigorate thinking about the novel within and without academia.

His novels treat issues that are central to our times: politics, and the promotion of vested interests; male violence and the problem of gender relations; science and the limits of rationality; nature and ecology; love and innocence; and the quest for an ethical world-view. Yet he is also an economical author, who 'writes only a few paragraphs each day', which he then 'works on intensively', paring them down, and allowing 'the spaces between sentences, the moments where the reader pauses, to do some of his work.'[2] McEwan's readers are called upon to attend, not just to the grand themes, but also to the precision of his spare writing.

From the perspective of an emerging twentieth-century literary history, McEwan occupies a central role in a new wave of British novelists whose mature writing began to emerge in the Thatcher era. McEwan stands alongside those writers mentioned above – Martin Amis, Graham Swift and Kazuo Ishiguro – a quartet of key writers who fashioned an ethical vision for the 'post-consensus' period. Grappling with the moral problems that present themselves in Britain in the 1980s and 1990s, a period characterized broadly by the growth of self-interest, the expansion of corporate power and the collapse of the Welfare State, these writers sought to forge (or resuscitate) the moral impulse in a period that was not conducive to such a venture.

If we are prepared to date the demise of consensus politics earlier than 1979, then the much-discussed literature of shock (especially evident in early works by Amis and McEwan) can be seen as one strategy for awakening the collective conscience. So, although McEwan's later works are more overtly political, more humane, and more ostentatiously literary than the early work, it is important to stress the continuity as well as the sense of evolution through the oeuvre. His quest to establish a viable ethical stance for the contemporary novelist is visible even in the disturbing early fiction.

Ian Russell McEwan was born on 21 June 1948 in Aldershot, the son of Scotsman David McEwan, a soldier in the British army (later an officer), and Rose Lilian McEwan, whose previous husband had died in the war, and by whom she had already had two children. In the early years of his childhood, McEwan lived at British military bases, at home, and abroad in Singapore and Libya. To this sense of geographical rootlessness was added the feeling of being in a form of class limbo when his father was 'commissioned from the ranks'.³ Because both parents were working class, the family experienced 'a curious kind of dislocated existence.'⁴ This is an important factor in McEwan's development as a writer, and one that enabled him to fly by the nets of traditional class affiliation in a way that marries with the broader dissolution of the traditional class model in British society.

Another important stage in the writer's emerging political consciousness stemmed from his experience as (in his words), an 'army brat':⁵ the Suez crisis of 1956, which emphatically demonstrated the waning of Britain as a world power, occurred when McEwan was eight years old and living in Libya. 'Anti-British feeling was naturally strong among the Libyans', he recalls, 'and Army families were herded into armed camps for protection.' Living in a tent with other children, 'not so very far from a machine-gun nest', and noticing the 'service revolver' strapped to his father's waist, McEwan claims to have 'understood for the first time that political events were real and affected people's lives' (*MA*, p. 27). Here, in McEwan's introduction to the screenplay for *The Ploughman's Lunch* (1983), in which parallels are drawn between Suez and the Falklands campaign, the writer retrospectively locates the birth of his political consciousness with the death of Britain as a colonial power (even if later adventures in British foreign policy did not acknowledge the fact).⁶

At the age of eleven, he was sent to a state boarding school in Suffolk, Woolverstone Hall, which he recalls as 'a rather successful experiment by a left-wing local authority in old-fashioned embourgeoisement.' Despite having 'the trappings of a public school', the 'ethos was rather stylishly undermined by the intake of mostly grammar-school level working-class lads from central London.'⁷ This unconventional institution, with its contradictory class and social signals, set the tone for McEwan's educational career, and his attendance at two new universities: the University of Sussex, where he read English and French as an undergraduate (1967–70), and the University of East Anglia, where he was the first student to study creative writing (with modern fiction), in 1970–71. Like Woolverstone Hall, the new universities of the 1960s and 1970s, which facilitated the expansion of

higher education, epitomized a society in flux. The University of
Sussex, which was associated with radical left-wing politics, was a
particular focus for new social and political thought. During his MA
year, at the University of East Anglia, McEwan was taught by both
Angus Wilson and Malcolm Bradbury.[8] This was not a course in
creative writing exclusively – it offered the facility 'to submit a little
bit of written fiction instead of the thesis'.[9] However, the experience
of being the first student *nationally* to take an emerging subject is a
key marker of another cultural change in which McEwan is a central
participant.

In 1972 McEwan experienced the counter-culture first hand,
following the hippy trail to Afghanistan. With hindsight, this might
seem another kind of convention. Certainly, his recollection of the
experience – 'boredom and smoking hash in huge quantities without
any real point' – would seem to suggest this.[10] Yet it is another instance
of the writer's direct experience of new cultural energies.

At the beginning of 1974 he moved from his flat in Norwich to
take an attic room in Stockwell, 'belonging to a one-eyed antiquarian
bookseller called Cyclops'. Cape was due to bring out his first collection
of stories, but not for eighteen months; and at this time, while working
on the second collection, he made contact with Ian Hamilton's *New
Review*, an important literary journal, funded by the Arts Council. In
'The Pillars of Hercules', the pub that 'was the *New Review*'s outer
office and unofficial club room', he reports meeting ' "my generation"
of writers – male, born in the late Forties', including Martin Amis,
Julian Barnes and Craig Raine. Most of the writers had yet to publish
their first books, but this was clearly a new literary establishment in the
making; 'a clique', perhaps, but also 'remarkably open', in the spirit of
a new meritocracy. Writers were drawn to the *New Review* and its
'fierce literary standards', recalls McEwan, 'because they respected Ian
[Hamilton]'s ideas of quality'.[11]

McEwan has been married twice; first in 1982, to Penny Allen, with
whom he had two sons. They were divorced in 1995, and the first
marriage ended in acrimony, with a dispute over custody of the
children. Allen, 'a trained spiritual counsellor and healer', bought a
farm in Brittany, with the intention of establishing a new family home.
At the end of a summer vacation, she initially refused to return the
boys (then aged thirteen and fifteen) to England despite a court ruling
in McEwan's favour.[12] Eventually, after the intervention of the French
legal system, McEwan was reunited with the youngest son, who had

remained in Allen's care, as she was apparently on the run from the police.[13] McEwan's second marriage, in 1997, was to literary journalist Annalena McAfee. Interviewed in 1998, and while avoiding any direct comment on his personal life, he remarked that 'no one . . . has an ordinary family life', given the 'incredible cross-alliances and third wives, second husbands, children by previous marriages, lovers who live in – mayhem, at street level.'[14] If the *extraordinary* domestic situation is becoming more commonplace – the new *ordinary* – then McEwan's domestic life corresponds with another important new social trend, which has gathered pace during his lifetime.

In a memoir of his mother, McEwan recalls that he read Germaine Greer's *The Female Eunuch* (1970), the flagship book of second-wave feminism, in 1971, and found it 'a revelation' because it 'spoke directly' to his family's life, and the problem of his father's dominance: 'my female characters became the repository of all the goodness that men fell short of. In other words, pen in hand, I was going to set my mother free.'[15] In a sense, this is a surprising claim. Feminism is engaged, in important preliminary ways, in both the screenplay for *The Imitation Game* (transmitted as a BBC 'Play for Today' in 1980) and *The Comfort of Strangers* (1981); but it is only in his work of the mid-1980s – in the words for the oratorio *Or Shall We Die?* (first performed in 1983) and in *The Child in Time* (1987) – that McEwan produces a sustained creative response to the implications of feminism. Nevertheless, the early encounter with feminism is another important formative influence, with an immediate experiential resonance.

The author's personal experiences, in short, have been affected by a variety of key social and political changes, including: fading colonialism; the dissolution of the British class structure; educational reform; the transformation of family life; and the second wave of feminism. It is a life that has been directly touched by those significant social trends that the fiction clearly responds to. That response is important; but it does not reveal dramatic technical innovations, where new fictional forms are moulded in direct response to new social energies. Like most significant literary developments, the work of those key British novelists who came to prominence in the Thatcher years is characterized by a combination of innovation and continuity. In McEwan's work, for example, there is evident continuity with an anxiety about the function of the novel that has been brewing for a significant period of time, through modernity and into postmodernity.

This is the wider intellectual context into which McEwan's particular preoccupations must be inserted.

Commenting on McEwan's first two books (both collections of short stories), Bradbury remarks that 'not since Angus Wilson had a major career started with two volumes of stories rather than a novel', and finds it 'significant' that Wilson had been his teacher.[16] One must allow for a degree of self-deprecation in Bradbury's comments: he also tutored McEwan at East Anglia. McEwan has, however, acknowledged the influence of Wilson on at least one of his stories.[17] The significance of the Wilson-Bradbury connection, in a broader literary-historical sense, is that McEwan comes out of a literary stable (so to speak), associated with the liberal identity in crisis. The 'disturbing and disruptive themes' of McEwan's early work seem to take him in an entirely new direction; but this work comprises an initial response to a time when 'the self was unable to define itself as a part of society' and 'moral coherence was gone.' Shock tactics can then be seen to embody the attempt 'to open the novel to a psychological realm in which the sense of crisis was felt.'[18]

McEwan's first book, the collection of stories *First Love, Last Rites* (1975) epitomizes the kind of reception he has always enjoyed: the book received critical praise – it won the Somerset Maugham Award (1976) – and also caused a stir, bringing the writer a reputation for shocking or macabre writing that was difficult to shake off. In 1983, the year in which he was named by *Granta* magazine as one of the 20 Best Young British Novelists, he began to produce more politically conscious work, and he was awarded *The Evening Standard* award for best screenplay for one such work, *The Ploughman's Lunch*. He has also won the 1987 Whitbread Novel Award for *The Child in Time*, and the Booker Prize in 1998, for *Amsterdam*. He has been short-listed for the Booker on three other occasions: for *The Comfort of Strangers* (1981), for *Black Dogs* (1992) and *Atonement* (2001), which won the W. H. Smith Literary Award. International prizes include: the 1993 French Prix Fémina Étranger; the Shakespeare Prize (Germany) in 1999; and the 2003 National Book Critics' Circle Fiction Award (USA) for *Atonement*. He was awarded the CBE in 2000. Although McEwan is now chiefly known as a novelist, it is worth remarking upon the versatility of his output: in addition to his film screenplays and short stories, he has also written scripts for TV, children's fiction, and the words for an oratorio by Michael Berkeley.

To advance the case for McEwan's prominence – pre-eminence, even – in the canon of contemporary British novelists, we need to consider more closely his serious anxieties about the function of the novel and the role of the novelist. One of the underlying premises of this book is that McEwan seeks to reconnect narrative fiction with moral sense, and that he therefore *develops* the sense of liberal identity crisis that one associates with Angus Wilson, or with the Malcolm Bradbury of *Stepping Westward* (1965) and *The History Man* (1975). In Bradbury's account, *The Child in Time*, 'a book of much greater sensitivities', marks a turning point in that 'what had essentially been private concerns, personal fantasies and psychic disorders become public and political ones.' Bradbury sees McEwan consolidating this shift of sensibilities, in works like *Enduring Love* (1997) and *Amsterdam*, to become 'the latter-day humanist, concerned with the need for the human spirit to confront its own dangerous impulses', the 'danger' comprising a threat to the social order as well as to the individual.[19]

This, however, may be to co-opt McEwan rather too easily into the literary tradition suggested by the Wilson-Bradbury East Anglia connection. Certainly, the development of the writer is usually thought to reveal significant differences between the first books and the more mature productions. Kiernan Ryan begins his excellent study of McEwan (1994) by responding to the 'received wisdom' which traces the trajectory of his career from an obsession with 'the perverse, the grotesque, the macabre' in his published work of the 1970s, through a 'marked evolution' consequent upon the writer's 'increasing involvement with feminism and the peace movement', which transforms his fiction of the 1980s. Ryan wryly observes the 'moral fable' that underpins this narrative, in which McEwan is cast as 'a kind of Prodigal Son', who matures into 'a responsible adult novelist', having burst onto the literary scene as the author of a series of 'nasty adolescent fantasies'. While crediting it with a degree of plausibility, Ryan resists the 'contrived and reassuring' air implicit in 'the exemplary tale of moral maturation', which obscures the ways in which 'nightmare and despair' return to undercut McEwan's evolving engagement with history and society. The simple narrative of linear development will not do to account for the recurring power in the novels 'to unseat our moral certainties'. It is this 'art of unease', in Ryan's phrase, that may be the key to McEwan's work.[20]

David Malcolm's study of 2002 suggests a further qualification to the moral fable account of McEwan's career. He does discern a trajectory of development in which the lack of moral judgement of character or situation in the early work is set against the more obvious moral positions taken in the work of the 1980s and beyond, notably in *The Child in Time, Black Dogs* and *Enduring Love*. Yet, Malcolm notes, 'the trajectory is not a prefect one', since it is complicated by a return to moral relativism in *The Innocent* (1991), and the amorality of *Amsterdam*.[21]

I began this introduction by acknowledging that writing about contemporary literature is a hazardous business, since judgements must be made in the absence of a critical consensus established over time. Narrowing my focus to offer a specific hostage to fortune, I should recall that I have suggested elsewhere that McEwan continues the tradition, associated most strongly with Iris Murdoch in British fiction since 1950, characterized by 'scrupulous thinking about the role of the novel and the novelist in the advancement of an ethical world-view'.[22] This is not to suggest that one can discern obvious examples of her influence in his work. It is true that McEwan has reported being, at the age of fourteen, 'an entranced reader of the handful of novels' she had published by then.[23] However, he has numbered her among those authors he felt himself to be reacting *against* at the start of his career.

In an interview conducted in 1994, McEwan considers his emergence as a writer, working 'very much in reaction against a certain kind of English writing which took the form of social documentary, and which was principally interested in the nuances of English class.' His early stories, he says in this interview, were dramatizations of the 'exclusion' and 'ignorance' that stemmed from his uncertainty about where he stood 'in relation to British society generally.' Because his parents were both working class, the family experienced 'a curious kind of dislocated existence' when his father was commissioned as an army officer, 'but not an officer of the middle class.' This, in McEwan's account, has a significant bearing on his own assessment of the English novel:

> I really didn't know where I fitted in. [. . .] when I read the fiction of Angus Wilson or Kingsley Amis or John Wain or Iris Murdoch – figures who were central to English writing at the time – I could find no way in for me there. I didn't really understand the middle-class world they described. Nor did I recognize the working-class world described by David Storey or Alan Sillitoe. I had to find a fictional world that was socially, and even historically disembodied.[24]

Struck by the 'uniform greyness of English writing at the time', and feeling dislocated by his own background, McEwan began writing his studiedly interiorized short stories, turning away from the kind of social embodiment current in the English novel. That sense of not fitting in with the rigid class structure of British society, however, was a common rather than an individual experience. Indeed, the theme of class mobility and the shake-up of society was a dominant literary theme from the late 1950s through to the 1970s, even if new forms of fictional social embodiment were yet to emerge. McEwan's personal experience, in short, left him well placed to speak to the experiences of a dislocated generation, for whom social change and, in particular, the demise of class as traditionally understood, was happening more rapidly than could be fully registered in the novel.

Curiously, in the same interview in which McEwan expresses bafflement about the work of prominent English novelists, including Iris Murdoch, he also enunciates something that is intimately related to her own convictions about human morality. Pondering the question of morality and writing, McEwan dismisses the view 'that language is a repository of moral values and there's no escape from it': 'true' but not very significant. Of far greater purport is the view he has arrived at (by 1994), that 'we are innately moral beings, at the most basic, wired-in neurological level.' Evolution produces instinctive social behaviour, made possible by the imagination and the ability to empathize. It is this 'wired-in' capacity that fiction both feeds and responds to: 'fiction is a deeply moral form in that it is the perfect medium for entering the mind of another. I think it is at the level of empathy that moral questions begin in fiction.'[25]

This is a view produced by McEwan's reading in popular science – particularly in evolutionary psychology – but it reveals a startling similarity with Murdoch's conviction about human goodness. In Murdoch's philosophy, human consciousness is so structured to generate for us a mode of moral being, in which we seek to find unity out of randomness, order out of chaos, and to pursue 'truth' in the process, thus distinguishing it from falsity. For Murdoch, the novel emulates this dynamic of moral thought, the tension between order and chaos, form and contingency, though in an ambivalent or provisional manner.[26] It is possible, perhaps, to see McEwan developing this conviction, but eschewing any form of mystical or religious explanation of the way in which human goodness might be 'wired-in', supplying in its stead an evolutionary explanation. The locus for this investigation is *Enduring Love*, a novel that explores this moral question in a more complex way than McEwan manages in his non-fictional ruminations on evolutionary psychology.

When McEwan remarks, in the 1994 interview cited above, that he began writing in reaction against those English novelists who seemed to be 'principally interested in the nuances of English class', he is partly articulating his family's experience of class dislocation, which fed the portrayal of 'exclusion' and 'ignorance' in his early work. This registers the vertiginous experience of social change in Britain after the Second World War, so the uncertainty about his standing 'in relation to British society generally' has a significance far beyond the personal. As the old tripartite class structure dissolved into more complex and fluid forms of social stratification, so did the experience of dislocation embody a new uncertainty about social affiliation and social responsibility.

Implicit in McEwan's feeling of dislocation is an intimation about British society that has some affinity, however unconscious this may be, with the complaints expressed by Murdoch in her famous essay 'Against Dryness'. Here, the Welfare State is her particular target, in representing 'a set of thoroughly desirable but limited ends'. This utilitarian political practice usurps political theory, she argues, inviting us to 'picture man as a brave naked will surrounded by an easily comprehended empirical world.' As a consequence, we are discouraged from developing 'a satisfactory Liberal theory of personality, a theory of man as free and separate and related to a rich and complicated world from which, as a moral being, he has much to learn.'[27]

The beneficent idea of the Welfare State was to provide a safety net for all, from cradle to grave, with regard to employment and health. For Murdoch, the problem with this paternalism, however laudable, was that it brought with it a moral lassitude, a failure to address the complexity of the social world and the responsibility of individuals within it: there is no onus on individuals to think about their social *selves* in this larger political sense, because the state has defined the empirical world, and (in principle) the safeguards needed for an acceptable degree of wealth redistribution. It then falls to literature, which 'has taken over some of the tasks formerly performed by phil-osophy', to supply 'concepts in terms of which to picture the substance of our being', or 'a new vocabulary of attention.' For the novelist, this project is figured as a necessary tension between 'the consolations of form' and 'a respect for the contingent', in the knowledge that 'only the very greatest art invigorates without consoling'.[28]

Certainly, McEwan's novels embody a marked tension between form and contingency, and (usually) betray a clear refusal of consolation.[29] The precise context of Murdoch's complaints, however, would seem to have no immediate relevance to his writing. McEwan's generation, after all, witnessed the gradual erosion of the Welfare State and, since Margaret Thatcher's era as Prime Minister, the adoption of a new language of individualism – of self-gain and personal advantage – that makes Murdoch's deliberations on personal responsibility seem to belong to an older age of idealism, impossible to recapture. Yet she describes the period of social dislocation in which McEwan grew up, and which had a formative influence on his work. The uncertainty, perhaps, stems from a paradox: the Welfare State safety net, in principle, supplies certain social safeguards to replace the older systems of class and patronage, but without encouraging any self-consciousness about social roles or networks. The older social fabric is replaced, not by recognized structures, but by legislation and institutions, against which it is impossible to define the self.

This is the era of social confusion to which McEwan deeply responds. It is not the case, of course, that all instances of social affiliation had disappeared. On the contrary, McEwan wrote through the final episode of the old-style British class struggle in the 1970s and 1980s; but, with hindsight, one can see how the workers/employers stand-off, traditionally defined in class terms, was becoming an anachronism, rapidly to be replaced by new, less identifiable forms of social inequality, such as the rapid rise of the underclass in a period of transition away from manual labour.[30] There is a sense, then, that the possibility of social affiliation is becoming problematic, if not illusory, in key instances. Even the dramatic success of the Women's Movement, to which McEwan responded positively, might be said to have brought with it an invitation to adopt a model of society wholesale, and without the need for complex self-examination. (This is the theme of McEwan's second longer work of fiction, *The Comfort of Strangers*.)

To argue that McEwan is Murdoch's natural heir is to suggest that he writes in a period in which the problem of identity – conceived as a problem of moral being – has become more acute. In connection with this, it is interesting that the formal tensions that Murdoch saw as a necessary aspect of the novel feature in a still more pronounced way in McEwan's work. There can be little doubt that one of his primary motivations as a novelist is to dramatize the emphatic impact of contingency on imagined lives, and to trace the personal tests and moral dilemmas that result from the unforeseen event: the abduction of a child in a supermarket; a ballooning accident; the appearance of threatening dogs on a mountain road; an encounter with thugs after a minor car accident, and so on. The fact that McEwan is renowned for his vivid rendering of such scenes suggests that a central impulse in his work is to emphasize randomness, chaos to an extraordinary degree. The necessary tension between form and contingency that characterizes the novel as a form of moral inquiry thus becomes, in McEwan, both more prominent than is customary, and a hallmark of the writer, a kind of self-conscious fingerprint.

When Murdoch wrote of the need to respect the contingent, she was suggesting how novels should be written, in a formal sense, to overcome the shortcomings of two types of twentieth-century novel: the 'crystalline' or 'quasi-allegorical novel' on the one hand; and the 'journalistic' or 'quasi-documentary' novel on the other. Where the former fails to produce characters in the manner of the nineteenth-century novel, the latter is a 'degenerate descendant' of the achievements of the previous century. In effect, Murdoch produces a manifesto for the kind of novel that will foster a complex moral and social identity.[31] The response to contingency, however, can also become a test for the characters within a novel (as is so often the case in Murdoch's own work).[32] The failure to respect (or manage) the random nature of experience is a recurring aspect of McEwan's treatment of character, leading, for example, to: Briony Tallis's crime (*Atonement*); the initial failure of Stephen Lewis to cope with grief (*The Child in Time*); and Joe Rose's problematic response to his stalker, Jed Parry – but especially to the delusional and destructive behaviour of Parry himself (*Enduring Love*).

The refusal of consolation is another exaggerated element of most of the fictions. Even the positive resolution of novels like *Enduring Love* and *The Child in Time* still leaves us deeply unsettled. Joe Rose may have been 'right' about Jed Parry, but the novel ends with several appendices attesting to the endurance of Parry's destructive delusion, as an emblem of failed self-identity. Similarly, the reconciliation of Stephen and Julie at the end of *The Child in Time*, and the birth of the new child, cannot console either parent (or the reader) for the traumatic abduction of the daughter Kate, which remains unresolved. The most dramatic refusal of consolation comes at the end of *Atonement*, with the revelation that the reuniting of the lovers, parted by Briony's misadventure, was her invention, a consoling feature of her latest draft, but not of McEwan's novel.

It is often claimed that the position adumbrated by Murdoch in 'Against Dryness' – that 'through literature we can re-discover a sense of the density of our lives'[33] – lays the foundation for subsequent discussion in the now burgeoning field of literature and moral philosophy, especially that branch defined as narrative ethics.[34]

Here I wish to observe a significant consonance between McEwan's extended fictional project, with its ongoing and often deeply troubled investigation of the self and morality (or the possible grounds thereof), and recent critical work in narrative ethics, which emerges in the 1980s and 1990s as a response to poststructuralism.[35] I observe this consonance for two reasons: first because wherever critics and writers appear to have similar concerns, this may suggest a deep and important response to a particular context (and not something to be immediately suspicious about); and, second, following from the above, this is a critical climate which now lends credibility to McEwan's project. Specifically, I refer to the relationship between *character* and moral exploration. Certainly, elements of poststructuralist criticism seemed profoundly antagonistic towards the idea that a moral dilemma could be encoded in the situation confronting a fictional character. The emphasis in poststructuralism on the primacy (and indeterminacy) of language suggests that the individual is comprised of a network of discourses, and it is this discursive interplay that demands our attention, and not a putative coherent self, since that self is an effect of language, merely.

Narrative ethics emerges on the far side of this debate to establish a position that occupies a mid-ground between the privileging of the autonomous speaking subject and the dissolution of the self into larger social and linguistic codes. Charles Taylor, in particular, has helped establish a complex mid-ground between these two positions, acknowledging on the one hand that our status as moral subjects indeed depends on the language community in which we participate, so that our 'moral intuitions' are inevitably sponsored, in part, by language and by culture. However, this is not the same thing as reducing 'moral intuitions' to effects of language. Taylor argues that our moral being is produced by the 'best account' we can give of 'the human domain', and that this account may well be given 'in anthro-pocentric terms', those terms, that is, 'which relate to the meanings things have for us'. This accords a significant degree of agency to the individual, whose own terms are rooted in thick lived experience, and whose intuitions about what is morally moving can be taken seriously.[36]

It is this kind of understanding that allows critics, inspired by moral philosophy, to reclaim the novel as a key site for the exploration of the human domain and moral being. As we have seen, this conception of narrative ethics takes due cognizance of debates about language and self and emerges on the other side of poststructuralism with an informed self-consciousness. It also acknowledges, however, the political and sociological attack on earlier manifestations of moral criticism. There is no attempt in criticism of this kind to suggest that a 'great novel' is an ennobling or civilizing force, and can always be taken as such. Rather, this kind of criticism establishes the capacity of the novel to treat moral concerns in a variety of ways.

The larger claim may be, in the spirit of Murdoch, that the novel has the capacity to achieve a unique form of moral philosophy, and particularly through its investigation of character, dilemma and moral agency; and that this capacity can and should be put to social uses. Yet this version of narrative ethics, with the emphasis on negotiation, and on lived experience, can be given the hue of postmodern relativism, especially insofar as it establishes the *constructed* nature of the dramatized self in the novel. This version of the role of narrative in the construction of the self is perhaps most commonly associated with Richard Rorty, who (in the words of Geoffrey Galt Harpham) places emphasis on 'self-understanding', which 'can only be reached by the construction of stories about the self': indeed, 'for Rorty, story-telling develops the indispensable ability to improvise an identity'.[37]

There is certainly an emphasis on self-understanding, a quest for identity, in many of McEwan's novels. However, this is equally true of many novels and novelists, and may reveal a truism about the novel, rather than something that is specific to McEwan's time. Yet, in his preoccupation with the improvization of identity, there is what appears to be a democratic postmodern tendency. The necessary invention of the self in the novel might partake of a wider postmodern emphasis on argument and discourse in social production, as societies are freed from the totalizing master narratives of modernity.[38] The self, 'decentred' in the sense that it is liberated from controlling institutional processes, can be defined in different ways to suit various circumstances and individual need.

The ethical dimension of the improvized self in McEwan might seem superficially to conform to this celebratory aspect of post-modernism.[39] This might also be a way of situating McEwan in contemporary British culture: the need for new forms of self-construction speaks to a society in flux in terms of its class, gender and ethnic composition, perhaps. The emphasis on self-construction, which is an aspect of the good life in ethical terms, is also a resolution to the 'dislocation' that many writers, including McEwan, have felt since the Second World War.[40] There is something unsatisfying about such a conclusion, however. The mere process of constructing and reconstructing the self implies a form of navel-contemplation that deserves fewer than three cheers, and which may not properly distinguish McEwan from his contemporaries, or, indeed, the postmodern novel from earlier manifestations. The novel has, surely, always been a crucible for the investigation of the self, and for examining the relationship between self and other, and between private and public realms.

There is another aspect of postmodern expression that cannot be found, unequivocally, in McEwan, and this may help to pin down his distinctiveness. I am thinking of Linda Hutcheon's classic account of postmodern narrative as a mode that combines realist reference and modernist self-consciousness, deploying and questioning these features simultaneously.[41] Where such a hybrid mode often develops a newly intensive form of self-reflexiveness that emphasizes textuality over reference, diluting the novel's capacity to illuminate the social world, McEwan, by contrast, is very much preoccupied with models of knowing. From the manipulation of quantum physics in *The Child in Time*, through the debate about rationality and religion in *Black Dogs*, to the investigation of biological and medical science in *Enduring Love* and *Saturday* (2005), respectively, McEwan's fictions betray an ongoing search for systematic ways of knowing the world.

This series of treatments, in which alternative explanatory systems become the narrative focus, reveals a keen anxiety in McEwan about the absence of foundational beliefs. Where systems of explanation are missing (as they are, for example, for the children in *The Cement Garden* (1978), and for the protagonists in *The Innocent* and *Amsterdam*), or are inappropriate or inadequate (as for Colin and Mary in *The Comfort of Strangers*, Jeremy in *Black Dogs*, Joe Rose in *Enduring Love*, or Briony Tallis in *Atonement*), the self is either destroyed or left floundering. There is no postmodern incredulity about metanarrative implied in this. The impossibility of finding coherent and enduring explanatory systems may be tacitly acknowledged in the series of different quests; but the absence is invariably shown to be catastrophic. Further, because it is this very absence that *necessitates* the process of self-improvization – that exercise in constructing the self that is a focus of postmodern liberation – we cannot see this process as anything other than ambivalent in McEwan. Systemic explanations are often exposed as limited or damaging; but without them, there is nothing against which the self can be measured or defined.

Critics of the novel, in the era of postmodernism, have often been treading parallel terrain to McEwan. For example, in his survey of postmodern narrative theory, Mark Currie suggests that critical perspectives since the 1970s have been 'implicitly dedicated to the proposition that personal identity is not inside us.' One line of argument pursues the notion that 'identity . . . inheres in the relations between a person and others.' This suggests that 'personal identity', rather than being 'contained in the body', is 'structured by, or constituted by, difference.' Currie's second line of argument is that 'identity is not within us because it exists only as narrative.' On the principle that 'the only way to explain who we are is to tell our own story', it follows that 'we learn how to self-narrate from the outside, from other stories, and particularly through the process of identification with other characters.'[42]

Currie reflects on the temptation to see characters in novels as having 'ready-made personalities', and our inclination, as readers, to understand our responses to character 'as individual and free judgements' resulting from 'an encounter between our own moral values and those represented by the character.' Partly, this is a consequence of the 'referential illusion of fictional narrative', which encourages us to 'make inferences about fictional characters no different from the inferences we make about real people.' These observations are prefatory to Currie's discussion of how narratology has explained 'the technical control of such responses and inferences', and how 'our responses are manufactured by the rhetoric of narrative.'[43]

A good deal is implied in these observations. Narrative theory might lead us to the conclusion that: readers may be duped by narrative rhetoric into making moral judgements they imagine to be independent; that, in doing so, they make deluded referential leaps of identification between text and world; and that the incremental sense of self a reader establishes through a lifetime of identifying with character (in other forms of narrative, if they are not novel readers) is constructed by external narrative forms fashioned by various ideologies. This summarizes an orthodoxy within narrative theory that must be seriously reckoned with. Indeed, in the analysis of any dense fictional work, it is important to identify those ideological factors that colour our reading. However, a systematic focus on the mechanics of how readers are manipulated, if conducted wholly by 'reading against the grain', will leave the literary effects of the work in question partially (or even entirely) unaccounted for.

The root of the problem, here, is a false conviction about the naivety of 'the reader'. There is, I think, much truth in the idea that our sense of self develops through a process of acculturation to narrative forms; but I do not think that leaves us blind to rhetorical effects, or to covert ideological influences. A lifetime of reading novels, for example, will often produce an intellectually formidable reader, whether or not he or she is well versed in narrative theory. Such a reader might well recognize a range of rhetorical devices and narrative strategies – and the ideological perspectives implicit within them – and may find that recognition a fundamental part of the pleasure in reading. At the same time, this may not deter our notional formidable reader from extending sympathy to particular characters, or from engaging with their theoretical dilemmas in such a way as to extract a moral lesson applicable to their own life in some way. Such theoretical moral debating, it seems to me, is an inevitable aspect of receiving fiction. Equally inevitable is the process of applying it to everyday experience.

In one sense, this summary might be seen to correspond to the trends in postmodern narrative theory identified by Currie. Certainly, if social life is seen as a fabric of ideologies and discourses, then familiarity with the formative impulses of narrative is a necessary social skill, an externalized survival mechanism that facilitates our role as social beings. There is an important point of divergence, however, and that concerns personal identity, the sense of self. If we learn to explain ourselves by the external process of narration – and if our identity is fashioned by our engagement with narrative forms – does that make us textual beings, merely, interpellated as subjects, entirely from without?

A reason for thinking otherwise – or, at least, for heavily qualifying this idea – is that every reader's sense of self is built from a body of narratives which are exclusive to them, and which have been internalized in highly individual ways – ways, moreover, that may not be fully communicable. The process of moral reading, and projection beyond the text, then emerges as a necessary attempt to externalize the highly individual and internalized self that has been constructed through personal narrative engagement. Our sense of self will develop, incrementally, every time we engage with and assimilate a novel, or other narrative, that we value: and that process of valuing is always internal and external, enhancing our unique intellectual identity, at the same time as it obliges us to bring our reading to bear upon the world we know, or the behaviour of individuals within it. And if our intellectual identity is indeed unique, then it may be impossible to say that it is clearly influenced by this or that ideology, this or that external factor. Moreover, even if we accept that our identity has been formed through a series of responses to external narratives – that it has an evidently textual basis – its individual nature, in the last analysis, produced through that unrepeatable cumulative series of narrative encounters, makes it legitimate for us to think of personal identity as specific to ourselves, and so *internal*.

What is established about the reader or receiver of narrative in this account – the possessor of a discovered and developing self with an identity more dense than the merely *textual* – is directly relevant to McEwan's portrayal of character and the quest for identity that underpins it. The emphasis is on the *quest*, however, betraying a developing concern about the efficacy of narrative fiction in the pursuit of resolution. Accurately registering the trend towards increasing anxiety about fiction-making, Jago Morrison observes that 'in all of McEwan's work after *The Child in Time*, the whole idea or possibility of narrative (and psychic) resolution becomes a central question.'[44]

McEwan's interest in science, and especially in scientific explanations for consciousness and emotional response, has an interesting bearing on the degree of credibility that can be attached to the self as a constructed phenomenon. Rather than turning to science for authoritative factual confirmation about consciousness in any simple sense, it may be that scientific models provide confirmation, on a best-that we-can-say-now basis, about the quests for selfhood that underpin McEwan's narrative.

Might this not imply a form of relativity in scientific understanding of the self to match the relativity of postmodern analysis, however? This is certainly the view of another British novelist, David Lodge. In his essay 'Consciousness and the Novel', Lodge indicates how certain branches of cognitive science, where consciousness is explained merely as neurological function, offer a challenge both to 'the idea of human nature enshrined in the Judeo-Christian religious tradition', and to 'the humanist or Enlightenment idea of man on which the presentation of character in the novel is based':

> This idea of the person, whether in real life or in fictional representations, has come under attack from both the humanities and science in recent times. There is, for instance, a certain affinity between the post-structuralist literary theory that maintains that the human subject is entirely constructed by the discourses in which it is situated, and the cognitive science view that regards human self-consciousness as an epiphenomenon of brain activity.[45]

Lodge defends the novel as 'arguably man's most successful effort to describe the experience of individual human beings moving through space and time'; and the reason why the novel can reveal aspects of human experience, where scientific disciplines cannot, is clear for Lodge:

> Science tries to formulate general explanatory laws which apply universally, which were in operation before they were discovered, and which would have been discovered sooner or later by somebody. Works of literature describe in the guise of fiction the dense specificity of personal experience, which is always unique, because each of us has a slightly or very different personal history, modifying every new experience we have.[46]

The unique and dense specificity of personal experience articulated here, corresponds to the individualized self of the notional formidable reader – or, simply, the receiver of narrative – I have argued for above. We should also note that Lodge sets up a preliminary opposition between science and literature, which he goes on to dismantle (arguing that 'literature constitutes a kind of knowledge about consciousness which is *complementary* to scientific knowledge'), a dismantling reinforced by the work of neurologist Antonio Damasio, whom Lodge cites in the essay.[47] Damasio, a direct influence on McEwan, has expressed scepticism about 'science's presumption of objectivity and definitiveness', intimating that 'scientific results, especially in neurobiology' should be seen as 'provisional approximations, to be enjoyed for a while and discarded as soon as better accounts become available.'[48] This opens up the possibility of a complementary dynamic between literature and science, with neither claiming definitive authority or access to consciousness; neither need it be read as a formula for indeterminate relativity about the composition of consciousness and the sources of the self.

For Damasio, neurological science points the way for a combination of scientific and cultural insights, positing 'an organism that comes to life designed with automatic survival mechanisms, and to which education and acculturation add a set of socially permissible and desirable decision-making strategies that, in turn, enhance survival, remarkably improve the quality of that survival, and serve as the basis for constructing a *person*.'[49] Again, this makes credible the idea of selfhood located within consciousness. Lodge slightly retreats from the implications of this idea of the self – as a credible force, even if it is constructed – when he concedes that 'the Western humanist concept of the autonomous individual self is not universal, eternally given, and valid for all time and all places, but is a product of history and culture.' He still insists that it is 'a good idea', and that 'a great deal of what we value in civilized life depends upon it.'[50] Yet this tacit admission of the artificiality of the self does not properly account for the unique nature of what is built through personal experience, the quest for which is a primary driving force in McEwan's fiction.

The very notion of locating the self, however, reinforces the idea that McEwan, far from being an exemplar of postmodernism, betrays much affinity with the realist models of the past. In summarizing his dismantling of the realism/experimentalism dichotomy that has influenced much thinking about fiction in post-war Britain, Andrzej Gąsiorek cites McEwan's comment that self-conscious formal experimentation is a cul-de-sac, that 'the artifice of fiction can be taken for granted', and that 'experimentation in its broadest and most viable sense should have less to do with formal factors like busting up your syntax and scrambling your page order, and more to do with content – the representation of states of mind and the society that forms them.'[51] Although this view was published in 1978, it has a lasting relevance to McEwan's position as a writer: despite some extravagant formal experiments (the timeslip in *The Child in Time*, for example, or the entire conception of *Atonement*), he remains focused on states of mind, and the shaping force of the social, and so precisely one of those writers whose works, as Gąsiorek puts it, 'make a nonsense of the realism/experimentalism opposition.'[52]

Quoting McEwan approvingly to read McEwan might raise a few poststructuralist eyebrows, much as my account of the common ground between narrative ethics and the author's mode of characterization may do. This should be taken to signal a critical approach that is not systematically symptomatic. However, I am not propounding a benign form of reading 'with the grain'. The procedure I follow is one in which the proper contextualizing of a work is deemed to involve a movement of reading sympathetic to a novel's apparent design. Against this backdrop, localized symptomatic observations, or informed instances of reading against the grain, become possible, or necessary, but in a way that responds to, or evaluates, the perceived original conception of a work.

Following this procedure, the book is organized in a conventional way to trace the chronological development of McEwan's oeuvre. Chapter 2 concentrates on the early work, the literature of shock embodied in the short story collections *First Love, Last Rites* and *In Between the Sheets* (1978), as well as the first longer fiction, *The Cement Garden*. Moving beyond the studiedly anarchic and iconoclastic element of the early work, the chapter considers ways in which the iconoclasm – a literary branch of the punk movement, perhaps – suggests the felt need to revitalize the British literary scene. Behind the immediate impact of these fictions, we can discern thoughtful deliberations on the role and function of literature, the germ of more extended deliberations in the later work. The readings given of stories such as 'Homemade' and 'Pornography', for example, reveal an implicit contribution to the debate about how literature may have supplanted the social function of religion.

A question that many of the stories pose, in fact, is how far literary art is an adequate response to instances of vacuous late twentieth-century experience. *The Cement Garden*, developing this response to wider social anomie, also extends the examination of literature's role, since the cement garden may be taken as a metaphor for the reputation of the British novel in the 1970s (however unjust the implication may seem, with hindsight).

The third chapter concentrates on *The Comfort of Strangers*, but begins with a discussion of the screenplay for *The Imitation Game*, McEwan's first explicit engagement of feminism. This is a wartime drama that uncovers a link between patriarchal power and secrecy, through the experiences of the protagonist, Cathy, at Bletchley Park. The drama is most notable for enacting a dialogue between two overlapping strands of feminism: the emergent feminism of the wartime era, viewed through the lens of 1970s feminism.

In *The Comfort of Strangers*, feminism is also engaged, but in a way that exposes its limits as a popular credo. Set in an unnamed city that is clearly Venice, the novella draws on the literary tradition of Venice as a brooding, threatening place as it exposes the failure of intellectual codes (feminism in particular) to relate to actual experience, when such codes are no more than an ideological veneer. The characters Colin and Mary are drawn into a trap of sexual violence, as culpable victims, chiefly, it seems, because of their own inner lack. *The Comfort of Strangers*, possibly McEwan's most disturbing book, marks the culmination of a phase of bleak early fiction.

Chapter 4 presents *The Child in Time* as McEwan's first sustained attempt at a novel of society, accepting the author's view that two expressly political projects – the words for the oratorio *Or Shall We Die?*, and the screenplay for *The Ploughman's Lunch* – prepared the ground for the more exploratory treatment of ideas in the novel.

The discussion draws especially on McEwan's sources in popular science to show how a post-Einsteinian conception of the plasticity of time and space allows the central character to intervene in the past and guarantee his own future. This he does by 'appearing' to his mother, while she is pregnant with him, and dissuading her from the abortion she is contemplating. This timeslip is the book's narrative fulcrum; and it is a thematic fulcrum, too, with regard to the topic of the child within, and to the idea that strong personal and intergenerational bonds are necessary in the healthy body politic. The timeslip is also a poetic development of a form of public discourse – the scientific attempt to understand nature – brought to bear on the most funda-mental aspect of personal experience, one's own conception. This grandiose and inventive reinvigoration of the bridge between the private and the public is both a direct response to the perceived social collapse consequent upon Thatcherism, and a dramatic reinvigoration of the novel of society.

The Innocent and *Black Dogs* are grouped together in the fifth chapter: they embody a significant phase of political writing in which McEwan takes cognisance of the historical trajectory of post-war Europe. These novels, which are also marked by a partial return to the early preoccupation with human depravity, are presented, in effect, as novels of ideas that dismantle their own scaffolding: the binary oppositions that order the works at the levels of argument, or ideas, are systematically and purposively unravelled. In *The Innocent*, for example, the dismemberment scene provokes in Leonard a definitive response of abjection – for Julia Kristeva, 'the corpse, seen without God and outside of science, is the utmost of abjection'[53] – and begins to undermine the symbolic order of identity upon which Leonard's emerging life depends. Now that he is unable to distinguish himself from the mutilated Otto ('the insult was . . . that all this stuff was also in himself' (*I*, p. 182)), the binary divisions that would enable him to marry Maria and condemn Otto – Englishman/German; lover/abuser – start to dissolve.

This unravelling of identities has a particular bearing on the larger binary opposition that structures the political divide of the Cold War. The resolution to this ideological strait-jacket, and a reassertion of a reinvigorated personal identity, occurs when Leonard betrays (or aims to betray) Operation Gold – the Berlin tunnel designed to tap telephone lines in the Soviet sector – in order to protect himself and Maria. In short, the novel adopts the framework of a spy novel to envisage the collapse of the individual identity that is finally reasserted in such a way as to undermine the basis of Cold War politics.

In *Black Dogs*, a similar process of unravelling complicates and enriches the fiction. The work is predicated on a thematic opposition between the rational and the spiritual life, presented as competing ways of facing up to the terror of human history; but this tidy structure is thrown into doubt by the questionable motives of the distinctly unreliability narrator, Jeremy. The impression grows that Jeremy's personal quest for meaning is the book's focus, rather than – or at least as much as – the war of ideas embodied in the ideological standoff of his parents-in-law, logical Bernard and intuitive June Tremaine. As in *The Innocent*, *Black Dogs* gestures towards the larger political context – the legacy of Nazism – by obscuring the rude binary structure. The problematic narrative frame makes us think less about rationality versus spiritualism, as a sensible debate that can be concluded, and more about the instability of Jeremy. His orphan mentality acquires a generalized significance, denoting the collective hunger of the post-war generation for social and political stability in Europe.

As the sixth chapter shows, McEwan had not finished his exploration of the emotional and the rational with *Black Dogs*: this recurring theme was to receive its fullest expression, in the form of a rigorous testing of scientific rationalism, in *Enduring Love*. Anticipating *Saturday* to a degree, the novel pits the relative merits of science and literature against each other, within the form of a thriller. The relationship between Joe Rose, a science journalist, and his wife Clarissa, an academic, is almost destroyed by the obsessive and delusional attachment of Jed Parry to Joe.

Underpinning this testing of character is McEwan's larger literary project, to consider the function of the novel when set against the claims of post-Darwinian science about the evolutionary basis of morality and judgement. Intrigued by evolutionary psychology, McEwan produces in Joe Rose a hero still more enamoured of the truth claims in this branch of science, but puts him in a narrative structure that tests to breaking point some of its central principles, most especially the notion that the habit of constructing 'morality' may be an inherited trait. The novel shows humanity to be at a stage of evolution and/or social complexity that puts us out of the evolutionary loop, and that demands of us an ethical sense that addresses the problem of self-interest with acute self-consciousness.

The shorter seventh chapter considers *Amsterdam*, which is often viewed as an inferior Booker winner, and reappraises it as an accomplished satirical novella. This social satire, a new departure for McEwan, is conducted through the portraits of newspaper editor Vernon Halliday and composer Clive Linley, projected as representative of the professional achievers of the Thatcher–Major era. The view emerges that, among the left-leaning intelligentsia – and even in the cultural sphere – professional standards have occluded ethical standards. However, this is not a stable social satire, consistent in its comic effects. The satire bleeds out into the contemporary world of literary culture, the culture of which this smartly composed novella is a self-conscious product.

In chapter 8 *Atonement* is examined as the creative equivalent or counterpart of narrative ethics, making explicit an intellectual journey that governs McEwan's career. Narrative ethics resuscitates an older conviction about the moral content of fiction, but with the hindsight bestowed by poststructuralist thinking. It establishes a position that represents a mid-ground between the privileging of the autonomous speaking subject and the dissolution of self into larger social and linguistic codes. In a similar process of repositioning, *Atonement* evokes a strong sense of lived experience that is morally moving, and yet insists on the constructed nature of fiction and the morally dubious authority wielded by the writer. This is an aspect of the novel's structure and narrative technique, which finally reveal Briony Tallis to be the 'author' of the work we have read, seeking to make a personal atonement that has wider ramifications for literary art.

With its literary allusiveness, *Atonement* has the air of an author writing himself, albeit problematically, into a literary tradition, a gesture that seems a world away from the 'shock-lit' of his early works. Yet this is a misleading impression. Where the early works made an implicit case for extending the literary, what is unsettling about *Atonement* is the manner in which its own aesthetic structure, and the inherited literary tradition on which it feeds, is partly undermined.

Against the horrors of the twentieth century, *Atonement* pits the empathetic creativity of complex fiction-making. This has the air of a grand, one-off (and, in one respect, consoling) gesture. One form of alternative creative social energy that is curtailed in *Atonement* is Robbie's desire to pursue medicine as a vocation. Reacting against the lectures of Leavis at Cambridge, Robbie wishes to acquire 'more elaborate' skills than those 'acquired in practical criticism' (*At*, p. 91). This desire to re-evaluate social and cultural work, post-Leavis, is cut short by Robbie's death at Bray Dunes; it is taken up, for a later era, with other ramifications, in *Saturday*.

In chapter 9 *Saturday* is shown to develop a comparable formal paradox to that discernible in *Atonement*: its treatment of the competing claims of literature and medicine is more thoroughgoing, even though still more extravagant claims for the literary are pressed, and also questioned. The celebration of neurosurgeon Henry Perowne challenges us because he is also characterized by an anti-literary 'philistinism'. Thematically, the novel casts doubt on the idea that literature matters, in a social or cultural sense: more explicitly than in his other novels, scientific discovery is lauded as having a far greater social significance.

However, in this novel championing medical advances in the understanding of consciousness, we realize, of course, that it is the narrative technique that permits special access to the consciousness of the protagonist. As the novel implies a new form of social accountability in the light of advances in genetic science, so is the question of a new model of responsibility for the novel tacitly posed.

How does this account of the writer's formal development reflect on those raw, early fictions? Without the complex layering of narrative perspective, what formal elements in the stories might imply a debate about the moral questions they seem otherwise to evade?

The value of the short stories is sometimes deemed not to depend on such layering. In his essay on violence and complicity in Martin Amis and Ian McEwan, Kiernan Ryan suggests that the shocking elements of McEwan's work may stem from an 'unnerving honesty about the secret ubiquity of depravity and its seductive appeal'; indeed, in this argument, 'it is only when the writer is let off the hook of moral responsibility, of conscious educative intent and political decorum, that he or she is apt to push back the frontiers of moral understanding'.[54] Ryan's defence of the short stories hinges upon McEwan's skilful use of confessional narrative, which effaces 'all signs of ulterior authorial intent' and 'compels our identification with his estranged soliloquists.' By this procedure, 'McEwan implicates himself and us through our confinement to the vision of this isolated voice.'[55] The question that the next chapter addresses is how far McEwan's early fiction progresses beyond this confessional mode, and the chilling affinity it elicits from us.

Notes

1 It is also possible that this surmise, which is framed by the projection of current models of literary history, may prove false. The current critical conviction that historical context is usefully illuminated by the literary response, may, over the next couple of generations, become less compelling in an era with other, pressing global concerns.

2 William Leith, 'Form and Dysfunction' (author profile), *The Observer*, 'Life' (20 September 1998), pp. 4–5, 7–8 (p. 8).

3 McEwan, 'Mother Tongue: A Memoir', in Zachary Leader, ed., *On Modern British Fiction* (Oxford University Press, 2002), pp. 34–44 (p. 35). The piece was first published in *The Guardian* (13 October 2001).

4 Liliane Louvel, Gilles Ménégaldo, and Anne-Laure Fortin, 'An Interview with Ian McEwan' (conducted November 1994), *Études Britanniques Contemporaines*, 8 (1995), pp. 1–12 (pp. 1, 3).

5 McEwan, 'Mother Tongue', p. 36.

6 In *The Child in Time* (pp. 69–74), Stephen Lewis's childhood recollections seem to be McEwan's.

7 McEwan, 'Mother Tongue', p. 36.

8 Malcolm Bradbury, *The Modern British Novel*, revised edition (London: Penguin, 2001), p. 437. Bradbury seems to mis-remember the dates, indicating that McEwan studied at UEA in the academic year 1969–70, rather than 1970–71.

9 Ian Hamilton, 'Points of Departure' (interview), *New Review* 5: 2 (1978), pp. 9–21 (p. 15).

10 Ibid., 17.

11 McEwan, 'Wild Man of Literature (c. 1976): A Memoir', *The Observer*, 'Review' (7 June 1998), p. 16. The context of McEwan's writing this memoir

is for inclusion in a festschrift for Ian Hamilton. Hamilton died in 2001, at the age of sixty-three.

12 Richard Reeves and Nicole Veash, 'A War of Words', *The Observer* (22 August 1999), p. 14.

13 See, for example, reports in *The Independent* on 28 August 1999, p. 4, and 4 September 1999, p. 3.

14 Leith, 'Form and Dysfunction', p. 8.

15 McEwan, 'Mother Tongue', pp. 41–2.

16 Bradbury, *The Modern British Novel*, p. 437.

17 In 1994 he acknowledged that ' "Disguises" owed a little to Angus Wilson's "Raspberry Jam", a strange and quite vicious story of his early writing.' See Louvel, *et al.*, 'An Interview with Ian McEwan', p. 2.

18 Bradbury, *The Modern British Novel*, p. 438.

19 Ibid., pp. 481, 536.

20 Kiernan Ryan, *Ian McEwan* (Plymouth: Northcote House/British Council, 1994), pp. 2, 4, 5.

21 David Malcolm, *Understanding Ian McEwan* (Columbia: University of South Carolina Press, 2002), pp. 6, 15–17.

22 Dominic Head, *The Cambridge Introduction to Modern British Fiction, 1950–2000* (Cambridge University Press, 2002), p. 258.

23 McEwan, 'Mother Tongue', p. 36.

24 Louvel, *et al.*, 'An Interview with Ian McEwan', pp. 1, 3.

25 Ibid., p. 4.

26 For a lucid account of the literary presentation of Murdoch's moral philosophy see Maria Antonaccio, 'Form and Contingency in Iris Murdoch's Ethics', in Maria Antonaccio and William Schweiker, eds, *Iris Murdoch and the Search for Human Goodness* (Chicago: University of Chicago Press, 1996), pp. 110–37.

27 Iris Murdoch, 'Against Dryness: A Polemical Sketch' (1961), in Malcolm Bradbury, ed., *The Novel Today: Contemporary Writers on Modern Fiction*, revised edition (London: Fontana, 1990), pp. 15–24 (pp. 18, 19).

28 Ibid., pp. 22, 23, 24. Murdoch's own novels, of course, enact this tension between form and contingency, whilst refusing to offer easy consolations to the reader.

29 The exception to this rule is *Saturday*.

30 A clear indication of the changing class structure is the way in which voting habits changed. Working-class support for Labour, determined by the voting habits of manual workers, ranged from 62% to 69% in the 1960s, but fell from 57% in 1974 to 50% in 1979 and then to 38% in 1983. See Dennis Kavanagh, *Thatcherism and British Politics: The End of Consensus?*, third edition (Oxford University Press, 1996), pp. 168–9.

31 Murdoch, 'Against Dryness', p. 20.

32 Murdoch's first novel, *Under the Net* (1954), for example, is structured to frame a lesson for its narrator, Jake Donaghue, who progresses from a solipsistic hater of contingency to someone who appears to be on the point of celebrating his place in a broader social network. (This novel predates 'Against Dryness', and so anticipates the kind of novel she describes in the polemical sketch.)

33 Murdoch, 'Against Dryness', p. 22.

34 See, for example, Jane Adamson, 'Against Tidiness: Literature and/versus Moral Philosophy', in Jane Adamson, Richard Freadman and David Parker, eds, *Renegotiating Ethics in Literature, Philosophy, and Theory* (Cambridge University Press, 1998), pp. 84–110 (p. 85).

35 As I was completing work on this book, Claudia Schemberg's short book appeared, in which this claim is also advanced: 'The ethical turn in McEwan's writing career . . . echoes the insights formulated by ethical critics in the late 1980s and early 1990s. It is thus part of a greater cultural movement which endeavours to open-mindedly address inescapable questions of value and which regards imaginative literature as an indispensable partner in this enterprise.' Schemberg goes further, however, advancing the intriguing idea that a later phase in McEwan's work parallels a later phase in narrative ethics: she finds 'a focus on character and emotion' in later McEwan (especially in *Atonement*) that corresponds with 'a subtle shift of emphasis' in ethical criticism, epitomized in Martha Nussbaum's *Upheavals of Thought* (Cambridge University Press, 2001) and the attention to 'an adequate theory of the emotions'. See Claudia Schemberg, *Achieving 'At-one-ment': Storytelling and the Concept of the Self in Ian McEwan's 'The Child in Time', 'Black Dogs', 'Enduring Love', and 'Atonement'* (Frankfurt: Peter Lang, 2004), pp. 28, 30–1.

36 Charles Taylor, *Sources of the Self: The Making of the Modern Identity* (1999; reprinted Cambridge University Press, 2002), p. 72. For an invaluable overview of this debate see David Parker, 'Introduction; The Turn to Ethics in the 1990s', in Adamson, Freadman and Parker, eds, *Renegotiating Ethics*, pp. 1–17.

37 Geoffrey Galt Harpham, 'Ethics and Literary Criticism', in Christa Knellwolf and Christopher Norris, eds, *The Cambridge History of Literary Criticism: Twentieth-Century Historical, Philosophical and Psychological Perspectives*, volume IX (Cambridge University Press, 2001), pp. 371–85 (p. 378). Harpham is discussing Rorty's well-known essay 'Solidarity or Objectivity?', in John Rajchman and Cornel West, eds, *Post-Analytic Philosophy* (New York: Columbia University Press, 1985), pp. 3–19.

38 See, for example, Ernesto Laclau, 'Politics and the Limits of Modernity', printed in Thomas Docherty, ed., *Postmodernism: A Reader* (London: Harvester, 1993), pp. 329–43.

39 This is how Claudia Schemberg seems to read McEwan. The 'central assumption' she finds 'borne out again and again', in *The Child in Time*, *Black Dogs*, *Enduring Love* and *Atonement*, is that 'the quest for the good life, for meaning, purpose, and "at-one-ment", constitutes an integral, ineradicable part of the characters' lives.' This emphasis on answering questions 'about who and what we are, about where we are and where we might be going' constitutes 'a good life' in itself, 'despite the absence of metaphysical foundations, and despite the precarious nature of all attachments and frameworks of belief'. See *Achieving 'At-one-ment'*, p. 97.

40 I discuss this issue further, and in several chapters, in *The Cambridge Introduction to Modern British Fiction, 1950–2000*.

41 See Linda Hutcheon, *The Politics of Postmodernism* (London: Routledge, 1989), p. 141.

42 Mark Currie, *Postmodern Narrative Theory* (Basingstoke: Macmillan, 1998), p. 17.

43 Ibid., pp. 17–18.

44 Jago Morrison, *Contemporary Fiction* (London: Routledge, 2003), p. 74.

45 David Lodge, *Consciousness and the Novel* (London: Secker and Warburg, 2002), pp. 2, 89.

46 Ibid., pp. 10–11.

47 Ibid., pp. 14–16.

48 Antonio Damasio, *Descartes' Error: Emotion, Reason, and the Human Brain* (1994; New York: Quill, 2000), p. xviii.

49 Ibid., p. 126.

50 Lodge, *Consciousness and the Novel*, p. 91.

51 Ian McEwan, 'The State of Fiction: A Symposium', *New Review*, 5: 1 (Summer 1978), pp. 14–76 (p. 51), cited in Andrzej Gąsiorek, *Post-War British Fiction: Realism and After* (London: Edward Arnold, 1995), p. 180.

52 Gąsiorek, *Post-War British Fiction*, p. 180.

53 Julia Kristeva, *Powers of Horror: An Essay on Abjection*, trans. Leon S. Roudiez (New York: Columbia University Press, 1982), p. 4.

54 Kiernan Ryan, 'Sex, Violence and Complicity: Martin Amis and Ian McEwan', in Rod Mengham, ed., *An Introduction to Contemporary Fiction* (Cambridge: Polity, 1999), pp. 203–18 (pp. 203, 204, 206).

55 Ibid., pp. 212, 213.

2

Shock-lit: the short stories
and *The Cement Garden*

McEwan's first three books made him notorious, as the author of
unpleasant – or challenging – shorter fictions (depending on your point
of view), which were preoccupied with violence and deviant sexuality.
This 'literature of shock' is at its most prominent in his two short story
collections, *First Love, Last Rites* and *In Between the Sheets*, as well as
in his first novel *The Cement Garden*. Various kinds of brutality and
dysfunctional behaviour – including incest, murder and paedophilia –
feature in these narratives. The visceral element of McEwan's earliest
work (which continues in *The Comfort of Strangers* and also resurfaces
later, most notably in *The Innocent*) seems, with hindsight, to have a
literary-historical significance: while McEwan's early readers might
have struggled to find the 'moral' content of these discomfiting fictions,
he was quietly playing his part in reinvigorating the British literary
scene, and unsettling expectations concerning the subject matter
appropriate for fictional treatment.

The importance of these first three books should not be overstated.
They do, perhaps, interrogate the line that divides reason from passion
in such a way as to lay bare some of the codes that regulate social
behaviour. This is especially true of *The Cement Garden*; but it is not
a prominent element or effect of the short stories, which merely anticipate the richer treatment of similar topics in later books. However, in
these early works it is possible to detect the first appearance of several
of McEwan's major themes, including: the troubling elements of
masculinity; the suggestiveness of the 'new science'; and the analysis
of attitudes to nature.

A measure of McEwan's early notoriety is the speed with which he
appeared in critical histories of the short story. In an account of the
English short story of the 1970s, for example, Walter Evans rates

McEwan as 'undeniably one of the decade's better writers'. His discussion of various practitioners establishes a number of categories, the second and third of which are relevant to his account of McEwan: 'the second involves those newer writers who focus on the individual and the individual's fundamental problems; the third concerns newer writers for whom an individual's conflicts with a given society seem to be of first importance'. Attesting to the incipient social vision of the author, Evans argues that, in McEwan's stories, 'the second category verges toward the third' without 'quite crossing the barrier'.[1]

The degree to which we feel that barrier to be crossed in the short stories – and whether or not we agree with Evans that they are 'unrelentingly moral' – will determine the extent to which the stories foreshadow the achievements of his mature fiction, where the personal and the social interact in rich and surprising ways. For Evans, the stories in *First Love, Last Rites* are variations on the general theme of the psychological distortions produced by a society that victimizes and oppresses: our expectations about who the 'victim' is may be challenged, or even reversed, in the process. For Evans, *In Between the Sheets*, though 'a fine collection', is less successful since it is concerned with the 'revelation of the mundane horror spawned in between the sheets'. This 'complements the more varied horrors exposed in the earlier and better book'.[2]

In Clare Hanson's history, McEwan's stories are considered in relation to postmodernist fiction, and particularly the way in which personality is eroded where 'radical uncertainty' is created concerning the status of 'narrator-figures'.[3] Her observation is perceptive: the radical uncertainty about personality, raised through the cultivation of ambiguous narrator-figures, now seems a hallmark of British fiction since 1980.[4] Whether or not one would wish to call this 'postmodernist', it has a particular pertinence to the later trajectory of McEwan's career.

When Hanson's history appeared, McEwan had published two longer works of fiction, *The Cement Garden* and *The Comfort of Strangers*, prompting her to observe that 'both McEwan's novels or novellas are organised around a central, compelling image: both deal with bizarre personal and sexual relations in a context far removed from everyday life.'[5] One implication of this is that McEwan's early work makes effective use of the modern short story's traditional capacities, since this is a literary form often deemed to work best with a central organizing image or idea, or 'single effect', in Edgar Allan

Poe's enduring formulation.[6] The reason Hanson marks McEwan out as a key practitioner of short fiction, however, is his subject matter:

> It could be argued that McEwan's adoption of the short fiction and novella forms is bound up with [his] focus on our most private and usually well-guarded feelings. While short fiction does not deal exclusively with private emotion – inevitably the sense of privacy and exclusion depends on an implied social context – it can shed the weight of social commentary which seems inherent in the novel form.[7]

There seems to be some affinity between this view and Evans's opinion that McEwan does not fully cross the barrier between the focus on the individual and the treatment of the individual's social tussles. In the judgement of these short story critics, then, McEwan's early work establishes him as a skilled practitioner in a form that may allude to a broader social context, but which is particularly well suited to the investigation of the private realm.

Of course, most novels approach the social realm through individual responses, so the implicit comparison between short story (the more insular form) and novel (the more expansive) would require greater elaboration to establish the point at which story*ness* becomes novel-*ness* in the identification of the public in the private. Without space to rehearse these arguments here, I will, for the purposes of this discussion, simply accept the obvious point that the longer the fiction, the more scope the writer has for engaging the reader in broader themes – social, philosophical or political. The questions to address then are: how far do McEwan's short stories foreshadow his later concerns? And does this make them accomplished works in their own right, or apprentice-pieces, merely?

A related question is why McEwan's early work came to be characterized by reviewers and critics as literature of shock. The way this is viewed will determine how this work is evaluated. In an interview with John Haffenden, published in 1983, McEwan records his surprise at the reception of the early stories and the way in which critics concentrated on their shocking and macabre side: 'My friends, most of whom had a literary education, seemed to take for granted the field of play in the stories; they had read Burroughs, Céline, Genet, and Kafka, so that lurid physical detail and a sense of cold dissociation did not stun them.'[8]

If this seems a little disingenuous, that may be because McEwan, knowing perhaps that he must shock the sensibility of some reviewers, also knew that this should not be so. He was writing, after all, in a literary terrain that was established in Europe and the US. The 'shock', that is to say, might have been to a conservative perception of the British literary tradition and what it might encompass.

If there is something wilfully anarchic and iconoclastic in the short stories, the iconoclasm carries the desire to open up British literary culture. Perhaps this is the intellectual wing of the punk movement, catching a mood in which raw cultural forms are generated to disturb the status quo. This need not imply immaturity, of course: the intellectual underpinnings of anarchy posit considered social alternatives to political structures deemed to be corrupt or outmoded. Possibly, McEwan's stories embody a parallel form of literary anarchy since they imply the need to resuscitate British fiction – which was widely perceived to be moribund in the 1970s.

The seriousness of McEwan's early work has very much to do with this process of revitalization. The 1970s has often been seen as the decade that represents the nadir of British fiction. It is undeniable, for example, that the gathering economic crisis had a deleterious effect on publishing, and on the range of fiction that found an outlet. In this view, the emergence of writers like McEwan and Martin Amis, at the end of the decade, signalled a new renaissance. From the longer perspective of literary history, however, when the immediate effects of economic recession fade from view, the 1970s will surely be remembered more favourably, as the decade that saw the publication of important novels by Iris Murdoch, John Fowles, J. G. Farrell and David Storey, among others. Rather than a period of suppressed creativity, we might now see the fiction of the 1970s as embodying the continuation of a tradition which McEwan has a role in developing.

This, however, is to anticipate the trajectory that McEwan's career was later to take. Here the focus is the impact of this early work. Apropos of *First Love, Last Rites*, but also in relation to the 'jolting scenarios' of *The Cement Garden*, *The Comfort of Strangers* and *The Innocent*, Jack Slay defends McEwan's 'desire to shock' in these terms:

> McEwan's fiction implies that without squirming (and occasionally revelling) in the brutalities of everyday life, we become blind to them; by forcing us to witness the atrocities of contemporary society, McEwan also forces us to acknowledge them. And acknowledging them, he asserts, is only a step away from reforming them.[9]

Slay goes on to situate McEwan's early literature of shock in an era where this kind of strategy was frequent, as witnessed in the work of

Angela Carter, Martin Amis and J. G. Ballard, among others. Pondering the 'line between the shock that draws a curious audience and the shock that enlightens', Slay justifies books like *First Love, Last Rites* and Amis's *Dead Babies* (1975) by virtue of their function as a prelude to something else for each writer:

> As sole works, Amis's and McEwan's books probably would have been quickly forgotten; however, both authors have succeeded in developing the darker themes of those early works, proving that these shocks into literature were, in fact, the origins of a more profound social consciousness.[10]

This does sound a little bit like special pleading, justifying the earlier shocks because they were to mellow into something more tangibly constructive. What we need to consider instead are those signals within the stories that betray the process of revitalization I have discussed above. Invariably, this reveals a literary self-consciousness that can be submerged by the shock impulse.

The story 'Homemade' is a good example of this pointed, but submerged, literariness. There is an arresting moment in the story where the fourteen-year-old narrator articulates the malign intent behind the game of 'hide and seek' he is playing with his ten-year-old sister:

> By the time I reached the top of the stairs, . . . the blood having drained from brain to groin, literally, one might say, from sense to sensibility, by the time I was catching my breath on the top stair and closing my moist hand round the bedroom door-handle, I had decided to rape my sister.
> (*FL*, p. 19)

The reference to Jane Austen's *Sense and Sensibility* – a very different treatment of love and manners – casts an instant ironic shadow on this scene. That word sensibility also carries a slightly earlier literary-historical resonance that is pertinent: Austen was responding to the novel of sensibility in the eighteenth century, which had caused a seismic shift in perceptions of what a novel could encompass, introducing a range of emotions hitherto restricted by the more moralistic conventions of a developing literary form. In 'Homemade', McEwan uses his knowing narrator to imply a new seismic shift: here is a literature of shock that inverts the convictions of the sentimental novel, where natural human emotions were deemed worthy of celebration. This 'sensibility', of course, is stripped of emotion, to reveal an ugly core of base human response.

Yet McEwan's vision is strangely in keeping with the sentimental novel, too: where Samuel Richardson presented human emotions in tension with the social order, the overwhelming effect of *First Love, Last Rites* is to present ways in which social organization distorts or destroys a propitious human response. In this sense, McEwan's is a later stage in the same debate, where civilization has all but corrupted the emotional life, which is no longer seen as a vital resisting force. The shock, then, resides in the defeat of sensibility, which is, as much as anything, a literary-historical shock. McEwan's early readers could not have been unaware of the factual basis of the brutish topics that characterize his first collection – incest, paedophilia, child-murder, and so on – so there is no shock of sudden recognition.[11] Neither are these matters presented in an obscene or lurid way. The shock has to do, rather, with the gesture of presenting this material as the stuff of serious fiction. Allied to this is the problem consequent upon the manner of presentation, especially where the narrator is also the perpetrator of the violence. In such instances, it is hard to locate a position outside the perspective of violence, an alternative to the amoral view.

In the case of 'Homemade' we have an older narrator reviewing an episode from his past, much in the manner of the boyhood stories in James Joyce's *Dubliners* (1914), using a sophisticated mode of expression that is inconsistent with his earlier self. What then arrests our moral attention is the fact that this narrator fails to pass judgement on his scheme to rape his sister. Through the story, in fact, he shows little sign of progression; but what he does do is reinterpret his adolescent obsession with all things sexual, adding a new layer of descriptive intensity, as in this recollection of the rumours about a local girl who is free with her favours: 'Lulu Slim – but how my mind reels – whose physical enormity was matched only by the enormity of her reputed sexual appetite and prowess, her grossness only by the grossness she inspired, the legend only by the reality' (*FL*, pp. 12–13). The willingness of the narrator to think himself back into the experience, at the time of narration ('my mind reels') establishes a principle that is sustained throughout: he adds an amoral layer of descriptive intensity to revivify earlier sensations, and so the principle of sensation supplants sentiment or sensibility. Thus, the sensation of his first masturbation is vividly recreated: ' I was lifted by the scruff of the neck, my arms, my legs, my insides, haled, twisted, racked, . . . producing for all this two dollops of sperm' (*FL*, p. 11). In a similar reimagining, he describes his virginity as 'a total anathema, my malodorous albatross' (*FL*, p. 13), which is significant since the dilemma of the story is predicated on social and peer-pressure concerning sexual experience. Here the narrator appears to accept the logic of this pressure, but in excessive terms that imply an ironic view that is never fleshed out.

The self-ironizing is easy to detect, as in this comment on the rape: 'I felt proud, proud to be fucking, even if it were only Connie, my ten-year-old sister, even if it had been a crippled mountain goat I would have been proud to be lying there in that manly position, proud in advance of being able to say "I have fucked"' (*FL*, p. 23). The irony, however, is rootless – in the absence of a retrospective orientation that is reflective – so any alternative perspective has to be supplied in other ways, most especially by the implicit deliberation on innocence.

Notionally, the narrator is introduced into the adult world – masturbation, alcohol, horror movies, shoplifting – by his older friend Raymond. Yet Raymond emerges as the innocent who cannot endure frightening films, or stomach alcohol, or distinguish semen from spittle, or steal without being detected. Similarly, Connie has to show the narrator how to finish their game of 'Mummies and Daddies' since he is unable to penetrate her without her assistance. This inverse motif of innocence and experience – another traditional English literary topic – obliges us to reconsider the narrator's status. In desperately seeking experience he is also an innocent suffering from the pressure to conform, and in ways that suppress his emotional being. The only hint of remorse occurs at the end of the story where the narrator reflects 'I had made it into the adult world finally, I was pleased about that, but right then I did not want to see a naked girl, or any naked thing for a while yet' (*FL*, p. 24). The element of remorse, however, is diluted by the egotistical sense of personal failure and inadequacy, even though this reinforces the sense of broader, distorting social forces.

Of the stories in *First Love, Last Rites*, 'Solid Geometry' has served to consolidate the sense of shock associated with the book, mainly because it was the subject of a BBC ban when it was adapted for television.[12] The story's chief interest is that it is an early treatment of the opposition between the mystical or intuitive and the rational, an idea that assumes great importance in McEwan's later work. The rationalist here is the narrator who lives a vicarious sense of self-importance through editing his great-grandfather's forty-five volume diary and surrounding himself with his ancestor's effects, which include a penis preserved in formaldehyde. His wife repudiates his preoccupation, his 'crawling over the past like a fly on a turd', while he is equally vituperative concerning her 'junk-shop mysticism' (*FL*, pp. 31, 30). This fantastic tale centres on the narrator's discovery in his grandfather's papers of the proof of a geometrical plane without a surface, which enables him to effect his wife's disappearance by 'folding her up' in a position of yogic contortion, on the pretext of foreplay.

This use of a scientific theory for fantastic fictional ends – in order to rein in the fantastic, as it were – points towards *The Child in Time*, where the novel's entire structure hinges on the reader's semi-credulity about just such a process. Here, the importance lies in how the stark opposition between the narrator and his wife is subtly undermined. In its first appearance in his work, the opposition between the rational and the intuitive is already fluid. As McEwan observes, the narrator and his wife are the 'exaggerated repre-sentatives' of 'the highly rational and destructive' and 'the loving but self-deluded'. What makes the opposition interesting is McEwan's 'intended irony' that his narrator 'uses the very system ("the mathematics of the Absolute") to dispose of her, that Maisie endorses and he has repudiated' (*IG*, p. 12).

The most problematic story in the collection, perhaps, is 'Butterflies', which is bleak in every sense.[13] The setting is a desolate part of London, with no parks ('only car parks'), traversed by a 'brown canal which goes between factories and past a scrap heap' (*FL*, p. 62). The narrator is a dysfunctional and isolated individual who recounts the episode in which he drowns a little girl after forcing her to touch his penis. He has enticed her to walk with him by the canal, claiming they will see colourful butterflies, even though he has never seen a butterfly (or even a flower) on this route. As they walk, they pass a gang of youths, apparently preparing to roast a cat alive (*FL*, p. 71).

The unpleasantness of the setting is matched by the way in which the narrator unselfconsciously explains the sensations he feels as he relates the murder episode. Pausing to wipe the girl's face free of ice-cream, for example, he attests: 'I had never touched another person's lips before, nor had I experienced this kind of pleasure. It rose painfully from my groin to my chest and lodged itself there, like a fist pushing against my ribs.' (*FL*, pp. 69–70) The narrator clearly sees himself as a social victim, who repulses others and arouses their suspicions, but he has no conception of personal responsibility.

We are enticed for a moment to think that he betrays a glimmer of responsibility, when we read: 'over and over again I ran through what had happened, and what I should have done.' (*FL*, p. 73) The reader's assumption that this is a murderer wrestling with his conscience is instantly quashed, however. He is reflecting on an episode that has just occurred in the notional present of the narrative, three days after the murder, when he fortuitously trapped a stone beneath his foot, attracting the approval of some boys playing football. This could have been an entrée to their game, he feels, and perhaps to longer-term friendships. He regrets missing the opportunity, since 'opportunities are rare, like butterflies' (*FL*, p. 74). The reader is doubly wrong-footed, here: first, by the blind self-interest that might initially be taken as remorse; and, second, by the appropriation of the title-symbol in the name of this self-interest.

An earlier connotation of the butterfly is suggested in the murder scene, before the little girl realizes the narrator's deception, that there are no butterflies:

> Where the sunlight entered the tunnel a little way there was a flower growing from between the bricks. It looked like some kind of dandelion, growing out of a small tuft of grass.
> 'It's coltsfoot,' she said, and picked it and put it in her hair, behind her ear. I said,
> 'I've never seen flowers along here before.'
> 'There have to be flowers,' she explained, 'for the butterflies.' (*FL*, p. 71)

In context, this reads like a parable gone awry. In a tunnel, very much like the one in which the girl is killed, a flower blooms unexpectedly, raising the possibility that the narrator's lie about the presence of butterflies by the canal might be transformed into truth. (If there is one flower, there might be others.) This possibility is also quashed; but the simple symbolic flower, flourishing in this bleak industrial landscape, almost out of the sun's reach, epitomizes the tenuous hope that McEwan just keeps in view throughout the collection, the promise of sensibility that balances the depiction of sensation.

The most positive moment in the collection comes at the end of the title story, 'First Love, Last Rites', which concerns a teenage couple living in a fourth-floor room by a quayside. The story spans a summer which the narrator spends making eel traps. He and his girlfriend Sissel are enraptured with each other, but are tormented by a scratching, scrabbling sound behind the wall in the room where they make love. The narrator has a bizarre sexual fantasy concerning the chemistry of procreation, articulated as a creature that he feeds in the sexual act, a creature he associates with the sound in the wall (*FL*, pp. 90–1). Lacking parental guidance, the sexual idyll of these innocents begins to collapse when their domestic ineptitude turns the love nest squalid, and this is compounded by Sissel's mind-numbing factory work and the constant interruptions of her younger brother, also seeking refuge from their broken home.

The source of the scratching is eventually found to be a large rat, which, when killed, splits open to reveal five unborn young. The moment of catharsis produces immediate results: the narrator frees the only eel he has caught; Sissel resolves to give up her factory work; and her brother departs for a summer holiday. This allows the couple to reclaim their idyll: 'Sissel said, This afternoon let's clean the room up and then go for a long walk, a walk along the river dyke. I pressed the flat of my palm against her warm belly and said, Yes' (*FL*, p. 99). The pregnant rat is the epitome of the instinctive and unstoppable life process that has tormented and intrigued the narrator in his sexual fascination with Sissel (*FL*, p. 90). In the conclusion, the careful disposal of the dead rat, Sissel's tenderness towards it, and the decision to free the eel, point towards the couple's more conscious understanding of their role in the generation of, and care for, life.

Critics have tended to emphasize how the dead rat reveals 'its consanguinity with its killers'.[14] Yet, in the tacit recognition implied in the characters' responses to the rat, they are distinguished from it, and the blind life force it represents, since the new mood of responsibility asserts a specifically human quality. In the final lines, the hints of fresh home-building, and Sissel's pregnancy, reinforce this implicit humanism and the progression from teenage sexual obsession it represents.

There is a related passage in 'Homemade' where the narrator recounts the experience of attending cross-country race meetings as a spectator, specifically to support his friend Raymond. The efforts of those runners who finish far down the field present 'a vision of human futility' (*FL*, p. 16), he feels, though this is complicated in his perception of Raymond's mediocre achievements:

> And there beneath the brooding metropolitan sky, as if to unify the complex totality of organic evolution and human purpose and place it within my grasp, the tiny amoebic blob across the field took on human shape and yet still it held to the same purpose, staggering determinedly

in its pointless effort to reach the flags – just life, just faceless, self-
renewing life to which, as the figure jack-knifed to the ground by
the finishing line, my heart warmed, my spirit rose in the fulsome
abandonment of morbid and fatal identification with the cosmic life
process – the Logos. (*FL*, p. 17)

In the fondness for Raymond, and the empathy for his pointless efforts,
the narrator's larger vision of human futility is qualified. The 'tiny
amoebic blob' becomes individuated as Raymond, and the narrator's
spirit is able to rise in response to particularized human endeavour
within the frame of 'the cosmic life process', even if this empathy, this
'identification' is still perceived as 'morbid and fatal'.

The use of 'Logos' in this passage seems deliberately to throw up
a problem of interpretation, which also takes us to the heart of
McEwan's writing. As the *Oxford English Dictionary* explains, 'Logos'
had metaphysical and theological applications in the hands of Greek
philosophers, applications derived from the ordinary senses of 'reason'
and 'word'. It was also used in the New Testament as a designation
of Jesus Christ. The succinct definition offered by the *New Oxford
Dictionary of English* (1998) is this: 'the Word of God, or principle of
divine reason and creative order, identified in the Gospel of John with
the second person of the Trinity incarnate in Jesus Christ.' 'Logos',
then, creates a connection between 'Word' and world which has
a primary religious significance; and this hovers ironically over
this secular passage in 'Homemade', where the agnostic narrator
empathizes with the human compulsion to participate in 'the cosmic
life process', even though he can discern no ultimate purpose in it.

For the writer, this is symptomatic of an era where the connection
between 'Word' and world is indistinct, where it no longer seems
possible 'to unify the complex totality of organic evolution and human
purpose'. This is not quite the same thing as the poststructuralist
critique of Western thought, where emphasis on words as the expression of external reality – logocentrism – is held up as a fundamental
flaw. McEwan is working in the same territory, however, though his
critique is oriented more towards the modern consciousness which
cannot bridge Word and world.

Here, at the beginning of his career, McEwan tacitly announces the
writer's quest to reinvigorate the Word – in a secular sense – in a society
without evident collective values. The literature of shock thus emerges
as the first response to the absent bridge, where the focus on sensation
at the expense of sensibility is an admission of the difficulty of the task.

The writer's struggle in writing about moral topics in the 1970s is thus akin to the unathletic competitor's efforts in a cross-country race. Like McEwan's narrator in 'Homemade', we are asked to identify with the effort of those who may 'run themselves into the ground for nothing at all' (*FL*, p. 17). Of course, the self-consciousness is, itself, a marker of progression beyond futility, a recognition of the crucial moral conundrum that confronts the contemporary writer.

This narrator's ambivalent abandonment to the Logos, emptied of its transcendent significance, forms a pointed parallel with McEwan's attempt to put narrative fiction to some moral or ethical purpose, and this, in broad terms, is an accurate way of describing his career-long quest as a writer. It is a focus which also represents an interesting intervention in the debate about how literature may have supplanted the social function of religion since the late nineteenth century. McEwan's career would suggest a later phase in this debate, projecting the view that literature can no longer be taken to function as a form of spiritual substitute. The validity of literature has to be established anew.

In 'Pornography' from the second short story collection, *In Between the Sheets*, the disused church, now used as a pornographer's warehouse, indicates a very different substitute for religion. The story is about the destructive consequences of the objectification of human sexuality. Ostensibly, it is a simple and gruesome revenge story, in which the seedy O'Byrne, who works in his brother's pornography outlet in Soho, receives his come-uppance. He is two-timing two hospital workers, a trainee nurse and a Sister, and after he has knowingly infected them both with venereal disease, they plan to castrate him, using borrowed surgical equipment.

The title of the story invites us to speculate on the extent to which the story mimics pornographic codes, and is 'pornography' itself. Certainly, the simple revenge story, in which a tale of sexual deceit and extreme sado-masochism is concealed beneath the thin veneer of a tale of female retribution, would seem culpable: pornography masquerading as a feminist fable. Yet the 'feminist' reading cannot be taken seriously since the air of corruption pervades the story, infecting the depiction of the 'wronged' women, too. McEwan makes us see a connection between the wares of the pornography store, with magazines containing such features as 'piss-in-her-cunt letters', and the predilections of Lucy, O'Byrne's older 'victim', whose dominating sexual preferences include striking and verbally abusing him, and, on one occasion, urinating on his head and chest (*IBS*, pp. 6, 11): the pornographic imagination, the story insists, reduces men and women to this debasement, urinating on each other, literally as well as metaphorically.

In the scene preparatory to the planned castration, Lucy stimulates herself, in her excitement at the violence she is to commit (*IBS*, pp. 15–16); and when the fateful moment is due, O'Byrne seemingly allows himself to be retied to the bed, even though he has apparently freed an arm and could strike out (*IBS*, p. 18). (Here the story ends.)

The mutual pleasure in inflicting harm, together with O'Byrne's possible compliance in his impending emasculation, give the story the outlines of a simple parable: mutual degradation and self-destruction are consequent upon the commodification of sexuality. However, these outlines are obscured by the extent to which the story courts pornographic codes. This fact, brazenly announced in the title, expresses the recurring uncertainty in early McEwan about the role of literature.

The story that perhaps best expresses this doubt is 'Reflections of a Kept Ape', narrated from the point of view of an ape who has been the lover of his keeper, a writer called Sally Klee. She has rejected him and now spends her time vainly attempting to write a second novel, to repeat the phenomenal success of her first. The ape, meanwhile, remains desirous of winning his way back into her affections. He is presented as having all the physical and behavioural characteristics of an ape, while also being intellectually advanced and well-read. For Slay, the significance of the story resides in these human qualities, which lend the ape the status of a 'scorned lover', revealing 'McEwan's purpose' as 'the exposure of the sexual politics of human relations'.[15] Similarly, Ryan finds within the story a 'critique of stale sexual idioms and attitudes', while Malcolm considers the lovesick ape to be a creation that 'both satirizes and strips a layer of familiarity off human behavior'.[16]

There is, of course, a tradition of 'simian literature' designed to defamiliarize in this way.[17] However, the significance of the ape in McEwan's story suggests a rather different purpose. This is a story about creativity and gestation in which the ape plays a symbolic role. Sally Klee's successful novel concerns 'the attempts and bitter failures of a young woman to have a baby' (*IBS*, p. 20). It was a chance blockbuster, despite the disparaging reviews it received, yet it is clear that it was not an insightful book. The quotations from it that the devoted ape has committed to memory are banal, despite his conviction about the book's worth; and when he discovers that her strategy for overcoming writer's block consists of typing out her published book verbatim, he experiences a crisis of conviction:

> Having crafted one novel, would it suffice to write it again, type it out with care, page by page? (Gloomily I recycled nits from torso to mouth.) Deep in my heart I knew it would suffice and, knowing that, seemed to know less than I had ever known before. (*IBS*, p. 32)

Just as Sally Klee's (apparently) uninspired book about maternity has proved an artistic dead-end, so has its author's sexual interest in her ape – a parallel form of procreative inspiration – soon waned. The parallel between book and ape is far from tidy, but it is prominent enough to make this clearly a story about the dubious nature of literary publishing, where a follow-up book may be more a recycling of nits than a significant cultural event. McEwan seems to be signalling personal artistic doubts about repetition in this, his second collection of stories, about 'shocking' subjects.[18]

Not all of the stories have such resonance. 'Dead as They Come', for example, is a relatively 'flat' story, which offers no way around the deranged perspective of its narrator, a millionaire who recounts his infatuation with a shop mannequin that he buys and takes home to his bed. Believing the mannequin, his 'Helen', to be having an affair with his chauffeur, he eventually decides to 'rape' and 'murder' her. It is not a 'real' murder, in the world of the story, but the culmination of the narrative enables McEwan to imagine the perspective of an unhinged sex killer, perceiving intense pleasure in his victim as he rapes and suffocates her, pleasure matched by his own 'transfiguration' (*IBS*, p. 76). It is an unpleasant story, but it does prepare the ground for the richer treatment of the psychology of sexual violence in *The Comfort of Strangers*.

Probably the most powerful piece in *In Between the Sheets* is the title story. It is a third-person narrative, but is presented entirely from the perspective of the central character, a divorced writer.[19] The story concerns his preoccupations before and during the visit of his fourteen-year-old daughter who comes to stay with him, accompanied by her short and unattractive friend. The personal insecurities and inadequacies of the protagonist – including his sexual performance in the failed marriage – begin to converge on sexual speculation about his daughter (and her relationship with the threatening friend), until he seems to be on the verge of violating the daughter. On a trip to the

bathroom in the early hours of the morning he pauses to listen at the
girls' door, imaging he hears the sound that is, for him 'the frame of
all anxieties': that is, 'the sound of his wife in, or approaching, orgasm.'
(*IBS*, p. 94) His daughter awakes, frightened in the strange house, and
confronts him as he stands naked in the hallway. 'She could be a child
or a woman, she could be any age', he reflects (*IBS*, p. 95). Paternal
concern asserts itself, and he tucks her back in to bed. Murmuring
reassuring words until

> she was asleep and almost smiling, and in the pallor of her upturned
> throat he thought he saw from one bright morning in his childhood a
> field of dazzling white snow which he, a small boy of eight, had not dared
> scar with footprints. (*IBS*, p. 96)

The father defeats the sexual predator that, in response to his life's
lessons in sexual inadequacy, had been growing within him. Thus, the
precarious innocence of father and daughter is re-established.

As a final example from *In Between the Sheets*, I will consider
'Psychopolis', a variation on the theme that runs throughout both story
collections and, in various forms, throughout McEwan's oeuvre: it is
an examination of how artistic endeavour might contest the futility of
human relations, articulated especially through debased sexual activity.
The narrator is an Englishman abroad in Los Angeles, observing the
absent core of Western civilization at the front line, it seems. In the
opening scene, he recounts the episode in which he chained to the bed,
at her own request, his part-time girlfriend, Mary, co-owner of a
feminist bookstore. He manages to keep the promise she has extracted
from him, to remain deaf to her pleas to be released, by practising his
flute. Here he articulates his feelings of ineptitude as a flautist,
confirmed by poor technique and musicianship. His worst failing,
however, concerns his limited vision as a musician: 'above all I have no
ambition to play any other than the same half-dozen pieces and I make
the same mistakes each time' (*IBS*, p. 108).

Later, he recounts his sense of aimless panic in Los Angeles, where
the boredom the suburban sprawl induces seems to him representative
of human existence generally (*IBS*, pp. 117–18). He turns to his flute,
not for respite, 'more to confirm [his] state of mind than change it',
and practises his favourite Bach sonata. Acutely conscious of his
inadequacy, he feels 'the coherence of the piece becomes purely
imaginary' in his rendition. Still, he regards the allegro as his
'showpiece', even though he plays it 'with expressionless aggression'
(*IBS*, p. 118).

The other protagonists in the story contribute to the theme of human futility. The narrator's friend Terence is characterized, chiefly, through the episode in which his girlfriend persuades him to urinate in his trousers while dining in a restaurant, apparently to test his declaration that he would do anything for love of her, but really because her detested parents have just walked in, and she seems to wish to offend them in some way (*IBS*, pp. 115–16).

The narrator's neighbour George asks him over for a farewell dinner before he leaves Los Angeles, and the invitation is extended to Mary and Terence. The crisis of the evening is a heated debate about Christianity: George, a non-believer, is raising his boys as church-goers since he believes this will provide them with a 'coherent set of values that are as good as any other' (*IBS*, p. 128). The others articulate familiar feminist and Marxist attacks on Christianity, while George, sticking to his conviction that 'God, Guts, Guns made America great' reveals that he keeps a gun.

Terence effects a stunt where he points the gun at George (who is the only one to observe him remove the bullets) and pulls the trigger (*IBS*, pp. 130–2). The narrator's 'quite irrelevant' remark of 'who is it?' (*IBS*, p. 132), made in panic as the trigger is pulled, actually pinpoints the identity crisis that confronts the four protagonists, each of whom adopts an identity that does not fulfil them: Terence's attempt to complete a thesis on George Orwell is undermined by his lack of constancy or conviction, while Mary's feminism cannot contain the irruption of a sado-masochistic desire. These contradictions are the equivalents of George's secular 'faith' in the efficacy of organized religion.

The narrator, as we have seen, turns to the music for which he has no feeling, at crucial moments. At the party, he entertains the other protagonists with his Bach sonata, after they have rehearsed the reasons for distrusting Christianity. The question McEwan is asking, again, is: can art really supply an alternative to religion? The narrator's weariness suggests not: 'Why did I go on doing what I couldn't do, music from another time and civilisation, its certainty and perfection to me a pretence and a lie, as much as they had once been, or might still be, a truth to others.' It is 'the vast, fragmented city without a centre' that generates the dissonance, where 'discord battened to bar after bar of implied harmony and inexorable logic' (*IBS*, p. 133).

As Los Angeles stands for the contemporary more generally, the narrator's pessimism suggests a bleak view about the function of art within fragmented urban existence.[20] George, Terence and Mary act in mock-appreciation, 'in parody of concert-goers', calling out 'Bravo! Bravissimo!' and presenting him with 'an imaginary bouquet' (*IBS*, p. 134). Going through the motions produces something positive, just as George believes that his sons, even without faith, 'have this whole set of stories, really good stories, exotic stories, believable stories', as a consequence of their Church going (*IBS*, p. 128). McEwan's short stories explore this area of agnosticism in a self-conscious way, and, by virtue of that very self-consciousness, identify the conundrum that is at the heart of much of his work: how can literary art contest the anomie of the contemporary?

This is also the emphasis of McEwan's first novel, *The Cement Garden*, though, as with the short stories, critics have sometimes struggled to discern a moral dimension to the novel. David Malcolm, for example, has argued that 'the most shocking aspect of McEwan's short stories is, paradoxically, their lack of moral judgment'. He does find 'hints' that invite certain moral responses from the reader, but maintains that the 'uncomfortable' nature of the stories stems from the fact that many 'lack any moral center at all'. He finds an 'equally disturbing lack of moral focus' in *The Cement Garden*.[21]

The problem centres on the lack of a clear moral position emanating from a narrative point of view located clearly beyond the perverse obsessions of successive protagonists and first-person narrators. Kiernan Ryan acknowledges that there can be a moral purpose to the resulting ambiguity, if it can be said to 'oblige us to reflect on the mixed motives governing our own response as readers'.[22] However, the effect of this may be confined to enticing readers to share dubious motives that remain unexamined. For David Malcolm, if there is 'very little overt disapproval of characters and actions' in the stories, then it is 'the reader who brings moral attitudes to the story', since 'they are absent in the text itself'.[23]

Understandable though this reasoning is, it makes little sense in the context of twentieth- and twenty-first-century fiction, where the use of a moralizing narrative perspective has all but disappeared from the serious novel, and where unreliable or suspect first-person narrators are extensively used, and where readers have become used to other devices that order the moral universe of fiction. A central feature of McEwan's fiction, which becomes especially prominent in his mature works, is an ongoing examination of the novel's capacity to treat moral questions. There is nothing new in this kind of agnostic self-consciousness: since Henry James and Joseph Conrad we have become used to extended implicit deliberations about the capacity of the novel to stage dilemmas of personal morality, linked to broader ethical questions. What is, perhaps, distinctive about McEwan's moral deliberations is the degree to which he underscores his own uncertainty in this area, in ways that make the reader complicitous in the desire for a pattern or a resolution that does not emerge, or which emerges in perverse ways.

In *The Cement Garden* a prominent interpretative signpost is bestowed by the literary allusion to the story tradition in which children are put into a situation in which they must fend for themselves.[24] The key reference here is to William Golding's *Lord of the Flies*, a pessimistic tale of the savage that emerges within the child when free of social controls. This opposition between the savage and the social stands as a backdrop to McEwan's novel, where the relationship between the two is made more complex. One complication is that McEwan's children are not entirely isolated from the social world. They are abandoned by the successive deaths of their parents and try to keep their sense of family together by entombing their dead mother in concrete in the cellar of their isolated house; but two of the children are on the cusp of adulthood, and all are influenced by adult codes of familial behaviour, which become distorted in their independent existence, a process which culminates in the incestuous involvement of the eldest siblings.

The novel thus seems to explore an ambiguous area somewhere between the poles of social control and unfettered impulse, and the effect of this can be to interrogate the nature of these social controls. The ambiguity that results from the interrogation of social norms and codes also complicates and obscures the moral stance, of course. Slay argues, for example, that it is possible to perceive the experience of incest to be presented as a 'completely positive experience', since it 'is seen as "sick" and unnatural only by Derek, an outsider'.[25] Within the novel, however, there may be sufficient evidence to suggest how the distortion of the children's experience results in something 'unnatural'.

An important aspect of the novel, at the simple narrative level, is that the apparently dysfunctional elements of the family are carefully traced. The father's lack of pride in his eldest daughter's achievements, his vindictive humour directed towards his wife and children (which brooks no reciprocation), his intolerance of children's 'noise and chaos', are precisely evoked (*CG*, pp. 19, 14–15). The parents, in Jack's

testimony, had no friends outside the family, and the children subscribe to the 'unspoken family rule' that they should never bring friends
home (*CG*, pp. 21, 19). The overwhelming sense of parental oppression
is confirmed when Jack's mother warns him that masturbation is
damaging, and that 'every time . . . you do that, it takes two pints of
blood to replace it' (*CG*, pp. 27–8).

Left to their own devices, the children's games result in the
infantilizing and gender transformation of Tom, the promotion of Julie
to the maternal role, and the eventual incest between Julie and Jack,
which is the culmination of the book's Oedipal theme, since Julie is
identified by all as a surrogate mother.[26] One reading of this is that the
over-dependence on the family unit as a source of reassurance and
repair is an extension, merely, of the parents' regime: by damaging the
children emotionally, while simultaneously cutting the family unit off
from outside contact, the parents have established a dysfunctional
home in which emotional need and emotional damage have become
inseparable.[27]

Another way of viewing this is equally plausible, however. In
'normal' family life the path to sexual maturity involves moving away
from the family and, in a sense, discarding the parents who cannot
supply the young adult's sexual needs: someone else must be enlisted
for this. In *The Cement Garden*, McEwan has conceived of a situation
in which the family unit dissolves at precisely the point where Jack and
Julie are discovering their emergent sexuality. For them, there is no
family left to move away from; so, to meet the psychological need
that sexual maturity demands, they must reconstruct the bedrock of
family security – as something to reject – by becoming 'mummy' and
'daddy'. Without this process of reconstruction, they cannot establish
their respective sexual identities; but, of course, they cannot achieve this
through incest, either.

The novel's psychological power comes from this inversion: Jack
and Julie are driven to construct a parody of the family structure they
needed to react against in order to achieve maturity. The perverseness
of the novel might then seem to emanate from the way in which its
situation is contrived. At the same time, however, we realize that there
is a perverseness, from the family perspective, in 'normal' sexual
development: childhood nurturing ends with the new needs of puberty,
which point to the necessary rejection of family.

In the few gestures to the wider context, the novel indicates that the
perverseness that is its focus may be a wider phenomenon, and not

just the consequence of activity in one dysfunctional family in extraordinary circumstances. Although the family house stands alone, it had once stood in a row of other houses that were subsequently knocked down to prepare for a motorway that was never built (*CG*, p. 21). In a neighbouring street a few more houses remain, where most have been cleared to prepare for the building of four tower blocks: 'They looked even older and sadder than our house. All down their concrete sides were colossal stains, almost black, caused by the rain. They never dried out' (*CG*, p. 22). The situation of urban desolation is established as general, and this makes the predicament of Jack and his siblings seem less extraordinary and more indicative, in extreme form, of a broader social malaise – or inherent destructiveness – rooted in human development.

The cement garden emerges as a very clear metaphor for this situation. It is the plan of the obsessive father – and, thus, an expression of the psychological disorder, concealed as order, that the family, as a whole, embodies. For Jack, 'mixing concrete and spreading it over a levelled garden was a fascinating violation' (*CG*, p. 16). The father's actions, especially the 'violation' of the family garden, actually antici- pate the rejection of family security that children must all move towards. The situation is then distorted only insofar as the father has, symbolically, anticipated the transgression that the children needed to achieve for themselves.

What is true for the situation of the protagonists in *The Cement Garden* has a parallel in the situation of the novelist. McEwan explores this question by the characteristic expedient of making one of his characters representative of the writer's situation, though this is done in a way that is not immediately obvious. Malcolm observes the mismatch between the spare, learned prose style that characterizes Jack's narrative, and Jack's putative identity as a callow, sexually obsessed fifteen-year-old who has never finished reading a book before becoming engrossed in the science-fiction novel he is given on his fifteenth birthday.[28] This is a significant stylistic feature, revealing a parallel between the character and author, both restricted by circumstance. Here we might detect McEwan's response not just to the anomie of contemporary society, but also to the novelistic tradition into which he is writing himself.

However, if the metaphorical cement garden stands for the tradition of the British novel at the end of the 1970s – or can be taken as an ironic figure for the way that tradition is perceived at the time – it also suggests a deliberate perverseness in the author, who has delighted in finding something disturbing and representative there. His next novel, *The Comfort of Strangers*, extends and concludes this phase of writing, in which a contemporary malaise is discovered beneath the violent, the perverse.

Notes

1 Walter Evans, 'The English Short Story in the Seventies', Dennis Vannatta, ed., *The English Short Story 1945–1980: A Critical History* (Boston: Twayne Publishers, 1985), pp. 120–72 (pp. 124, 140).
2 Evans, 'The English Short Story in the Seventies', pp. 140–3.
3 Clare Hanson, *Short Stories and Short Fictions, 1880–1980* (London: Macmillan, 1985), p. 142.
4 Other names that spring immediately to mind in connection with the uncertain narrating-persona are Martin Amis and Kazuo Ishiguro.
5 Hanson, *Short Stories and Short Fictions*, p. 165.
6 Edgar Allan Poe, 'Review of *Twice-Told Tales*', *Graham's Magazine*, May 1842, reprinted in Charles E. May, ed., *Short Story Theories* (Ohio University Press, 1976), pp. 45–51 (p. 48).
7 Hanson, *Short Stories and Short Fictions*, p. 165.
8 'John Haffenden Talks to Ian McEwan', *The Literary Review* (June 1983), pp. 29–35 (p. 29). This interview was reprinted in Haffenden's *Novelists in Interview* (London: Methuen, 1985), pp. 168–90.
9 Jack Slay, *Ian McEwan* (New York: Twayne, 1996), p. 9.
10 Ibid., p. 11.
11 It is true, however, that child abuse was not prominent in the public consciousness of the 1970s to the degree that it was in the 1990s and beyond.
12 McEwan adapted the story in 1978 when it was commissioned for a series called 'The Other Side'. (It was written in 1973.) The ban, of March 1979, made reference to 'grotesque and bizarre sexual elements in the play'. See the 'Introduction' to *The Imitation Game: Three Plays for Television* (1981; London: Picador, 1982), pp. 12–13. A later adaptation of 'Solid Geometry', starring Ewan McGregor, was screened on Grampian Television and Channel 4 in 2002.
13 In the interview with Haffenden, McEwan was later to brand the story as 'appalling', 'a story written by someone who had nothing to do with children.' He went on to explain how the writer's imagination is crucially shaped by parenthood: 'As children come more into your life the possibility of their death is not something you can play with lightly.' See 'John Haffenden Talks to Ian McEwan', 30.
14 Ryan, *Ian McEwan*, p. 10.

15   Slay, *Ian McEwan*, p. 54.

16   Ryan, *Ian McEwan*, p. 16; Malcolm, *Understanding Ian McEwan*, p. 42.

17   Ryan suggests that McEwan's story 'began life as a pastiche of Kafka's "Lecture to an Academy"'. See *Ian McEwan*, p. 16. A more recent example of this genre is Will Self's *Great Apes* (1997).

18   Slay explains the different order in which McEwan's early work appeared on each side of the Atlantic: 'Released by Jonathan Cape in January 1978, *In Between the Sheets* was McEwan's second published work (in the United States, the collection was published as McEwan's third work, with Simon and Schuster releasing it in August 1979, almost a year after the publication of the American edition of *The Cement Garden*).' See Slay, *Ian McEwan*, p. 51.

19   The fact that this character has written a book about 'evolution' suggests an interest in popular science, an enduring preoccupation for McEwan.

20   Richard Brown offers an intriguing account of how America might stand for the contemporary more generally in this story, and in other earlier work by McEwan: as the epitome of an irrational postmodern urban capitalism. See Richard Brown, 'Postmodern Americas in the Fiction of Angela Carter, Martin Amis and Ian McEwan', in Anna Massa and Alistair Stead, eds, *Forked Tongues? Comparing Twentieth-Century British and American Literature* (London: Longman, 1994), pp. 92–110.

21   Malcolm, *Understanding Ian McEwan*, pp. 42, 44.

22   Ryan, *Ian McEwan*, p. 13.

23   Malcolm, *Understanding Ian McEwan*, p. 43.

24   Jack Slay's list of novels based on 'the familiar plot of children suddenly abandoned and isolated' includes R. M. Ballantyne's *The Coral Island* (1857), Richard Arthur Warren Hughes's *High Wind in Jamaica* (1929), and Arthur Ransome's *Swallows and Amazons* (1930). See Slay, *Ian McEwan*, p. 36. In children's literature the situation of isolated children is more or less the norm, in fact.

25   Slay, *Ian McEwan*, p. 46.

26   For a fuller treatment of the Oedipal and other psychoanalytical themes in McEwan see Christina Byrnes, *The Work of Ian McEwan: A Psychodynamic Approach* (Nottingham: Paupers' Press, 2002).

27   Ian McEwan has suggested that the drought of 1976 had a significant impact on his conception of this oppressive novel. (From a radio interview: 'Out of the Blue: How Writers Gain Inspiration From Weather', Radio 4, 3 March 2005.) The oppressiveness of the work is caught well in the 1992 film version, written and directed by Andrew Birkin.

28   For Malcolm, the 'slippage' between stylistic levels 'can be seen as a self-referential device, advertising the figure of the implied author behind all the verisimilar details of the text'. See *Understanding Ian McEwan*, p. 51.

3

Dreams of captivity:
The Comfort of Strangers

The Comfort of Strangers, McEwan's second longer work of fiction, is an enactment of the inner lack that results when individuals adopt value systems or codes by which to live, having paid little heed to their own desires and needs. Simultaneously, it addresses the problematic relationship between values, ideas and literature. The novella is profitably considered alongside the screenplay for the film *The Imitation Game*: together these pieces comprise a significant intellectual phase in McEwan's work. The screenplay is an explicit attempt to address the impact of the Women's Movement of the 1970s; but both works point to a cul-de-sac in his career as a novelist: the screenplay is the result of a project that was originally planned as a novel, while the novella, *The Comfort of Strangers*, though a fine piece of writing, demonstrates that the author is unable, as yet, to generate vital social resonances through the medium of fiction. This work – perhaps his most disturbing book – is the culmination of his bleak early fiction, with its emphasis on violence and psychosis.

The screenplay for *The Imitation Game* contains McEwan's most explicit treatment of feminist issues. The social issues that inspire the piece have a broader relevance to the post-war period, but the author's comments clearly indicate that the feminism of the 1970s was a direct influence. 'The Women's Movement', he writes in the introduction to the published screenplay, 'had presented ways of looking at the world, both its present and its past, that were at once profoundly dislocating and infinite in possibility'. In response, his aim was to write a novel 'which would assume as its background a society not primarily as a set of economic classes but as a patriarchy.' Patriarchy, he felt, 'could be a still richer source' than the English class system – which 'had once been a rich source for the English novel' – since 'men and women

have to do with each other in ways that economic classes do not.'
(*IG*, p. 14)

The novel that McEwan wanted to write, partly out of a sense of
dissatisfaction with his fiction up to *The Cement Garden*, evolved into
The Imitation Game (*IG*, pp. 14, 18). The historical dialogue opened up
by the Women's Movement is enacted in McEwan's screenplay, with
a central female character who carries contemporary standards, and
demands for equality, back into the wartime era. Rather than producing
a sense of anachronism, this is an economical route to a familiar kind
of feminist rethinking of the post-war period, in which the war emerges
as a watershed in female ambitions: having carried the war effort on
the home front, even if only in menial labour, women would baulk
at those social pressures that might seek to reconfine them to the
domestic sphere. As part of his research for the film, McEwan
interviewed ex-Auxiliary Territorial Service (ATS) and Women's Royal
Naval Service (WRNS) women, and found that ambivalent memories
about the war were a commonplace: 'despite the hardships of military
life, the crowded living quarters, low wages, lack of privacy, exhausting
work, occasional bullying, the one word which recurred in their
reminiscences was "independence". Without the war they would
normally have expected to move straight from their father's house to
their husband's' (*IG*, p. 17).

That sense of the right to economic independence is one aspect of
Cathy Raine's expectations in *The Imitation Game*; but there is a
further demand that takes the screenplay in a more complex direction.
The piece centres on Cathy's refusal to accept that her contribution
to the war effort should be limited to repetitive labour in a munitions
factory. She decides to join the army, and then opts to be a wireless
operator (intercepting enemy code) rather than a cook or a driver.
At each stage her ambitions are hampered by an external sexual
appraisal of her role. Her mother thinks that the ATS has a bad
reputation and is no place for 'a respectable girl' (*IG*, p. 94). Similarly,
her boyfriend Tony thinks her decision signals the end of their
relationship, partly on account of 'the kind of temptations' he feels she
will encounter (*IG*, p. 95).

While working as a code interceptor, Cathy has an altercation with
a publican who feels that Cathy and her friend Mary, drinking alone,
are lowering the tone of his 'respectable pub'. He slaps Cathy's face –
'*the cure for hysteria*', as the stage direction puts it – and she knees him
sharply in the groin in response (*IG*, p. 117). This is the most pointed

moment where behavioural codes of the 1940s clash memorably with those of the 1970s or 1980s.

Escaping a court martial for assault, Cathy is demoted and sent to work as a general skivvy at Bletchley Park. Here, however, she is closer to the heart of the code-breaking process that fascinates her, and which seems to represent genuinely important war work. She responds to the advances of Turner, partly modelled on Alan Turing, the brilliant mathematician who worked on the German Enigma codes at Bletchley. Following an unsuccessful sexual encounter, Turner feels humiliated and reacts venomously to Cathy, accusing her wildly of plotting his inadequacy out of jealousy for his position: 'you know all the secrets', she had said to him, pillow talk to forgive him for his nervous lie about prior sexual experience, but which he chooses to reinterpret as vindictive (*IG*, p. 139).

Left alone in Turner's room, Cathy is found perusing secret files and is locked up on suspicion of spying, partly on Turner's testimony. She comes to the conclusion that her crime is to have exposed Turner's sexual inadequacy (even though she found his weakness endearing), and that the defensiveness about the exposure of this secret parallels the general conspiracy to keep women out of the war, confined to the status of passive sexual objects: 'if the girls fired the guns as well as the boys', the male sense of the 'morality' of war would evaporate; men 'would have no one to fight for' and 'war would appear to them as savage and as pointless as it really is.' (*IG*, p. 142)

Cathy's earlier elation at the war is explained by the screenplay's feminist dimension. This apparently inappropriate response, which causes her to wake early with excitement each morning, 'like a seven-year-old on Christmas day', is rooted in her intimation that 'everything is about to change forever.' (*IG*, p. 90)

The title was inspired by 'a magazine piece on machine intelligence' written by Alan Turing, and published in 1950, in which 'he proposed the "imitation game" as an operational procedure for approaching the question Can Machines Think?' (*IG*, p. 15) In the playscript Turner expounds the theory: there are three players in the imitation game, a man and a woman, hidden from the third player, their interrogator. The interrogator's task is to establish which is the man and which is the woman; the man's task is to try and confuse the interrogator, while the woman's is to assist. The purpose of the exercise is to answer the question: 'what will happen when a machine takes the part of the man in the game?' Turner asks: 'will the interrogator decide wrongly as often when the game is played like this as he does when the game is played with a man and a woman?' (*IG*, pp. 125–6).

The imitation game, underpinned by a preconceived expectation of gender traits, is clearly a metaphor for the imposition of set gender roles. Cathy's crime has been to confuse the identification of these roles, when it was her place to assist the process of recognition. The idea of the interchangeability of man and machine in the game, in the context of wartime code-breaking, makes a neat connection between patriarchal power and secrecy, and this is clearly the link that inspires the writing. In his introduction McEwan ponders the traditional exclusion of women from warfare, 'just as they had been excluded, by clearly stated rules written by men, from government, higher education, the professions, trade guilds, the priesthood and from inherited property; in effect, until recent times, from citizenship.' McEwan's observation of the circularity of patriarchy is the most arresting aspect of his analysis, notably where he suggests why women were necessary for the conduct of war: 'their moral and emotional commitment was vital, for they were the living embodiment of what the men fought to protect from the Enemy' (*IG*, pp. 16–17). Patriarchy is here presented as a self-perpetuating and self-justifying system: the secrecy and power of patriarchy governs the conduct of war; it also determines the subjugation of women, and marks them out as 'other' in moral and emotional terms, and in a way that produces the rationale for war.

This is, of course, a familiar feminist understanding of the relationship between patriarchy and power which, in the treatment it gives rise to, seems rather blunt: Cathy functions as a representative woman, punished by agents of a larger system, and this is not a treatment that facilitates more subtle or nuanced interactions. Later, in 1989, McEwan was to characterize *The Imitation Game* as 'a polemic about gender and power.' (*MA*, p. xxiv) However, it is enriched by the dialogue between two overlapping versions of post-war feminism: the politicized feminism of the Women's Movement in the 1970s, with its specific demands for equality, contained within the longer, historical account of how wartime experience accelerated the process that made second-wave feminism inevitable. This produces apparently anachronistic moments – such as Cathy kneeing the publican in the groin – that serve to emphasize the change in perceptions over a forty-year period, as well as the connections between women's experiences in the two eras. Even so, despite these admirable effects, there is a bluntness about the politics of McEwan's screenplays which he has made the subject of an important deliberation on forms of writing.

Speculating on 'why writing dialogue in play form should encourage an engagement with social conflicts and values', McEwan wonders if the concentration on 'what people say and do' means that the writer is 'drawn into behaviour and motive, and through them to underlying values.' (*MA*, p. xxiv)[1] Novel-writing emerges from this discussion as a different process, in which the writer ought not to begin with underlying ideas or values:

> The problem with starting out with an idea you want to sell, however decent and ennobling it may be, is that it reverses the imaginative order from which the novel takes its life; a moral or political scheme draws you away at the very beginning, at the moment of inception, from the specific, from the detail, from the strange combination of details that give novels their curious power. (*MA*, p. x)

McEwan is insistent that this principle, far from denying the novel's capacity to engage with the political, is actually the guarantor of its political potency. For the novel,

> it is precisely its expressive freedom and the capability it has of naming everything, exploring every corner of human experience, that make it a natural opponent of political systems, tyrannies and cant. The successful or memorable novels we think of as 'political' are always written against a politics. (*MA*, p. xi)

This bears some resemblance to that familiar and long-standing aesthetic conviction, which has been voiced by critics as well as novelists, that literary effects are destroyed by partisan political writing. Perhaps the best known of these critiques is Engels' appreciation of how Balzac reveals the weaknesses of royalist feudal France, despite the fact that he was a loyalist.[2]

In McEwan's statement, however, it is not the suppression of the writer's intention or affiliation that is identified as the key to successful political writing; rather, it is the necessarily exploratory – or anti-systemic – nature of novelistic discourse that is deemed capable of producing something more richly 'political'.

The Comfort of Strangers is a conscious enactment of this principle, and an interesting work to compare with *The Imitation Game*. The politics that it is superficially written 'against' – the left-liberal thinking about society and about gender that may be more of a badge of identity than a response to personal experience – yields to a more problematic picture of gender relations.

Set in Venice (the reader is left to deduce this), the novella draws on a long literary tradition in which that city is a mysterious and sometimes threatening place. Here the claustrophobic city backdrop mirrors the inner malaise of protagonists Colin and Mary. McEwan is interested in how the veneer of ideology – the assertion of an insubstantial intellectual feminism – fails to control or suppress deeper, destructive sexual desires. It is this lack of self-knowledge that facilitates the destruction of their relationship, and the death of Colin at the hands of the murderous patriarch, Robert. The work's principal theme is psychological, but it also contains an early observation about the political failure of liberal sentiment in the Thatcher era.

A summary of *The Comfort of Strangers* may suggest a salacious horror tale. It tells the disturbing story of a couple on holiday in Venice, whose aimlessness and evident lack of inner resource mark them out as victims. Colin and Mary have been together for seven years, but do not live together. She has children by an earlier marriage, but seems strangely disconnected from them: her postcards home remain unposted. Colin and Mary hold strong left-liberal political views – his more socialist than feminist, hers more feminist than socialist – but seem lacking in conviction, or even understanding, about their private lives. They are stalked by the sinister English expatriate Robert, whose Canadian wife is confined to their upstairs flat, having been invalided by Robert's sexual violence. Unable to resist the strange allure of the machismo Robert, Colin and Mary willingly go back to Robert and Caroline's flat, after an unnerving earlier visit, and Colin is murdered in front of a drugged Mary, who then, in her befuddled state, witnesses some kind of depraved sexual activity that involves the corpse.

The novel contains what is probably the most disturbing moment of violence in all of McEwan's work; but the power of the narrative resides not in its ability to shock; rather, the truly disturbing element – and the locus of the book's seriousness – lies in the psychological anatomy of a type. McEwan traces the psychological vacuum that necessarily results when individuals order their lives according to codes of behaviour that are untested at a personal level: where, that is, public convictions obscure private needs.

In the interview with John Haffenden (1983), McEwan gives an account of having recently attended 'a *Marxism Today* conference about eroticism and the Left'. This account is revealing because the conference produced a situation in which McEwan had the opportunity to articulate some of the ideas that had inspired *The Comfort of Strangers*, and to present them in debate with the kind of audience the novel seems designed to reach ('a broad coalition of socialists and feminists'). McEwan acknowledges the clumsiness of the 'extempore' speech that he gave, but it is the reaction to the broad point 'about eroticism not being totally amenable to rationalism' that is instructive:

> I got on to incredibly dangerous ground when I suggested that many women probably have masochistic fantasies and that many men probably have sadistic fantasies, which are acted out in private but never spoken about in any kind of public debate.

McEwan went on to suggest that 'it would be far better in a relationship to embrace this than to deny it, and that true freedom would be for such women to recognise their masochism and to understand how it has become related to sexual pleasure. The same was no less true for male masochists.' The response to this account of 'sexual fantasy' was predictable: 'the whole room exploded' and McEwan was accused of 'providing a "rapist's charter" and for poaching on forbidden territory – women's experience'. He 'came away feeling terribly bruised because I had been very inarticulate, as one is when speaking against such hostility'.[3] The hostility of the closed mind assumes increasing importance in McEwan's work; but it is important, here, to avoid the label 'political correctness', which assumed currency in the 1990s, and to put this experience in the context of McEwan's evolving response to certain oppositional tendencies in British social and political life in the broader post-war context.

The 'very difficult argument' that McEwan was trying to make to the delegates at the *Marxism Today* conference concerns those 'desires – masochism in women, sadism in men – which act out the oppression of women in patriarchal societies but which have actually become related to sources of pleasure.'[4]

An important issue is the extent of McEwan's feminism. In a thoughtful application of a feminist psychoanalytical perspective, Judith Seaboyer finds in the novella 'an exploration of the violent psychic dreams through which we imagine ourselves into existence as gendered subjects.' Seaboyer's is a detailed reading that finds fertile material, for the particular critical orientation, in such things as the depiction of Venice as a confusing, labyrinthine space, and the treatment of voyeurism and photography.

I am not convinced, however, that that the novella reveals an urgent 'polemic' to correspond with 'the narratives of psychoanalysis' that disrupt the 'dominant fiction' of Western patriarchy. Such a reading is certainly possible – forceful, even; but it would be a symptomatic reading of McEwan's more opaque treatment of gender politics, rather than one that tallies with any discernible polemic.[5] Indeed, while recognizing that Seaboyer is persuasive in her suggestion that Robert's trauma parallels 'the trauma faced by patriarchal culture at the end of the twentieth century', disrupted by 'feminism and the development of gender politics', we should remember that the novella is premised on the intellectual limits of these developments.[6] There is also the hint that Robert's father is just as confused about his gender identity as his son – for example, when Robert recollects that his father touched up his greying moustache 'with a little brush . . . such as ladies use for their eyes' (*CS*, p. 32): Robert's trauma may be a historical repetition, rather than a consequence of second-wave feminism. Through Colin and Mary, however, the focus is on that intellectual moment. Both are in favour of feminist principles; but their engagement with gender politics has taught them nothing about how their fantasies have been constructed. They stand for a brand of 'progressive' thinking that is confident in discussion, but useless in practice.

The novella's setting is well suited to this purpose of exposing psychological inadequacy since the evocation of Venice as a menacing and claustrophobic city is well achieved. Indeed, the brooding presence of the setting inspires Slay to suggest that it 'is portrayed as the fifth character of the novel'.[7] The most obvious twentieth-century literary antecedent in which Venice is presented as a place of malaise is probably Thomas Mann's *Death in Venice* (1912).[8] Like Aschenbach, Colin and Mary seem to desire their own destruction at some deeper level, and this makes the parallel striking. It is Daphne du Maurier's story 'Don't Look Now' (1971), however – and the still more sinister film by Nicholas Roeg that it inspired – that seems to many readers to lie behind the novella. However, it is important to note that McEwan, responding to a question about this apparent influence, claimed not to have seen the film or to have read the du Maurier story when the novella was written.[9] There is, in any case, a long Western tradition of writing about Venice as a place of labyrinthine danger.[10] Because the setting is unnamed, however, we are tacitly instructed not to associate the sense of threat with a particular location: the threat, rather than an attribute of place, is human sponsored; and it comes from within, as well as without.

It is easy to view Robert as simply the embodiment of an extreme patriarchal principle. Indeed, McEwan has indicated that he thinks of him 'more as a cipher than as a character', and there is a sense in which his exaggerated masculine views help establish 'the premise of the novel'.[11] Robert's reverential collection of his father's and grandfather's effects – which Colin ironically calls 'a museum to the good old days' – functions as a kind of shrine to a particular kind of patriarchal thinking. After showing Colin the assorted artefacts – his grandfather's seal and opera glasses, his father's brushes, pipes and razors, the favourite novels of both men, in first editions, bearing 'the mark of a distinguished bookseller' – Robert is moved to lament the passing of an age when men 'understood themselves clearly' and 'were proud of their sex' (*CS*, pp. 74–5). For Robert, the changes that feminism has brought involve a confusion of roles, producing unhappiness for all – self-loathing for men and self-deception for women: 'even though they hate themselves for it, women long to be ruled by men. It's deep in their minds. They lie to themselves. They talk of freedom, and dream of captivity' (*CS*, p. 76).

This scene ends with Robert punching Colin in the stomach with 'a relaxed, easy blow which, had it not instantly expelled all the air from Colin's lungs, might have seemed playful' (*CS*, p. 77). The sudden violence, which causes Colin to collapse, and from which he takes some time to recover, punctuates the scene by undermining Robert: his conviction of the rightness of masculine impulse seems, in his mind, to sanction unpredictable violence. The relationship between Robert and Caroline is also constructed through Robert's distorted masculinity. They have embraced their respective roles of aggressor and victim, and embark on a spiral of sexual violence that culminates, Caroline reports, in Robert breaking her back in the apparent attempt to kill her (*CS*, p. 118).

Robert's condemnation of feminism is based on the view that something fundamental and permanent in gender identity has been overlaid by something ephemeral: that a false kind of socialization has obscured a deeper psychological need. McEwan sidesteps the nature versus nurture impasse this implies by presenting Robert as the product of key instances of socialization, rather than as the embodiment of a monolithic masculine principle that is, at least, coherent on its own terms. Robert recounts to Colin and Mary the episode from his childhood where his sisters, paying him back for his insufferable priggishness, stuff him with laxative, chocolate and lemonade before locking him in his father's study. The predictable results leave the study in the state of a 'farmyard', and earn Robert beatings and prolonged disfavour (*CS*, p. 39).

Robert is a victim in this episode in various ways. The sisters hate him because, as his father's favourite, he is made to pronounce the father's strict judgements, at the age of ten, on his older sisters' clothing and leisure activities, 'without knowing' that he is 'being used' (*CS*, p. 33). A complex of inequality and patriarchal control generates Robert's unpopularity. The scene of revenge is also shaped by the father's control, since he has forbidden Robert from having 'sweet things, especially chocolate' on the grounds that they make boys 'weak in character, like girls' (*CS*, p. 36). Thus, the temptation that makes him vulnerable to the vengeful sisters is sponsored by the father, and the episode is presented as formative of his misogynistic world-view.

Reading the scene from a psychoanalytical point of view, the defiling of the father's inner sanctum might suggest a repressed desire to displace the father. For Seaboyer, in the later murder scene Robert 'defiles the patriarchal house as he had once defiled his father's study', as a subconscious drive towards self-destruction becomes manifest. In this reading, Robert's conscious desire to destroy the effeminate Colin enables him 'to step into his father's shoes and punish his failed, effeminate self' in an act of 'ultimate transgression' that 'will guarantee the ego's exposure and destruction at the hands of the law, as the symbolic father.'[12]

McEwan certainly places emphasis on the element of self-defeat in the patriarchal control of the father. Robert's inability to stomach sweet things, as well as his yearning for them, are both produced by the father's strictures, so in this sense the father is responsible for the defilement. And, of course, the challenge is a conscious act by the disgruntled daughters who plan the flouting of the father's rules and the defilement of his study. Robert's recollection implies an understanding of the father's cruelty; yet the identity he has established for himself implies a reverential embrace of his example. The episode condenses a sense of disastrous gender confusion. There is clearly significance in his hankering as a boy for that which his upbringing brands as feminine: it is the repressed feminine aspect of his identity that he simultaneously yearns to foster and deny.

Once this principle has been installed, it is easy to see that Robert's psyche is governed by gender confusion stemming from his failure to live up to his own masculine ideal. Caroline confides to Mary that

Robert's sexual violence began when his infertility was diagnosed (*CS*, p. 116). While she is in hospital with her broken back, Robert buys a bar (*CS*, p. 118) that is presented as a stereotypical gay bar in the scene where Robert invites Colin and Mary for a drink: the customers seem exclusively male, dressed in tight clothes and favouring a particular 'virile, sentimental song' on the juke-box. 'Thank God I'm not a man', jokes Mary, when she has assessed the clientele (*CS*, pp. 28, 29, 110). When Robert takes Colin back to the bar, he holds his hand, parades him in front of his acquaintances, telling everyone that they are lovers (*CS*, pp. 108, 110).

Of course, Robert's indoctrinated sense of male superiority does not necessarily preclude a theatrical and virile form of homosexuality; but it seems significant that the aggressiveness to Caroline dates from the discovery of his own infertility, and that the purchase of the bar dates from Caroline's hospitalization, when they had agreed 'to be sensible' in future, and when 'Robert was putting all his energy into the bar' (*CS*, p. 118). In each case, his masculinity seems to be channelled into an extreme or exaggerated form of sexual expression.

Mary and Colin's shared lack of purpose stands in marked contrast to the volatile assertiveness of Robert, a contrast that produces the dramatic tension in the book. Their malaise has literary antecedents for characters visiting Venice, but McEwan is really interested in other, identifiable causes for their inner vacuity. Each one has a strong theoretical position that informs their perception of society. For Mary, patriarchy is 'the most powerful single principle of organization', while for Colin 'class dominance' is 'more fundamental' (*CS*, p. 84). (This is the same competition for authority that McEwan claimed to have resolved – in favour of the feminist model – in composing *The Imitation Game*.) They are presented as left-liberal thinking people, whose ideas are dry, theoretical, untested: 'when they talked of the politics of sex, which they did sometimes, they did not talk of themselves' (*CS*, p. 17). The presence of Robert soon begins to affect their unconscious lives. Indeed, before they have met him, his stalking activities seem already to have alerted them at some deeper psychological level to the sexual fascination they are beginning to exert: they dress for dinner 'meticulously and without consulting the other, as though somewhere among the thousands they were soon to join, there waited someone who cared deeply how they appeared' (*CS*, p. 11).

Colin and Mary find their sex life reinvigorated after their encounter with Robert. A four-day spell confined to their hotel ensues, their lives governed by a new-found sexual intimacy that is also tainted by sadistic and masochistic fantasies: Mary imagines having Colin's limbs amputated so that she can keep him indoors 'exclusively for sex', while he imagines a machine that 'would fuck her, not just for hours or weeks, but for years, on and on . . . till she was dead . . . till Colin, or his solicitor, switched it off '. McEwan emphasizes the mutual fascination with these 'stories that came from nowhere, out of the dark, stories that produced moans and giggles of hopeless abandon' (*CS*, p. 86).

It is possible to see Colin and Mary as, essentially, empty vessels whose sexual imagination is led in the direction suggested by the influence of Robert, before whom they are 'mesmerized' (*CS*, p. 54). There is certainly an impression in the book that the pair are unable to react assertively to their circumstances, or, in their dazed state, to interpret what is happening around them. This is mainly due to the studied, external third-person narrative that leaves the reader as uncertain about Colin and Mary's motivation and feelings as they are themselves; indeed, the opacity about motivation is established in the opening pages where, we read, 'for reasons they could no longer define clearly, Colin and Mary were not on speaking terms' (*CS*, p. 9).

This does not mean, however, they are merely passive and do not wish to interpret their surroundings. When Colin witnesses an episode from the hotel balcony, he is eager to generate an interesting narrative from it. The episode is anodyne enough: an elderly gentleman's attempt to take a spontaneous snapshot of his wife is humorously undermined by the table of young men drinking beer in the background, who insist on raising their glasses at the camera pointing their way. In an apparent attempt to regain Mary's attention, Colin reinvents the scene, exaggerating 'its small pathos into vaudeville':

> He described the elderly gentleman as 'incredibly old and feeble', his wife was 'batty beyond belief', the men at the table were 'bovine morons', and he made the husband give out 'an incredible roar of fury'. In fact the word 'incredible' suggested itself to him at every turn, perhaps because he feared that Mary did not believe him, or because he did not believe himself. (*CS*, p. 16)

The self-doubt and uncertainty in the ability to read events does not suggest an atrophied desire to interpret, or a disinclination to offer forceful interpretations. It is the waywardness and unpredictability of the interpretive skills that is emphasized. This is especially clear in one

memorable passage when Colin and Mary are sitting at a café in what
is evidently St Mark's Square, and Colin 'followed Mary's gaze to a
nearby family whose baby, supported at the waist by its father, stood
on the table, swaying'. He notices how the baby's dummy 'obscured its
mouth, giving it an air of sustained, comic surprise'. In Colin's view,
the baby's 'head wobbled quizzically', and 'its fat, weak legs were
splayed round the massive, shameless burden of its nappy'. Colin's
perspective now follows the baby's gaze:

> The wild eyes, round and pure, blazed across the sunlit square and fixed
> in seeming astonishment and anger on the roofline of the cathedral
> where, it had once been written, the crests of the arches, as if in ecstasy,
> broke into marble foam and tossed themselves far into the blue sky in
> flashes and wreaths of sculptured spray, as if breakers on a shore had
> been frost-bound before they fell. (*CS*, pp. 50–1)

Colin is clearly signalled as the focalizer of this passage, presented
in a form of indirect free discourse that, quite subtly, expresses a
significant feature of the character's perspective. First, and most
obviously, there is the implied inner lack that permits Colin's attention
to wander to the object of Mary's attention, and then to where the baby
seems to be looking. Yet there are implied judgements in this passage,
notably in the ambivalent appraisal of the baby. The emphasis on bodily
functions, and particularly the 'shameless burden' of the nappy,
suggests distaste; yet the eyes, though 'wild', are also 'pure'. As Colin's
attention wanders, following the baby's gaze, a paraphrase from John
Ruskin describing the splendour of St Mark's cathedral – signalled by
'it had once been written' – is dutifully and seamlessly introduced.[13]

For David Malcolm, it is the narrator's ironic juxtaposition of the
drooling baby with the cathedral's architecture that is noteworthy.
Malcolm, who has made an attentive investigation of McEwan's source
in Ruskin's *The Stones of Venice*, judges that 'the passage from Ruskin
is not entirely dissimilar to many of the narrator's own descriptions'.[14]
In the passage quoted above, however, it is plausible to read the
paraphrase as indicative of the respectfully informed, but unenthused
tourist. The celebrated passage from Ruskin, we can infer, is the kind
of thing Colin has imbibed in preparation for the trip (which 'had been
his idea' (*CS*, p. 52)). The incongruous juxtaposition of baby with
architecture, together with Colin's ambivalence about the baby, and his
dry, second-hand appraisal of the sublime architectural phenomenon,
all contribute to our sense of Colin's inability to discriminate, or, indeed,
to become involved with external reality.

At this point we might reconsider the different kind of openness that McEwan associated with the exploratory political novel in the Preface to *A Move Abroad*. There is clearly a distinction to be drawn between, on the one hand, that exploratory open-mindedness that can (for example) generate the kind of discoveries that McEwan associates with the fiction-writing process; and, on the other hand, the failure of perception and discrimination that characterizes the 'openness' of Mary and Colin. Immediately before the account of their sado-masochistic fantasies, the narrator makes a distinction of this order, summarizing the couple's attitude to 'conversations about important matters', and their 'unspoken assumption . . . that a subject was best explored by taking the opposing view, even if it was not quite the view one held oneself'. However, for this pair, the result of the process is not to enhance clarity and understanding:

> The idea, if it was an idea and not a habit of mind, was that adversaries, fearing contradiction, would be more rigorous in argument, like scientists proposing innovation to their colleagues. What tended to happen, to Colin and Mary at least, was that subjects were not explored so much as defensively reiterated, or forced into elaborate irrelevancies, and suffused with irritability. Now, freed by mutual encouragement they roamed, like children at seaside rockpools, from one matter to another. (*CS*, p. 85)

Intellectually, Colin and Mary betray infantile qualities; which is to say that neither of them have a sufficiently developed sense of mature selfhood to feel personal *investment* in an intellectual terrain. Rather than innocence, the intellectual whimsy of the pair suggests anomie, and this has an important bearing on the book's treatment of selfhood and sexuality. When Colin and Mary go back to Robert and Caroline's flat, they go without having made a conscious decision to do so. Like sacrificial victims, they seem powerless to resist, and in this respect the book conforms to McEwan's conviction that 'an unconscious contractual agreement . . . can exist between oppressor and victim'.[15] The novella illustrates that gulf between theory and experience that makes Colin and Mary vulnerable and which shows how ill-equipped they are to recognize their plight. Again, McEwan's own observation is instructive:

> There is something intractable about the sexual imagination, and what you desire is not very amenable to programmes of change. You might well have grown up deciding that you accept certain intellectual points of view, and you might also change the way you behave as a man or as a

woman, but there are also other things – vulnerabilities, desires – within you that might well have been irreversibly shaped in childhood.[16]

This last sentence, with the stress on how both vulnerabilities and desires are *shaped*, is very important to understanding *The Comfort of Strangers*. The logic of the narrative is not simply to demonstrate how repressed desires become dangerous or unmanageable for those unwilling to pay attention to them. Desire (like vulnerability) is not a dormant quality waiting to be unleashed. The novella shows very clearly how desire can be shaped or distorted, as in the case of Robert whose career seems to have taken several curious turns, stemming from the strictures about gender imbibed in childhood, before he turns into a sex murderer.

In the light of this important qualification, we have to read the last page of the narrative very carefully, for it seems to contain a kind of summary of the principal theme, presented through Mary's thoughts as she poignantly formulates an explanation for Colin, while examining his corpse:

> She was going to explain it all to him, tell him her theory, tentative at this stage, of course, which explained how the imagination, the sexual imagination, men's ancient dreams of hurting, and women's of being hurt, embodied and declared a powerful single organizing principle, which distorted all relations, all truth. (*CS*, p. 134)

The novella shows, rather, how stereotypical strictures about gender identity produce imbalances that can distort or neglect the sexual imagination leading to violent or unpredictable results. This applies to Mary's untested theoretical feminism as much as it does to Robert's inherited perception of traditional manliness, or his later cultivation of aggressive homosexuality.

The gender issue can obscure the wider application of the novella's chief impression. What the book really explores is the moral chasm that opens up when there is no discernible basis or foundation for actions or convictions. The ungrounded individual is free of responsibilities, or can fantasize that he or she is (as when Mary dreams of her children as her contemporaries (*CS*, p. 10)). In the final scene Mary is in a state of shock, but this is really an extension of her original state of existence. She is ready with a pat theoretical explanation of Colin's death, after all, even though (in a superbly understated passage), she has only 'the briefest intimation of the grief that lay in wait' (*CS*, p. 134).

Her 'lack of affect' (*CS*, p. 131), ostensibly occasioned by shock, is her principal characteristic (and Colin's, too) before the murder. Here McEwan produces a fictional enactment of the 'waning of affect' articulated in theories about postmodernism: Colin and Mary, archly self-conscious postmoderns, outwardly confident in their political convictions, and their capacity to argue a point, are likened to 'children at seaside rockpools', untroubled by the absence of an intellectual foundation or belief to underpin their thinking.

Speaking in 2005, in interview with Melvyn Bragg on *The South Bank Show*, McEwan described *The Comfort of Strangers* as 'the darkest thing I ever wrote'.[17] It certainly contains the most disturbing moment of violence in all of McEwan's work. In the murder scene, the drugged Mary is the focalizer, and her nightmare state of immobility produces a stylized description of the killing of Colin, who falls in front of her. It is what happens after the killing, in the room soaked with Colin's blood, which is the true horror, however:

> All through the night that followed she [Mary] dreamed of moans and whimpers, and sudden shouts, of figures locked and turning at her feet, churning through the little pond, calling out for joy. (*CS*, p. 130)

This single sentence suffices to communicate the indescribable. A psychopath's depraved orgy, presumed to be a real event in the world of the novel, is presented as if it had been a vague nightmare, too awful to comprehend fully. Only in the word 'joy' is there a hint of the psychopath's ghastly perspective; and it is this single word that makes the passage hard to stomach – and so much more uncomfortable than, for example, the dismemberment scene in *The Innocent*, where the horror is also the perpetrator's – Leonard's – horror.

The book conveys the irrationality of violence; but this can make the violence seem gratuitous, or implausible in the narrative context. If one reads Robert's actions as the result of a subconscious self-destructive impulse, then the contradictions that surround him need no explanation. Yet readers will still find something unsatisfying in the portrayal of Robert and Caroline, who have made careful plans to leave Venice permanently, having committed their murder, even though Robert is rooted to the city through his identification with his father and grandfather, and, especially, through inheriting his grandfather's house (*CS*, p. 73).

The 1990 film version of the book, with Harold Pinter's screenplay, ameliorates the problem by stressing Robert's insanity. At the end of the film Robert and Caroline have been caught, and the final shot is of Robert, repeating to a detective his mantra about his father's black moustache, kept black by means of 'a little brush . . . such as ladies use for their eyes' (as a signifier of his impressive masculinity, but with the pointed hint of femininity). The film starts with this recollection, as a voice-over, and so in the final shot the viewer is made to feel the emphatic circularity of Robert's derangement, his development arrested by the lesson in power learnt from his father.[18]

McEwan's retrospective assessment of *The Comfort of Strangers*, in *The South Bank Show* interview, reveals a crisis for the author: 'I thought that I was coming to the end of what I could do in fiction', he said, 'I felt as if I was only writing out of a tiny corner of my mind.' Fearing that he was writing himself 'into silence', he then fortuitously had opportunities to write in other modes – an oratorio and a screenplay – and to rediscover his central mission as a novelist: the engagement of society.

As a bleak enactment of violence, and a depressing representation of intellectual vacuity, *The Comfort of Strangers* embodies a creative cul-de-sac for McEwan. At the same time, the book can be taken to demonstrate the need for balance between the masculine and feminine principles, and in this sense it anticipates the oratorio for *Or Shall We Die?*, which, as the following chapter shows, also serves to articulate McEwan's view that 'male and female should exist in balance within individuals and within society.'[19]

Notes

1 The context of the speculation is McEwan's Preface to his oratorio *Or Shall We Die?* (1983) and the screenplay for *The Ploughman's Lunch* (1983), published together as *A Move Abroad* (London: Picador, 1989).

2 For an account of this, see Georg Lukács, *Studies in European Realism*, trans. Edith Bone (London: Merlin Press, 1989), p. 10.

3 'John Haffenden Talks to Ian McEwan', p. 32.

4 Ibid., p. 32.

5 Judith Seaboyer, 'Sadism Demands a Story: Ian McEwan's *The Comfort of Strangers*', *Modern Fiction Studies*, 45: 4 (1999), pp. 957–86 (pp. 958, 981).

6 Ibid., p. 980.

7 Slay is suitably conscious of McEwan's lack of specificity, however: 'ultimately, the unnamed city becomes a symbolic Everycity, representative of all that is foreign and strange', he writes. See *Ian McEwan*, p. 73.

8 Slay's list of earlier antecedents includes Dicken's *Pictures from Italy* (1845), Byron's *Childe Harold* (1812–18), and Ruskin's *The Stones of Venice* (1851–53) (to which McEwan alludes, in fact). *Ian McEwan*, p. 73.

9 'John Haffenden Talks to Ian McEwan', p. 32.

10 For a discussion of this tradition see George B. von der Lippe, 'Death in Venice in Literature and Film: Six Twentieth-Century Versions', *Mosaic*, 32: 1 (March 1999), pp. 35–54. The bulk of the essay is an account of McEwan's novella, Mann's *Death in Venice*, du Maurier's 'Don't Look Now', and the films they inspired.

11 'John Haffenden Talks to Ian McEwan', p. 32.

12 Seaboyer, 'Sadism Demands a Story', p. 979.

13 See John Ruskin, *The Stones of Venice, Volume 2: The Sea Stories*, chapter 4. Reference for the edition I have consulted: (London: George Allen, 1906), pp. 67–8.

14 Malcolm, *Understanding Ian McEwan*, p. 71.

15 'John Haffenden Talks to Ian McEwan', p. 33.

16 Ibid., p. 32.

17 Interview with Melvyn Bragg, *The South Bank Show*, ITV1, broadcast 20 February 2005.

18 *The Comfort of Strangers* (MGM, 1990), directed by Paul Shrader, screenplay by Harold Pinter, starring Christopher Walken as Robert, Helen Mirren as Caroline, Rupert Everett as Colin, and Natasha Richardson as Mary. Aside from one or two changes, the film is faithful to the book, evoking the menacing atmosphere, especially in the dimly lit scenes at Robert's house. This is not a narrative that translates particularly well to film, however: the way in which film renders characters' exteriors makes Colin and Mary seem wooden, where they are convincingly presented by McEwan as entrapped in a form of *ennui*.

19 'John Haffenden Talks to Ian McEwan', p. 33.

Towards the 'implicate order':
The Child in Time

The Child in Time marks a turning point in McEwan's career: it was his first fiction to be clearly longer than novella length, and his first sustained attempt at a social novel, in which the private and the public are systematically intertwined. It is categorizable as a 'Condition of England novel' in some respects, with its projection of a fourth or fifth-term Thatcherite government becoming increasingly authoritarian;[1] yet McEwan produces a unique way of tracing the connections between the personal and the political, most notably through a poetic application of post-Einsteinian physics. This is a crucial moment in his career, since it enables him to bring his established qualities to bear upon wider concerns, especially the rendering of intensely individual and insular experience. Moreover, it is a strategy that enables him to eschew the pitfalls he associates with 'political' writing. In short, he re-invents the novel of society on his own terms.

The novel was written between 1983 and 1986;[2] and for McEwan, it was the culmination of his investigation of the relationship between 'ideas, opinions, politics' as one force working on the writer, and 'the imagination' as the other imperative. In the author's account, this investigation was carried out through the writing of the words for the oratorio *Or Shall We Die?* and the screenplay for *The Ploughman's Lunch*. These projects were 'the groundwork' for *The Child in Time*, by virtue of the 'move abroad' they represented for McEwan: they were, that is, 'tactical evasions of novel writing' (*MA*, p. vii). More particularly, they seem to have afforded McEwan the opportunity to express 'ideas, opinions' with an immediacy that he was coming, increasingly, to feel to be inappropriate in a novel.

This brings us back to the aesthetic of fiction that was emerging in *The Comfort of Strangers*. For McEwan, the problem with dominant ideas is that they prevent the novel from being 'an exploration or investigation', turning it instead into 'an illustration of conclusions already reached'. Following Milan Kundera, McEwan expresses the view – and it is a recurring conviction in his writing about fiction (and in the history of the novel) – that the discoveries possible in the novel form 'come about, if at all, despite your convictions rather than because of them' (*MA*, p. x). This is not to say that writers are apolitical creatures, without views – rather, their opinions must be 'held in abeyance', says McEwan. Neither is the political realm beyond the reach of the novel; but it is best approached through the interweaving of public and private worlds: 'by measuring individual human worth, the novelist reveals the full enormity of the State's crime when it sets out to crush that individuality' (*MA*, pp. xi, xii). This is actually a very good account of *The Child in Time*; or, perhaps it is more accurate to say that *The Child in Time* itself serves as an exploration of how successfully the novel can treat this conflict.

In McEwan's recollection, in 1980 and 1981 he was investigating the 'new cold war' emerging at that time, with a new novel in mind (*MA*, p. xviii). His research was thorough, but debilitating:

> Armed to the teeth with my facts and figures, histories, moral revulsion and precarious moral hopes, desperate to engage and persuade everybody in what I took to be the single most important issue to face humankind, I was all set to write the worst novel imaginable. (*MA*, p. xx)

Michael Berkeley's invitation to write the words for the oratorio *Or Shall We Die?* supplied the way out: McEwan was able to rechannel his 'moral argument' and to make it 'directly and without embarrassment'. The piece is an assault upon unfettered scientific rationality, and a lament for the ravaged natural world – the nuclear threat being one aspect of this – which poses the question: 'shall we change, shall there be womanly times, or shall we die?' (*MA*, pp. xxi, xxiii).

It is indeed a very direct piece of writing, in which the nuances come, as is appropriate in this kind of composition, from the way in which the musical settings and inversions work with the words, which are stark read in isolation from the music. The sleeve notes from the LP recording, written jointly by McEwan and Berkeley, reveal an interesting aspect of this phase in McEwan's career. *Or Shall We Die?* is a simple expression of fear and horror at the prospect of nuclear devastation. There is one very affecting section in which a woman is searching for her daughter in the aftermath of a nuclear attack: the child, when found, is beyond help and is cradled by the mother until she dies. The notes indicate that the woman's words 'are those of an actual Hiroshima survivor who lost her family in the attack.'[3] However, aside from this section, and some choral elements where McEwan draws on William Blake, the writing is blunt. This befits the urgency of the topic, but is quite opposed to the non-partisan spirit that McEwan sees as the vital ingredient of the aesthetic of the novel.

McEwan summarizes the libretto as exposing the insufficiency of the Newtonian paradigm, in which detachment and objectivity are privileged over emotion (*MA*, pp. 11–12); McEwan presents Blake as the 'presiding spirit' of the piece in the sleeve notes, as 'an early and fierce opponent of Newtonian science' whose writing returned 'again and again to the perils of divorcing reason from feeling'.[4] Connected to the poles of reason/feeling were 'the male and female principles' which took 'many forms in his writing' (*MA*, pp. 12–13). Coloured by his developing interest in feminism, and by a particular generational mood in which nuclear fear (quite reasonably) sometimes seemed overpowering, McEwan produced a cautionary work about science in which the sections jointly sung by 'Man' and 'Woman' spell out a clear message. There is the current bad science:

> Our science mocks magic and the human heart,
> Our knowledge is the brutal mastery of the unknown.

But science could become a force for good:

> The planet does not turn for us alone.
> Science is a form of wonder, knowledge a form of love.
> Are we too late to love ourselves?
> Shall we change, or shall we die? (*MA*, pp. 23, 24)

In the 'Introduction' to the libretto in *A Move Abroad* – which is dated 1982, before the first performance of the work, but which is more expansive than the LP sleeve notes – McEwan has the freedom to expound in more personal terms about the process of composition. He points out, for example, his desire 'to write about those private fears while they were still fresh.' The music, he suggests, translates the writing 'to another realm, abstract, beyond definitions, and yet with direct appeal to feelings' (*MA*, pp. 5, 6). Interestingly, he articulates an appreciation of science here that anticipates his later interests in a way that the libretto does not. He comments, for example, that 'increasingly the talk of physicists has come to sound like theology', and that science 'might no longer be at odds with that deep intuitive sense . . . that there is a spiritual dimension to our existence' (*MA*, pp. 13, 14). Indeed, the enthusiasm for 'the new physics' expressed here leads McEwan to characterize it as a world-view to set against the Newtonian one, the 'female principle' to oppose the male, objective Newtonian universe (*MA*, p. 15): already he seemed to be thinking beyond the cautionary note of the libretto.

The Ploughman's Lunch presented McEwan with the prospect of a different kind of immediacy. It was his most overt critique of the Thatcher government to that date: it draws a parallel between the Suez crisis and the Falklands War in its powerful treatment of private and public morality. The piece began as a parallel between a man's personal and public duplicity, the latter explored through 'the opportunistic rewriting of the history of the Suez crisis' (*MA*, p. xxv). After the first draft was completed, however, the Falkland's War was in the offing; the final film embraced this last gasp of British imperialism, and addressed the triumphalism of Mrs Thatcher after the war, and the new tide of nationalism that she sought to cultivate.

In his own account, it was after realizing these projects, with their moral and political directness, and two months after the release of *The Ploughman's Lunch* in 1983, that McEwan turned, in the summer of that year, to writing *The Child in Time*, a project he was not to complete until 1986. He began with the fragment that was to become the episode at 'The Bell', a fragment the appeal of which 'he was not yet able to explain.' With retrospect, McEwan presents the oratorio and the screenplay as preparing the way for the novel, and as a demonstration of the fact that 'novels take longer to cook' (*MA*, pp. xxv, xxvi).

The Child in Time is McEwan's first truly substantial novel. It is a focused critique of Thatcher's Britain (conducted in the form of a near-future political fable, apparently set in 1996);[5] but it is also a moving depiction of love, loss and reconciliation, centred on the profoundly painful topic of an abducted child. In the 1990s and beyond, British society became deeply preoccupied with child abduction and paedophilia – indeed this became a media obsession – and McEwan's novel anticipates the way in which this topic has become a central issue in the society's struggle to understand itself. The novel achieves a very effective interweaving of its private and public themes, especially through the business of the 'Authorized Childcare Handbook', which draws in all of the principal characters, and which reveals the collision of personal and political concerns.

Slay sees the novel as an amalgamation of old and new concerns for McEwan, combining 'the political and social concerns of his film scripts with the darker, more visceral edge of his fiction.'[6] The new direction that results from this amalgamation also draws in another crucial element: the enthusiasm for the new physics expressed in McEwan's account of *Or Shall We Die?*, which leads the novel to gesture towards the 'womanly times' of the libretto, conceived as a perfect balance of the rational and the intuitive.

The science is one element that gives licence to a fluid perception of time, which suits McEwan's purpose admirably, of course, in a novel about the child within us all, and the need to foster strong personal and intergenerational bonds as a necessary component of the healthy body politic.[7] Beyond this, the treatment of time is also fashioned by McEwan's allusion to the post-Einsteinian notion of the plasticity of time and space. There is a particular locus of this (though its implications reach out into the rest of the novel). This is the fantastic episode at 'The Bell' (the fragment with which McEwan reports having started the novel), which appears to allow the central protagonist to intervene in the past and secure his own future.

This is an extraordinary moment in a novel that otherwise follows the codes of realism. Yet this is not simply the instance of magic realism that Henry Perowne assumes it to be (in an arch allusion in *Saturday* (*S*, p. 67)): McEwan may be chiefly interested in the capacity of fiction to render personal time in a fluid way, but he also sees connections between the speculative understanding of time in contemporary physics and the ways in which narrative fiction can productively cheat a strict chronology. He goes to some lengths, in fact, to make a timeslip faintly plausible.

At the beginning of the novel Stephen Lewis, a successful children's writer, is on his way to a weekly meeting in Whitehall. He is a member of a sub-committee on reading and writing that will make recommendations to an 'Official Commission on Childcare', informing the 'Authorized Childcare Handbook' the Commission is tasked to produce. The committee meeting does not hold his attention, and the recollection that occupies his thoughts reveals the incident that establishes the terms of the novel's action: two years' ago his three-year-old daughter Kate was abducted from a supermarket checkout while he was momentarily distracted with the business of packing his goods.

The novel treats narrative chronology in an assured and fluid way, with flashbacks appearing seamlessly within the episodes that give rise to them, or dexterously juxtaposed with the later scenes they elucidate. The notional present of the novel, at the outset, finds Stephen in a state of despair, still struggling to come to terms with the loss of Kate, and now separated from his wife, Julie, who has gone to live in an isolated cottage thirty miles from London.

On his way to visit Julie in her cottage, after an extended separation, Stephen experiences the decisive moment in his self-transformation. This is also the fulcrum of the book (and the episode that gives readers most trouble). Stephen espies his parents – or, rather, the younger selves of his parents – through the window of a pub called 'The Bell'. In a later conversation with his mother, she confirms the experience and amplifies its significance: she was pregnant with Stephen and decided to keep the child upon seeing 'the face of a child' at the window, 'sort of floating there' (*CT*, p. 175). In an apparently fantastic moment, Stephen experiences a timeslip that enables him to secure his own existence. He goes on to visit Julie, and they conceive a new child (who is born in the uplifting final episode), with Stephen certain that their renewed intimacy, 'and what would happen as a consequence', is connected with the episode at 'The Bell': 'the two moments were undeniably bound, they held in common the innocent longing they provoked, the desire to belong' (*CT*, p. 63).

The presentation of familial hopefulness, in a treatment conditioned by the needs of the paternal figure, has given rise to some criticism, it should be noted. The most famous discussion of the novel in this connection is Adam Mars-Jones's, in his essay 'Venus Envy'. Mars-Jones discusses *The Child in Time* (alongside *Einstein's Monsters* by Martin Amis (1987)) to illustrate an aspect of how masculinity has been redefined in response to feminism. He detects a 'new style . . . of faintly synthetic introspection' that, in McEwan's case, contributes to the identity of 'New Man'. Mars-Jones's essay is curiously coy: he admits to the hobbyhorse that drives him, and to the defensiveness of his writing; yet his central complaint about *The Child in Time* is hard-hitting and, if accepted in full, serves to undermine the novel's chief effects. He finds in Stephen's redefinition of fatherhood a *couvade*, a term drawn from anthropology, denoting the upstaging of 'potent moments in the lives of women'. Julie's new pregnancy occurs 'off stage', and unknown to Stephen; moreover, when the baby is due, their love-making seems to trigger the birth, and Stephen must stand in for the midwife. In this 'suppressed drama of symbolic ownership', 'the male, all the while loudly extolling the sanctity of her privileges, usurps the female.'[8]

Still more damaging to the structure of the book is Mars-Jones's quibble with the child abduction. In his account, the disappearance of Kate becomes a device to promote the standing of the father: 'only in the absence of the child does it become possible for the father's claims to be heard so favourably.' This seemingly odd suggestion is only explicable in the light of Mars-Jones's further claim that Kate is tainted with 'imperfection': while she was 'fully mothered', she was only 'imperfectly fathered'. The birth at the end of the novel then redresses the 'imbalance', the 'flaw' located 'at the very moment of [Kate's] coming into being.' To advance this idea, Mars-Jones suggests that the abduction is 'curiously unconvincing, as most readers of the book have acknowledged.' He immediately admits, however: 'that is a flat lie – I know of no one who was even faintly troubled by the passage – but critics get lonely too.' This is a bizarre admission, again, of the essay's polemical intent, which does not prevent him from stressing the implausibility of the episode. Rather distastefully, he puts the abduction at the 'master-criminal end of the scale' due to the level of difficulty, which makes it comparable to an abductor placing, in the grasp of a parent, 'a small artificial hand, cunningly weighted, in a brightly coloured glove'.[9]

The essay is avowedly polemical, and it explicitly raises the question of personal experience and the subjectivity of the observer. Mars-Jones refuses to empathize with the imagined position of a father of small children, partly out of irritation with the smugness he has observed from life, the 'habit of wearing paternity as a medal', a habit that fathers of teenagers lose, he feels.[10] Yet the 'implausibility' that Mars-Jones detects in relation to aspects of parenthood in the novel, and which leads him to his suspicion about the male *couvade*, may not be felt by other readers. McEwan trades on a fear that all parents experience, for small children *do* have a habit of getting lost in the twinkling of an eye, for instance. It is also worth noting that love-making *is* said to induce a biological response that can trigger birth.[11] It is true that Stephen is unaware of Julie's pregnancy, but that is because McEwan chose to write a book chiefly about a father's grief, rather than a mother's. Logically, the complaint would censor such an approach. The book is certainly written from the experience of a father;[12] but that should not make it unavailable to a responsive reading from those who are not fathers.[13]

Still more troubling for some readers is that episode at 'The Bell', an apparent instance of time travel that sits oddly with a novel that is otherwise a realist, near-future dystopia. How should we account for this disruption to the codes of realism? For Slay, it amounts to 'an episode of magical realism';[14] while for Ryan, the episode is 'paranormal' in that it suggests that 'mother and son communicate telepathically across time'.[15] In Malcolm's account, it is the element of 'metaphysical, supernatural experience' that contributes to the generic complexity of the novel.[16]

In what manner, however, are the lines of realism blurred in the novel? Malcolm's further observation points the way: 'Stephen's supernatural experience is confirmed and validated, and certainly not explained away as hallucination.'[17] Indeed, it is the extraordinary level of credulity that McEwan seems to establish for the episode at 'The Bell' – the attempt to render it something other than 'paranormal' or 'supernatural' – that often grates with readers, for whom the episode must remain incredible. It is worth investigating McEwan's motives, here.

In the exchange between Stephen and Thelma about the apparent timeslip, she waxes lyrical about the achievements of twentieth-century physicists, arguing that they have 're-invented the world and our place in it' in ways that are more radical and bizarre than the reconceptions envisaged by Luther, Copernicus, Darwin, Marx or Freud. Tellingly, she laments the fact that the implications of these theories have not significantly influenced twentieth-century literature, arguing that earlier writers would have been inspired by this 'stupendous shake-up':

> Shakespeare would have grasped wave functions, Donne would have understood complementarity and relative time. They would have been excited. What richness! They would have plundered this new science for their imagery. And they would have educated their audiences too. (*CT*, pp. 44–5)

Thelma, it should be said, is apparently ignorant of the ways in which literature has repeatedly been influenced by science, most notably in the Victorian period, but also in the modernist era (about which she is particularly scathing (*CT*, p. 45)). In one sense, this is McEwan setting himself a personal challenge, and Thelma's blind spot is a way for the author to project (and examine) his own prejudices: 'we have to be very careful in a literary culture not to believe we have a key to all mythologies', he has said, in the process of re-evaluating his own erstwhile sense of the relative claims of literature and science.[18] From the publication of *The Child in Time* onwards, contemporary science becomes a more prominent influence in his novels. This affects his imagery only locally, perhaps; and the 'education' he is able to offer is sometimes embedded in surprising ways, as in this novel, where the timeslip is only really explicable after one has gleaned a rudimentary knowledge of the scientific ideas that influenced the author. Indeed, the understanding of this moment, which mars the novel for some readers, is significantly altered when one grasps the scientific underpinning – however loosely it is interpreted – that might make it credible, at least to a degree.

The timeslip is the pivotal moment in the book, both in terms of the novel's development – it is a turning point in the plot and in Stephen's personal repair – and in relation to the experimental direction of the novel. In her response to Stephen's query about his 'hallucination' (as she calls it), Thelma indicates that physics is a divided subject, and cannot furnish him with an explanation:

> The twin pillars are relativity and quantum theories. One describes a causal and continuous world, the other a non-causal, discontinuous world. Is it possible to reconcile them? Einstein failed with his unified field theory. I side with the optimists like my colleague David Bohm, who anticipates a higher order of theory. (*CT*, p. 118)

The esteemed scientific thinker and philosopher, David Bohm, who died in 1992, is here imagined as the colleague of a fictional character.[19] This gesture is far more than the novelistic conceit in which the fictive and the real are elided, though this blurring of worlds may be significant, a way – by extension – of underscoring the problem of individual being conceived as a separate entity.[20] Thelma's hint that 'a higher order of theory', anticipated in the work of David Bohm, is also McEwan's hint, for the only work of science that he refers to in his Acknowledgements is Bohm's celebrated book, *Wholeness and the Implicate Order* (1980).

In a later essay, Bohm succinctly describes this book as concerning 'the relationship of mind and matter', with the aim of 'understanding relativity and quantum theory on a basis common to both', thus bringing together Thelma's 'twin pillars' and supplying the possible foundation for that higher order of theory. Bohm goes on to explain the book's fascinating concept of 'the enfolded or implicate order':

The essential feature of this idea was that the whole universe is in some way enfolded in everything and that each thing is enfolded in the whole. From this it follows that in some way, and to some degree everything enfolds or implicates everything, but in such a manner that under typical conditions of ordinary experience, there is a great deal of relative independence of things.

This means that the 'unfolded or explicate order' – 'the external relationships' in the physical world – ensures that things are seen to be 'relatively separate' and so 'related only externally to other things'. However, this explicate order of ordinary experience 'cannot be understood properly apart from its ground in the primary reality of the implicate order', where 'each thing is internally related to the whole, and therefore, to everything else'.[21]

Bohm's theory is particularly suggestive for McEwan where it defines consciousness and time. For Bohm, mind and matter are both characterized by 'flow', so, although we can separate out particular thoughts and ideas, our thinking is more properly described as a stream of consciousness. This is more than an analogy for Bohm, since the more mystical direction of his thinking suggests that we cannot separate mind (one part of reality) from matter (other aspects of reality): both should be seen as part of the same flow. Relevant here are Bohm's thoughts on meditation as a striving for 'the immeasurable', or a state of mind where a man 'ceases to sense a separation between himself and the whole of reality.'[22]

Time is considered briefly in the last few pages of Bohm's book, in an inconclusive discussion that seems to have been especially intriguing for McEwan. Here Bohm observes the paradox that, in common experience 'physical time' seems 'absolute', and yet it is equally common knowledge that the impact of time on consciousness 'is highly variable and relative to conditions' which can mean that 'a given period may be felt to be short or long by different people'. (The 'slowing of time' experienced by Stephen as he tries to avoid crashing into an upended lorry is an obvious example (*CT*, p. 94).)[23]

Bohm links this paradox directly to the theory of relativity, with its implication 'that physical time is in fact relative, in the sense that it may vary according to the speed of the observer.' Simultaneously, however, he distances the theoretical physics from the experience of consciousness by pointing out that 'this variation is . . . significant only as we approach the speed of light and is quite negligible in the domain of ordinary experience.' Yet Bohm seems to be striving for that higher

level theory, applicable to both space and time, that might embrace
ordinary experience: 'since the quantum theory implies that elements
that are separated in space are generally non-causally and non-locally
related projections of a higher-dimensional reality, it follows that
moments separated in time are also such projections of this reality.'

For Bohm, 'this leads to a fundamentally new notion of the meaning
of time', no longer seeming to be 'a primary, independent and
universally applicable order', he proposes that it should be seen as
'secondary', derived, like space, 'from a higher-dimensional ground'.
The hypothesis that follows is the one that inspires *The Child in Time*:
Bohm is 'led to propose that this multidimensional reality may project
into many orders of sequences of moments in consciousness.' The
illustration he chooses is the common experience of people who meet
up after a long separation – long 'as measured by the sequence of
moments registered by a clock' – to find they 'are often able to "take up
from where they left off" as if no time had passed'. In proposing 'that
sequences of moments that "skip" intervening spaces are just as
allowable forms of time as those which seem continuous', Bohm
produces 'a consideration of time as a projection of multidimensional
reality into a sequence of moments.'[24]

It is important to realize that there is a factual basis – or, at least, a
basis in scientific theory – in the apparently fantastic moments in
the novel. When one looks at the more prosaic details, the author's
scrupulous attention to the laws of the physical world are clear. In the
episode of the lorry accident, for example, the lorry blocks Stephen's
way, leaving him aiming for a six-foot gap 'from a distance of less than
a hundred feet and at a speed which he estimated . . . to be forty-five
miles an hour' (*CT*, p. 94): that is (according to a *genuine* HMSO
publication, the *Highway Code*) too fast to stop in time, but slow
enough to make finding the gap a plausible feat.[25]

Of course, the attraction of Bohm to McEwan is evidently that his
work introduces an element of intuition into rational reasoning,
unsettling the factual basis of it. Much, in fact, as the timeslip unsettles
the 'rational' realist code of the novel. The same kind of combination – still more pronounced – is a characteristic of *Magical Child*,
by Joseph Chilton Pearce, one of the other two books cited in the
Acknowledgements.

Pearce makes a compelling case for home childbirth, as a 'natural,
euphoric, and ecstatic experience', free from the damaging assump-
tions and practices of medical science. This distinction between the

'naturally delivered and nurtured child and the technologically delivered and abandoned child' identifies the first (though crucial) of many phases where the child's natural development can be seriously impaired.[26] In one telling contrast, Pearce compares the bonding observed between Ugandan mothers and infants, in one survey, with the nursery culture of US society, where parents leave baby to cry him- or herself to sleep, oblivious to the abandonment of which they are guilty and the nature of the infant rage they are producing. The long-term consequences of such abandonment, argues Pearce, are 'a breakdown of interpersonal relations and an obsessive-compulsive attachment to material objects' by way of compensation. In the abandonment of the infant, Pearce sees the seeds of 'a collapsing social order, on the one hand, and a generation with an increased passion for consumer goods, on the other'. A further consequence of the breakdown of interpersonal relations is 'the attempt to turn the other person into an object'.[27]

Pearce's book is a plea for an approach to parenting and education which, on the bedrock of unconditional love, gives free reign to the child's innate intelligence, and which enables the child to develop through natural curiosity, play and imagination. Because the emphasis is on creative thinking, learning how to process information, rather than learning facts, there is a point of contact with Bohm's implicate order. For Pearce and Bohm, self-realization involves a process in which mind and matter are brought together in ways that are usually dismissed in Western culture.

An analogy that Bohm uses, and which also appears in Pearce's book, is the hologram, the three-dimensional photographic image generated using light from a laser. When the photographic plate is illuminated with laser light, the whole structure of the image can be seen in three dimensions and from different perspectives. What is particularly important about the hologram, however, is that the whole image is also manifest when only a small region of the plate is illuminated. The detail is less clear, but information about the whole is contained in each region of the plate. Bohm suggests that 'physical law should refer primarily to an order of undivided wholeness . . . similar to that indicated by the hologram'. The analogy leads Bohm to his grand claim for a 'whole illuminated structure' that 'extends over the whole universe and over the whole past, with implications for the whole future.' This is 'the germ of a new notion of order' in which 'a *total order* is contained, in some *implicit* sense, in each region of space and time.'[28]

On the connection between mind and matter, and the topic of human potential, Pearce makes explicit that which is perhaps implicit in Bohm's theory when he suggests that the human brain, at birth, might be conceived as 'a hologram fragment' that 'must have exposure to and interact with the earth hologram to achieve clarity, to bring the brain's picture into focus, so to speak.' For Pearce, experiments pointing to shared hypnotic dreams suggest that it is 'feasible to share a hypnagogic kind of creativity with another mind.'[29]

It does seem in this novel that McEwan has pieced together his ideas about childhood and personal development, consciousness and time, from these sources. A local example is Stephen's memory of building a sandcastle on holiday in Cornwall, and of Kate's immersion in the game, which surely draws on Pearce's account of the importance of play and imagination in childhood development. Kate's conviction that the sandcastle can keep the sea at bay, and that it might really become the family's new home (*CT*, p. 106), is an aspect of the fantasy play described by Pearce, in which the child is 'bending the world to his/her desire', practising the capacity and the power that children believe adults to have.[30]

The child psychologist who makes a representation to the sub-committee about the dangers of 'premature literacy' – whose testimony Stephen is called upon to refute – clearly echoes Pearce in his idealistic enthusiasm for 'all forms of intelligent play' in younger children (*CT*, p. 77). The mind–matter connection, which the speaker calls 'the dancing interpenetration of the physical and the psychic', is interrupted, he argues, by the desire to 'inflict literacy', and so to 'dissolve the enchanted identification of word and thing and, through that, self and world' (*CT*, pp. 76–7). McEwan has this expert draw on a model of language acquisition that is very similar to Pearce's, in which language, in the infant mind, forms together with bodily movements (the word 'hot' includes a physical recoil where necessary), in such a way to establish a 'word-thing unity' in the brain's developmental interaction with the world. For Pearce, a later 'logic of differentiation', which enables a word to be 'abstracted from this unity', begins at the age of eleven. Thus, biological imperatives dictate the rate at which the child moves 'from concreteness to abstraction': 'the biological plan strives to get physical learning accomplished and out of the way so that more abstract learning might take place.'[31]

Another important influence on McEwan's thinking about the novel is Pearce's account of how play disappears from adult identity: this has a direct bearing on the portrayal of Charles Darke. Pearce sees play as adaptive, part of the development through which the individual 'moves toward autonomy', acquiring 'the intelligence to survive'. The ability to play 'on the surface' ensures the success of 'the nonconscious conceptual work' of development going on underneath, though the two levels are interdependent. However, a time comes when the surface play is destroyed, displaced by 'work on the surface' which becomes 'the aware self's drive'. Then, for Pearce, 'the inner work of intelligence breaks down . . . anxiety takes over, joy disappears, and the avoidance of death becomes the central issue of life'. By this apocalyptic account, Pearce means, simply, 'we grow up'.[32]

This puts a fresh perspective on Mars-Jones's comments on the portrayal of Darke, which extends his suspicion of McEwan's dramatization of the quest 'to make fatherhood a binding contract'. Darke, argues Mars-Jones, 'is not a real father, and his sponsorship of Stephen is a manipulative perversion of the real thing. The conclusion of the novel's Darke-strand is that men who do not produce children are condemned to become them.'[33] An acquaintance with McEwan's sources suggests that the characterization of Darke is an exploration of the failure of childhood, rather than the failure of adulthood; or, perhaps, an exaggerated depiction of how the work of childhood development might be adversely affected by the intrusion of adult concerns.

Many readers would probably concur with Slay's account of how the novel 'portrays the search for the child that exists in every individual'.[34] Again, an acquaintance with McEwan's sources suggests a way of enriching that observation.

The third book cited in the Acknowledgements is Christina Hardyment's *Dream Babies: Three Centuries of Good Advice on Child Care*, which examines baby-care manuals from the mid-eighteenth century through to the 1980s. (The starting point for the survey identifies the historical moment when such manuals began to be written for intelligent parents and not just for medical practitioners.) The sceptical spirit of Hardyment's survey is intended to encourage parents to be more selective in their perusal of modern manuals, and to place greater 'trust in their own feelings towards their children'. A prescriptive approach to parenting, she suggests, 'is arguably as silly as sending false teeth through the post and hoping that they will fit.'[35]

There is certainly resistance to a particular kind of prescriptive approach in McEwan's fictional HMSO childcare handbook; yet the book strives for a synthesis of ideas, which makes *The Child in Time* implicitly prescriptive in its own way. Perhaps the most significant influence McEwan draws from Hardyment is her authoritative demonstration that there are fashions in parenting, and that childcare manuals are subject to diverse social and cultural influences.

In preparation for his work on the sub-committee, Stephen has read the background material (evidently inspired by McEwan's reading of Hardyment), extracted from 'three centuries [of] instructions and ever-mutating facts for the benefit of mothers.' The relativity of 'absolute truth' is the lesson that emerges from these judgements, which demonstrate the folly of each generation's pretensions 'to stand on the pinnacle of common sense and scientific insight to which its predecessors had merely aspired' (*CT*, p. 80).

McEwan projects his authoritarian childcare handbook as the logical extension of unchecked Thatcherism. The epigraphs to each chapter, comprising extracts from this fictional government handbook, serve two purposes: first to satirize Thatcherite policies, making explicit the fear that a government concerned with promoting individual self-interest and competition probably *is* in the business of infiltrating private consciousness with ideological propaganda; and, second, to offer an ironic contrast with aspects of the narrative development, which sometimes undermine the position taken in the handbook.

The ironic counterpoint is thorough, in some cases. For example, the epigraph to chapter 2 emphasizes the importance of clock time as a way of reinforcing discipline, routine and predetermined adult roles (*CT*, p. 27). The chapter, however, treats the indeterminacy of time and identity: the scientific theme of relative time is introduced (*CT*, pp. 43–5), and the first hint of Stephen's timeslip, or hallucination, is given in his 'unplaced memory' of being with his parents cycling in Kent, even though this does not seem possible, and this 'memory' provokes thoughts on the hidden histories of parents which can make them 'strangers to their children' (*CT*, pp. 47–8). The spectre of Armageddon, the end of human time, is raised in a projected repetition of the Cuban missile crisis, the stand-off this time stemming from a fracas at the Olympic Games involving two sprinters, a Russian and an American (*CT*, pp. 34–6). Stephen's adult role is shown to be determined by cultural whim – he aspires to be a writer in the 'European cultural tradition' of Joyce, Mann or Shakespeare, but is redefined by his publisher as a children's author (*CT*, pp. 28–34); and Charles Darke's arbitrary decision to pursue a political career on the right rather than the left is recalled (*CT*, pp. 37–8).

In its cultivation of a political dystopia, the novel has sometimes been criticized for a political commentary that is too overt, which is interesting in the light of McEwan's own convictions about the need to keep authorial opinions in check, and his view that those two works of political ideas written in other media – the oratorio and the screenplay – had paved the way for the more exploratory work of this novel. Certainly, the dystopia is a projection of Thatcherite policies, presented through such features as the cynical opportunism of Darke.[36]

For D. J. Taylor, there is a marked contrast between the 'political debate', which is 'sheer caricature', and 'the novel's informal scenes' concerning, for example, the relationship between Stephen and Julie, and the lost child, scenes that 'strike a consistently relaxed yet forceful note.' For Taylor it is 'masterly' in its examination of the family, yet 'as an examination of the way in which people formally react to political contingency . . . fundamentally flawed.'[37] Taylor was later to reinforce his critique of the book's political content, writing that it 'makes its points with the grace of a meat-cleaver.'[38] The contrast detected by Taylor between the success of the family strand and the failure of the political element stands in opposition, of course, to my reading of the novel as a reimagining of the private–public nexus in fiction.

Agreeing with Taylor to a degree, Ryan feels 'the novel is indeed scarred by passages where McEwan does too much expounding and not enough implying, where the discursive scaffolding of the book has been incompletely dismantled.' On balance, Ryan feels that 'the flaws of the novel are far outweighed by its accomplishments';[39] but these harsh criticisms of the political element of the novel need to be addressed. What is revealing is that these early assessments no longer carry the weight they would have had closer to the date of the novel's publication.

From the perspective of the twenty-first century, the dystopian elements of the novel are far less pronounced than they were in 1987 for the simple and depressing reason that some of McEwan's projections have become recognizable aspects of contemporary experience. All readers are now familiar with the presence of beggars on British streets, and with the kind of aggressive begging experienced by Stephen (*CT*, pp. 8–9, 102). We may not have badge-wearing, licensed beggars, working 'authorized thoroughfares' (*CT*, p. 101), but the familiar sight of homeless people selling *The Big Issue* – purposeful, but obliged to occupy designated sites and to wear official badges – makes the invented policy of a scheme of licensed begging to save social security expenditure seem distinctly less fantastic (*CT*, p. 39).[40] The dystopian element of the novel with which we are now most familiar is climate change. Of course, the predictions of dramatic climate change, such as those summarized in the novel (*CT*, p. 123), were etched in the popular consciousness; but the freak hot summer described in the novel, followed by severe winds and gales that effectively bypass autumn (*CT*, p. 123) – an 'abnormality' which now seems representative, merely – would have seemed more darkly predictive in 1987.[41] Another example is the government-sponsored (but still commercial), all-day TV channel, specializing in game shows, chat shows and phone-ins: this inevitably seemed more sinister at a time when satellite broadcasting in Britain was relatively new (*CT*, p. 124).[42]

These unsettling dystopian elements have become less remarkable as the times have caught up with the novel; and this does have an effect on its reception. In particular, the timeslip, read without a knowledge of McEwan's sources, now seems a moment of pronounced unevenness in a novel that, originally, was more uniformly discomfiting.

Ben Knights reads the novel sympathetically as 'a sort of green parable addressed to the late 1980s', in which 'the collective fears haunting the moment of writing' – the fear of nuclear conflict, environmental degradation, the rise of the underclass, and so on – amount to more than 'a gratuitous or alarmist setting'; indeed, for Knights, 'the narrator's pessimistic assessment of the social and environmental moment contours the structure of the novel as a whole.' Knights picks up on Stephen's reflection that 'the art of bad government was to sever the line between public policy and intimate feeling' (*CT*, pp. 8–9), and argues that 'the whole novel appears to be a symbolic attempt to redress that severance'.[43]

The way in which this is done, in Knights' account – given the overt 'critique of mainstream masculinity and patriarchal power' – is through a development of masculinity, signalled by Stephen's recognition of how men might learn from a female 'principle of selfhood in which being surpassed doing.' (*CT*, p. 55) With Stephen deputizing for the narrator is such moments, Knights suggests that the novel's project 'may be to reclaim for men – through the agency of the male author – a share of that plasticity and that creative inner space.'

But this is also a strained attempt to right the wrongs of patriarchy, and to co-opt the work of the male author in the spirit of productive reconciliation, an idea which culminates in Stephen acting as mid-wife to his new child in the closing scene, with its hopeful 'saviour' motif.[44]

As a green parable, denoting the necessary reorientation of masculinity, and positing the role of the male author within this process, the novel is avowedly optimistic. The difficulty of the task, and the effort of credulity required, is tacitly acknowledged in the arrested moment of the novel's end, with the sex of the new baby left indeterminate (*CT*, p. 220). A parallel effort of credulity, of course, is asked of the reader in accepting the timeslip, which we might now present as a crucial bridge between public discourse in its most grandiose form – the scientific attempt to understand Nature – and the most essential aspect of individual being: the progression from conception to birth. It is an extraordinary artistic conception, and a stunningly inventive rearticulation of the materials that might comprise the novel of society.

The considerable effort of credulity that the novel self-consciously asks of the reader ensures that there is no easy consolation to be taken from it, however. Indeed, when the new child is born, we cannot help but recall the abducted Kate, whose disappearance, so terrifyingly depicted at the outset, is never explained, and who remains lost to us.

Notes

1 The book was finished before Margaret Thatcher's third election victory in 1987. Allan Massie, for example, suggests that the book 'belongs to the tradition of the "Condition of England novel" '. See *The Novel Today, 1970–89* (London: Longman, 1990), p. 51.

2 McEwan supplies these details in the Preface to *A Move Abroad: 'Or Shall We Die?' and 'The Ploughman's Lunch'* (London: Picador, 1989), pp. vii–xxvi.

3 Sleeve notes to Michael Berkeley's, *Or Shall We Die?*, words by Ian McEwan, London Symphony Orchestra, conducted by Richard Hickox, Heather Harper (soprano), David Wilson-Johnson (baritone), EMI 1984 (ASD 2700581). In the longer 'Introduction' to the piece in *A Move Abroad*, McEwan reveals his source for this section: 'Mrs Tomoyasu was a young woman in 1945 whose nine-year-old daughter died in her arms. She told her story to Jonathan Dimbleby in his film *In Evidence: The Bomb*' (*MA*, p. 7).

4 Sleeve notes to Michael Berkeley, *Or Shall We Die?* In *A Move Abroad*, however, McEwan observes that the stanzas from Blake were only inserted after he had finished a first draft of the libretto (*MA*, p. 12).

5   Adam Mars-Jones gives a persuasive account of the date in 'Venus Envy', printed in *Blind Bitter Happiness* (London: Chatto and Windus, 1997), pp. 128–56 (p. 142).

6   Slay, *Ian McEwan*, p. 115.

7   In Peter Childs' account, childhood figures prominently in McEwan's work, as a governing idea. Apropos of *The Cement Garden* and *Atonement*, but with regard to the oeuvre more generally, Childs finds a treatment of childhood as 'a sleep from which everyone must awaken to face an adult world where their former actions will have unforeseen consequences.' At the same time, childhood is 'a realm adults seek to control but to which they also seek to return.' See Peter Childs, *Contemporary Novelists: British Fiction Since 1970* (Basingstoke: Palgrave, 2005), p. 173.

8   Mars-Jones, *Blind Bitter Happiness*, pp. 129, 151, 128–9, 148, 152.

9   Ibid., pp. 148, 149, 142, 143.

10 Ibid., p. 153.

11 Sheila Kitzinger observes that 'some women are thought to be especially sensitive to prostaglandins in semen. (Prostaglandins cause the uterus to contract, and semen has a higher proportion of them than any other body substance.)' See *The New Pregnancy and Childbirth* (London: Penguin, 1997), p. 168.

12 McEwan became father to two sons during the writing of the novel, and it is clear that the anticipation and then the experience of fatherhood had a profound effect on his creativity. (See Jonathan Noakes, 'Interview with Ian McEwan' (21 September 2001), in Margaret Reynolds and Jonathan Noakes, eds, *Ian McEwan: The Essential Guide* (London: Vintage, 2002), pp. 10–23 (p. 12).) If *The Child in Time* is McEwan's first novel of maturity, then it is hard not to see a connection between fatherhood and his enlarged social vision.

13 The popularity of the novel as an A Level set text in England tends to suggest this.

14 Slay, *Ian McEwan*, p. 124.

15 Ryan, *Ian McEwan*, p. 52.

16 Malcolm, *Understanding Ian McEwan*, p. 98.

17 Ibid., p. 100.

18 Interview with Melvyn Bragg, *The South Bank Show*, ITV1, broadcast 20 February 2005.

19 Thelma is a lecturer in Physics at Birkbeck College, London (*CT*, p. 32), where David Bohm held a Chair from 1961 until his death in 1992. (See Will Keepin, 'Lifework of David Bohm: River of Truth', www.satyana.org/html/bohm3.html (accessed 12 January 2005), also posted elsewhere on the internet.)

20 For Brian McHale, references to actual people/places/ideas mean that these are incorporated rather than reflected in fiction: they comprise areas

of ontological difference within a fictional heterocosm that is otherwise homogeneous. See *Postmodernist Fiction* (1987; reprinted London: Routledge, 1991), p. 28.

21 David Bohm, 'A New Theory of the Relationship of Mind and Matter', *Philosophical Psychology*, 3: 2 (1990), pp. 271–86; reproduced at: http://members.aol.com/Mszlazak/BOHM.html (accessed 12 January 2005).

22 David Bohm, *Wholeness and the Implicate Order* (London: Routledge, 1980), p. 31.

23 Students of literature are more commonly referred to Henri Bergson's ideas about consciousness (which may have inspired Proust), as a continuous and unmeasurable flow. See Henri Bergson, *Time and Free Will: An Essay on the Immediate Data of Consciousness*, trans. F. L. Pogson (1889; third edition, 1913, reprinted New York: Dover, 2001).

24 Bohm, Wholeness and the Implicate Order, pp. 267–9.

25 The relevant 'typical stopping distances' given in the *Highway Code* are 120 feet for 40 mph, and 175 feet for 50 mph. See www.highwaycode.gov.uk/09.shtml (accessed 19 January 2005).

26 Joseph Chilton Pearce, *Magical Child* (1977; London: Plume, 1992), pp. 47, 59.

27 Ibid., p. 62. The good nurturing work done by Ugandan mothers, in the survey alluded to, is destroyed, however, by the cultural imperative that obliges a mother to give up her child to relatives or neighbours at the age of four (pp. 63–4).

28 Bohm, *Wholeness and the Implicate Order*, pp. 183–4, 186, 188.

29 Pearce, *Magical Child*, pp. 6, 209.

30 Ibid., p. 143. Pearce is drawing on the ideas of Jean Piaget here, and elsewhere, in his book.

31 Ibid., pp. 196–7, 171.

32 Ibid., p. 171.

33 Mars-Jones, *Blind Bitter Happiness*, pp. 152, 146.

34 Slay, *Ian McEwan*, p. 115.

35 Christina Hardyment, *Dream Babies: Three Centuries of Good Advice on Child Care* (New York: Harper and Row, 1983), p. xv.

36 The Prime Minister's obsessive fondness for Darke may be an exaggeration inspired by Mrs Thatcher's reputed fondness for Cecil Parkinson: he is said to have been 'a favourite' of hers. (See, for example, www.bbc.co.uk/politics97/news/06/0603/hague.shtml (accessed 19 January 2005).) Parkinson resigned from the government in 1983 over his affair with his secretary Sara Keays, and the 'lovechild scandal' that ensued. He was 'the fourth Tory MP . . . to hit the headlines for scandal since Thatcher gained power in 1979'. See http://news.bbc.co.uk/onthisday/hi/dates/stories/october/14/newsid_2534000/2534615.stm (accessed 19 January 2005).

37   D. J. Taylor, *A Vain Conceit: British Fiction in the 1980s* (London: Bloomsbury, 1989), p. 59.

38   D. J. Taylor, *After the War: The Novel and England Since 1945* (1993; London: Flamingo, 1994), p. 270.

39   Ryan, *Ian McEwan*, p. 51.

40   *The Big Issue* was launched in September 1991 – initially, as a monthly publication in London only. See www.bigissue.com/aboutmag.html (accessed 14 January 2005). Aggressive begging has been a prominent topic in headline politics for several years, and throughout the New Labour administration. Tony Blair was answering questions on this topic from 1997. For example, see www.bbc.co.uk/politics97/news/06/0613/answers.shtml (accessed 14 January 2005).

41   In the Great Storm of 16 October 1987 eighteen people were killed in England (the casualties would doubtless have been greater had the storm struck during the day), and 15 million trees were lost in southern England. See www.metoffice.com/education/historic/1987.html (accessed 14 January 2005). This storm probably represents the watershed in British public perceptions about climate change, and marks the growing realization that inclement weather will be the future norm. *The Child in Time* was published the previous month, in September 1987.

42   Sky TV had been launched in 1984, but BSB (British Satellite Broadcasting) did not begin transmission until April 1990. (It was later merged with Sky to form BskyB.) See www.makingthemodernworld.org.uk/learning_modules/history/04.TU.04/?style=expander_popup&filename=expandables/04.EX.12.xml (accessed 22 April 2005).

43   Ben Knights, *Writing Masculinities: Male Narratives in Twentieth-Century Fiction* (Basingstoke: Macmillan, 1999), pp. 207, 209.

44   Ibid., pp. 208, 215, 220.

5

Unravelling the binaries:
The Innocent and *Black Dogs*

In the next two novels, the private–public nexus is extended in different ways. Both works engage with international politics, and particularly with the collapse of communism in Eastern Europe. In this respect, *The Innocent* and *Black Dogs*, taken together, represent a significant phase of political writing. At the same time, there is a retreat from the extraordinarily empathic treatment of the personal in *The Child in Time*. This is understandable in the sense that the literary gesture that determines that effect – the timeslip, embedded in the context of the novel – is probably a once-in-a-career invention. There is a retreat from that resonant opening out of the personal in this next phase of writing, and a partial return to the earlier emphasis on the exploitative nature of the individual psyche.

As an illustration of how this theme creates a new personal–political dynamic, there is a rape fantasy in *The Innocent* that introduces an element of political allegory about the domination of weak nations by strong ones;[1] and in the novel's dismemberment scene – a clear return to the shock tactics of the early works – McEwan makes a gruesome point about the carving up of the global body politic in the Cold War period. However, the personal theme of the loss of innocence predominates. In *Black Dogs*, too, the treatment of individual motivation and choice becomes crucial, finally modifying and enriching the surface novel-of-ideas (suggested by the ideological antagonism in the marriage of June and Bernard). Against a backdrop that posits inhumanity as the sponsor of political conflict, McEwan conducts an exploration of narrative reliability, thus tying in the business of writing to the larger deliberation about ethics and responsibility.

The Innocent

The Innocent represents a stylistic departure for McEwan, since its mood and plot is directly influenced by the Cold War spy novel. Malcolm Bradbury feels the presence of the spy novels of Len Deighton and John Le Carré (and behind them the influence of Graham Greene), and suggests that these writers have a bearing on McEwan's treatment of 'the moral state of post-war Britain', and the paranoia that a corrupted Establishment invokes.[2]

The novel is set in 1955–56, and focuses on Leonard Marnham, the 'innocent' of the novel's title, who goes to Germany to undertake electronics work in the Berlin Tunnel, or Operation Gold, a joint American and British espionage venture, designed to lay secret underground taps on Russian communication lines. The narrative, part thriller, part psychological novel, presents a series of tests of Leonard's innocence. He has to negotiate the flagrant anti-Britishness of his superior, Bob Glass, and is persuaded to undertake some minor (but ineffectual) espionage himself, rooted in Anglo-American distrust.

The personal and the political strands come together through Leonard's relationship with, and engagement to, Maria. His awakening is sexual, emotional and political, and the tension between these pulls is highlighted in the novel's focal dramatic scene and its aftermath. This is the killing of Maria's former husband, the violent Otto. Leonard and Maria conclude that any plea of self-defence will not be taken seriously, and so decide to dismember the corpse and dispose of it in a railway locker. In a nightmare sequence, the plan is thwarted, and Leonard decides to secrete the cases containing Otto in the tunnel. In the desperate hope of covering up the action, he betrays the tunnel to the Russians, convinced that they will conceal the discovery.

The postscript, a letter from Maria, written thirty years later, reveals that the tunnel was actually betrayed by the double-agent George Blake, who appears as a character in the novel, and who chooses this moment to advise that the tunnel be 'uncovered' (the Russians were aware of it from the beginning), because he believes Leonard has deposited valuable decoding equipment there (rather than a dismembered corpse). The postscript also reveals that Maria and Glass had married, after the estrangement of Maria and Leonard caused by the guilt each comes to represent for the other following the butchery of Otto.

It is the psychological and moral ramifications of the events that make them resonate. The horrifying dismemberment scene comprises the most arresting such event. Equally significant, however, is the situation that pushes Leonard to the expedient of betraying his country, in order (he hopes) to save himself and Maria. The fact that George Blake had got there before him does not ameliorate the decision to betray, which is a straightforward decision to privilege the personal over the political, in a definitive scenario.[3]

The mutual antagonism between the Americans and the British has, at its root, a distinction between amateurism and professionalism. The novel's opening underscores this idea, where Lieutenant Lofting meets Leonard, and is more concerned with the double-dealing of the Americans over the planning of an inter-section swimming match than he is with explaining Leonard's duties (*I*, pp. 1–2). 'You're not serious the way we are', Glass complains to Leonard, bemoaning the miscalculations of John MacNamee on heat output, done 'on the back of an envelope', and which may betray the tunnel when the autumn frosts come. The Americans, claims Glass, 'would have had three independent teams. If they hadn't come up with the same result, we would have wanted to know why' (*I*, p. 119). The unpreparedness or immaturity of the British for the emerging Cold War is signalled economically by choice symbolic details. MacNamee's crooked teeth, for example, are his milk teeth: 'the other lot never came through', he explains: 'I think perhaps I never wanted to grow up' (*I*, p. 71).

Leonard is a representative of this other kind of innocence – that of the amateur. When MacNamee – 'a senior government scientist', in Leonard's estimation (*I*, p. 69) – conscripts him for a spot of spying, the ineffectiveness of the amateur is made explicit. Leonard's attempts to glean technical information about the American code-breaking system is confined to trying a couple of locked doors, and 'one unsuccessful minute in Glass's office' (*I*, p. 105). The tough-mindedness of George Blake – who, for instance, seems more security-conscious than Glass at the engagement party (*I*, p. 135) – only serves to emphasize the routine dilettantism of the British (and, we infer, the ease with which their cause might be betrayed). As the novel progresses, however, the distinction between what is innocent or amateur, and what is knowing or professional, becomes acutely problematic.

There is an allegorical dimension to the novel that invites an equation between individual action and international politics. Kiernan Ryan observes that one of the novel's main concerns is to show 'the eclipsing of Britain by the USA, both as a political and as a cultural force.'⁴ It is quite pointed, for example, that the suggestible Leonard is open to being 'colonized' by US culture, most especially popular music, the temptation of which defeats his English restraint. Leonard and Maria initially disapprove of couples jiving on the dance floor; he thinks it is 'showy and childish, typically American.' However, 'once they had succumbed to the music, there was nothing for it but to turn up the volume of Leonard's wireless set and try the steps' (*I*, p. 130).

McEwan convincingly claimed to have conceived Leonard's susceptibility to US culture, 'overcoming his distaste for rock and roll and beginning to like freezing cold Coca Cola, and accepting that grown men might drink chocolate milk', as a marker of political change, and literary-historical change, simultaneously. In the year before the Suez crisis, with British imperial power and dominion in terminal retreat, McEwan projects a character who 'goes abroad for the first time in his life and is rather unconfident, rather in the way his country is so recently unconfident.' This is quite unlike the Englishman abroad in the work of earlier English novelists: where Evelyn Waugh in *The Loved One* (1948), McEwan suggests, could plausibly invent a hero who 'would've felt he belonged to a superior race', viewing American habits as 'fundamentally empty and vulgar', Leonard feels 'the Americans offer a world he'd rather like to enter.'⁵

The sense of Leonard's rudderless impressionability affords the opportunity for McEwan to bring political allegory and personal psychology together in compelling fashion, as he does in the dismemberment scene. In asserting his intention 'to show the brutality man can aspire to by comparing the dismemberment of a corpse to the dismemberment of a city: the bomb-devastated Berlin of the post-war', McEwan emphasizes a continuity between the public and the private that Leonard also observes:⁶ in the middle of the process, after Leonard has severed Otto's head, he reflects that 'what was on the table now was no one at all. It was the field of operations, it was a city far below he had been ordered to destroy' (*I*, p. 178). Leonard desensitizes himself in order to proceed, principally by taking frequent swigs of gin, but also by the mental trick mentioned here. The image evokes that haunting wartime footage of the nuclear attacks on Japan that became an integral part of twentieth-century consciousness. Following the order, and letting the bomb go, is an impersonal act if one sees the city far below as a map, a plan of campaign, rather than as a populated place.

Leonard's mental trick is a conscious act of self-deceit, of course, and it opens up a profound rift in his psyche. In order to reduce Otto's corpse to manageable sections that will fit the two cases obtained to remove the evidence, it is necessary to saw the torso in half. As Leonard bungles this operation, Otto's innards disgorge onto the carpet: 'the insult was, Leonard had time to think, as he stepped hurriedly round the up-ended halves of the torso that were still joined, that all this stuff was also in himself' (*I*, p. 182). The 'insult' is the reminder of the common human biology that links Leonard to Otto.

The larger connotation of this insult is the affront to our emotional and spiritual aspirations, shown to be constrained by the corporeal; but within the scene, the offence is also the evidence that makes Leonard's distancing strategy ludicrous: he is cheated of his mental self-protection. Later, when Leonard has a vivid dream of opening the cases and putting Otto back together again, we have a sense of how deep the psychological scar may be. Leonard and Maria's estrangement from each other has its roots in their shared transgression, and the reminder of it that each represents to the other. It begins in the aftermath of the dismemberment, when 'everything between them, every detail, every transaction, chafed and irritated, like grit in the eye' (*I*, p. 184). The sense of guilt permeates the language at times, as in the scene at the train station where Leonard is thwarted in his intention of leaving the cases containing the dismembered Otto in a locker: the observation that 'his thoughts were oozing quickly' leaves us in no doubt about the urgent need to dispose of the cases (*I*, p. 191).

Such a straightforward 'moral' reading, however, may not do full justice to the episode. The effect of the dismemberment on Leonard is both profound and ambiguous. It propels him, in fact, into a state that corresponds very closely to *abjection*, as articulated by Julia Kristeva. For Kristeva, the abject is the horrified response to the threatened collapse of meaning when the distinction between self and other is blurred. A corpse, which instantly reminds us of our own mortality, is Kristeva's chief example of that which triggers the abject: 'the corpse, seen without God and outside of science, is the utmost of abjection. It is death injecting life. Abject.'[7] The 'insult' Leonard feels at the sight of Otto's innards (*I*, p. 182) opens him up to an appreciation of the breakdown of meaning in abjection, where the threatened collapse of 'borders, positions, rules' emphatically 'disturbs identity, system, order'.[8] The uncertainty of the Englishman abroad is here exacerbated in the most radical fashion: the visceral demonstration of mortality dissolves the line between Englishman/German and lover/abuser, upon which his sense of self as an agent, with moral rectitude, depends. Leonard's predicament is perfectly understood through this under-mining of the symbolic order of identity, and the collapse of those binary opposites upon which it is built.

There are other aspects of Kristeva's account of abjection that seem relevant to Leonard's state. For Kristeva, the abject is more than an expression of horror or trauma: it also marks the moment in an individual's development when he or she begins to recognize the distinction between self and *m*other. Yet the desired moment of separation is irreducibly ambivalent, since it is also the primal moment of expulsion. In tune with this ambivalent aspect of abjection in the psychoanalytic tradition, Leonard's childish turn of mind sometimes seems to hint at a psychological need for regression.

A further complication is that we are drawn to the abject, despite the horror that it arouses. For Kristeva, literature is an ideal site for the exploration of the abject, that is, for an aesthetic experience of the abject that is also a form of catharsis, of '*purifying* the abject'.[9]

In this light we need to consider Kiernan Ryan's worry about the dismemberment, which, he suggests, implies a Chinese-box structure to the novel that effectively dissolves its narrative structure. The 'spy yarn' conceals 'a wry historical novel about the twilight of British supremacy, the triumph of American cultural imperialism and the ice age of the Cold War.' Then, however,

> the bottom slides out of this chronicle to reveal a *Bildungsroman*, in which a young man barters his guiltless heart for bittersweet carnal knowledge and a gruesome schooling in the craft of the abattoir. Squatting at the heart of this tale is the appalling spectacle of the demystified body, the black hole in the text through which meaning itself threatens to bleed away.[10]

In Kristeva's account of abjection, the meaning that threatens to bleed away might be conceived as the social identities that permit the skewed self-justification that Maria and Leonard indulge in, and which the reader is also invited to invest in: the projection of them as an engaged couple, with their future under threat. They act in self-defence, and *circumstances* drive them to butcher the corpse of the violent ex-husband, wrongly identified as a war hero by the local police. If the corpse triggers the abject, and the potential collapse of those identities upon which their future as a couple depends, then Leonard's dream of reassembling the corpse has potentially opposing meanings: the apparent workings of a guilty conscience might also be read as a denial of the abject, as a reassertion of the separate identities that are being effaced in the reaction to the corpse.

What also begins to break down in the dismemberment scene is any easy parallel between private and public realms. Immediately before, at Leonard and Maria's engagement party, Glass makes an idealistic speech about how personal relationships signal a process of political healing, and, of course, the prospect of a marriage between an Englishman and a German woman in 1956 is particularly symbolic, in this regard: 'their marriage, and all others like it, bind countries tighter than any treaty can', says Glass (*I*, p. 134). However, his is an orthodox American, Cold War view, where the personal is deemed to be benign only insofar as it corresponds to current foreign policy. Later, to Leonard, Maria outwardly condemns Glass's view: 'Does he think I'm the Third Reich. Is that what he thinks you are marrying? Does he really think that people represent countries?' (*I*, p. 139). Leonard doubts Maria's convictions, here; but he is prone to consistent jealously about Glass and Maria which, ultimately, seems to be a reasonable apprehension about Glass, but not Maria. In her letter to Leonard, written thirty years later, she explains that her affair with Glass began nine months after Leonard's departure from Berlin. Yet she also reveals how Glass had used his position to cover up the killing of Otto, but had sworn her to secrecy. Circumstances had presented him with an opportunity to bind her to him, to use the machinations of political secrecy to advance his own personal cause, in a cynical manipulation in which the personal is artificially tied to the political (*I*, pp. 239–40).

The central question that the book poses is 'what is innocence?' Leonard's initial attributes – bestowed, for example, by his sheltered background and his virginity – mark him out as an empty vessel. This can make him seem to be someone with humble expectations, and whose impact on his environment is minimal, benign.

When he is introduced to the repetitive work of his early days in Berlin, for example, the prospect makes him 'unaccountably happy' (*I*, p. 22). However, the extent to which Leonard's status as a novice generates innocence is soon called into question. When he parrots the opinion of two Englishmen about the behaviour of the Russians in 1945, the ease with which his 'emptiness' can be filled is disturbing. In the manner of a child, Leonard wants his American drinking companions to be fooled by the 'quiet authority' he seeks to project by suggesting that, in the wake of the savage behaviour of the Russian troops, the memory of rape and brutality ensures that men of other nations have a greater opportunity of sexual success with Berlin women (*I*, pp. 29, 33). The expectation of sexual conquest reveals a degree of continuity with the posited rapists, of course, and the failure to examine this, coupled with the sexual bravado of the innocent, makes us realize that Leonard's initiation into both private and public worlds might well unleash unpleasant tendencies.

The most shocking element of Leonard's sexual initiation is the speed with which he progresses from the fear of the insecure novitiate to the desire of the would-be rapist. When his rape fantasy first materializes – he imagines himself as a victorious, heroic soldier, and Maria as the defeated conquest – he tries to reject 'these formulations' when he reflects on them: 'they were alien to his obliging and kindly nature, they offended his sense of what was reasonable' (*I*, p. 83).

In Leonard's desire to dominate Maria there is, of course, an element of political allegory. Slay points to the apparent intention that Leonard should 'represent the moral anarchy that entices stronger nations to force their world views on weaker countries'.[11] Yet this protracted episode is also a grim investigation of personal psychology. Unable to contain his rape fantasies, Leonard desires to express his domination outwardly and to involve Maria in the role-play. Wilfully, he persuades himself that her reluctance to succumb to his unwanted sexual demand will evolve, if he persists, into an acceptance of her role in his fantasy. When he dimly perceives he is wrong, and that he may have destroyed their relationship, a telling thought comes to his mind:

> There came to him an image of a blue clockwork locomotive, a present on his eighth or ninth birthday. It pulled a string of coal trucks round a figure-of-eight track until one afternoon, in a spirit of reverent experimentation, he had overwound it. (*I*, pp. 88–9)

A little earlier, the sight of power lines and the technical paraphernalia in the tunnel makes him think of 'the gigantic train set in Hamleys' (p. 71). Then, as here, the infantile thought might seem to indicate personal failure, rather than innocence. The failure to register adequately the signs of each situation – the trappings of the Cold War, the torment of a violated woman – ensures that we begin to see Leonard's 'innocence' as insular to the point of stupidity and brutality. The broken toy that Leonard sees as an image of his shattered relationship suggests continuity with the selfishness of the disappointed or thwarted child. Maria's 'more burdensome' memory from ten years before, as she recoils from Leonard, emphasizes the extent of his immaturity: she remembers the rape by a Russian soldier, in an air raid shelter, of a woman who had been shot in both legs (*I*, p. 89).

This reading is not stable, however. Indeed, part of the unsettling nature of the novel is that quite opposing readings of such details as the clockwork locomotive are possible. Here, Leonard's self-pitying childhood memory of the over-wound toy is an interesting moment of regression. This is not exactly that aspect of abjection which preserves the connection between infant and mother; but it is a pale echo of the pre-objectal relationship preserved in the abject, in the sense that the self-pity is predicated in that state where the child's emotional needs assume central significance. This trace of abjection, with its inherent challenge to adult selfhood, displaces the constructed adult identity, here – the Englishman fantasizing about rape in post-war Germany.

In such moments, the novel might be said to illustrate the more radical and purposive aspects of abjection that are sometimes claimed for Kristeva. In 'focusing on those "borderline practices" that disturb notions of identity, system and order', does she not, in the words of Joan Brandt, advance a 'project to undermine a culture whose social systems are seen as totalising and repressive'?[12]

Yet Leonard's innocence in his relationship with Maria functions, primarily, as a measure of how his immaturity leaves him ill-equipped to deal with situations of emotional and psychological complexity. Or, in other words, innocence leaves him acutely susceptible to the repressive effects of acculturation, in the context he is thrown into. His rape fantasy is the product of an 'innocent' imagination in the sense that it is arrived at by a series of steps in which powerful external influences act upon Leonard's undeveloped moral self. In beginning to see Maria as an object of conquest, he discovers that the word 'German', in his mind, 'had not been prised loose of its associations after all. . . . German. Enemy. Mortal Enemy. Defeated Enemy.' (*I*, p. 83) A contributory factor, then, is the impact of wartime ideology on Leonard in his impressionable boyhood. Maria herself comes to the view 'that Leonard was not malicious or brutal, and that it was an innocent stupidity that had made him behave the way he had' (*I*, p. 111). The possibility of losing Maria marks a key stage in Leonard's development and, making his apology, he finds himself acknowledging 'a serious emotion' in himself for the first time. His emotions are mixed – 'shame, desperation, love' – but out of the personal need comes the beginning of his capacity to identify with another (*I*, p. 107).

This does not entirely absolve Leonard from responsibility for his dubious acts, of course; and the ambivalence surrounding his innocence is most pronounced in the episode culminating in the killing and dismemberment of Otto. In a reiteration of the stage-by-stage rape fantasy, a series of steps – each one of which 'had seemed logical enough, consistent with the one before' (*I*, p. 182) – leads Leonard and Maria to the decision to try and dispose surreptitiously of Otto.

A central aspect of assessing Leonard's innocence or culpability is to establish the submerged moral code against which his actions may be measured. The novel, in fact, teases us with some clues about the moral code that might be applied. Thus, Leonard's assault on Maria becomes a kind of Fall, before which 'it had seemed possible to make their own rules, and thrive independently of those quiet, forceful conventions that keep men and women in their tracks'. Leonard's 'naughtiness', as Maria terms it, 'forced them back', and obliges them to settle for 'blissful ordinariness' (*I*, pp. 117, 118). However, if it is the pronounced innocence of his social disengagement and inexperience that makes Leonard especially susceptible to selfish and harmful impulses, it seems to follow that the enforced experience of social contingency is the primary element of his personal growth.

Late in the novel, we are presented with Leonard's rationale for his actions, his self-justification as he wrestles with his guilt. Here there is another attempt to suggest the inevitability of each 'logical step' and 'sad necessity' that justifies the killing of Otto, the concealment of the killing, the dismemberment, the deception of his superiors and, finally, the betrayal of the tunnel (*I*, p. 216). He imagines himself making a courtroom defence of his actions, and prepares a speech in his mind in which he might '*plead guilty to the charge as described* ', and yet prove, to judge and jurors, '*that I am no different from you, that I am not evil, and that all along I acted only for what I took to be the best* ' (*I*, p. 217; original emphasis).

There is a clear indication, however, that the course of events is by no means inevitable. When the drunken Otto is discovered asleep in the wardrobe, Maria and Leonard spend time arguing about him, rather than acting to evict him, or to take themselves out of danger. Their 'sense of violation' is displaced by 'householderly outrage'. Maria dismisses the suggestion that the police (who know Otto) should be called, and they are then distracted by mutual annoyances, and then accusations which cast doubt on their bond. As their argument flares, there is another conflagration, a bizarre prelude to the book's central scene of violence, as Maria is set on fire by a dropped cigarette (*I*, pp. 144–50).

Distracted by this drama, and having failed to evict or escape from Otto, Maria and Leonard must now confront him. It soon becomes clear that Otto intends to push a claim to Maria's flat, and Leonard's first reaction is that this is a solution: Otto can have Maria's flat, she can move in with him, since 'they did not need two places'. Maria, however, reads Otto's actions as a continuation of his desire to control her; though he does allude to a process of arbitration that makes it clear he is involving the appropriate authorities, however dubious his motivation may be. Once Otto attacks Maria, the violence is inevitable; but she has helped to goad him in an argument where she shows herself to be 'ferocious . . . a fighting cat, a tiger' (*I*, p. 154).

After the killing, Leonard's assumption is that they will call the police and explain how they acted in self-defence. However, Maria indicates that the local police, for whom Otto is a war hero, have been, effectively, in collusion with him in her oppression (*I*, pp. 160–1). Finally, and partly because of the extremity of the violence Otto appears to have suffered, Maria leads Leonard to share the conclusion she initially made: that the corpse will have to be disposed of surreptitiously (*I*, p. 169).

The sequence of choices and responses is a process of asserting self-interest. Leonard's suggestible innocence here makes him a convenient tool for Maria. There is no sense of a conscious plan on her part; but it is she who delivers the fatal blow to Otto, even though Leonard also has his hand on the cobbler's last as it crashes into Otto's skull, which is symbolic of their shared plight (*I*, p. 155). It is also interesting that she remonstrates with Leonard for his restrained response to Otto's presence, attacking his masculinity and ridiculing him for wanting a peaceful solution: 'you should be breaking the furniture. And what are you doing? Scratching your head and saying nicely we should get the police!' (*I*, p. 146). Maria's irrationality, and her vehement outbursts, form a convincing response to the scene; but her response is a contributory factor in the violence that ensues, and in which she participates.

The business with the corpse leads to Leonard's 'betrayal' of the tunnel, an apparent – and emphatic – loss of innocence. The fact that it is not really a betrayal, as its existence is known to the Russians, seems to demonstrate McEwan's view about spying as 'a curiously useless thing . . . an oddly circular, self-contained, self-referential system'.[13] Yet Leonard is unaware of this: as far as he is concerned, the imperative of self-protection outweighs any sense of international political allegiance. Even here, however, the idea of innocence is partially preserved. It is possible to weigh the element of self-interest in the balance against the image of the abject Leonard, scheming to have Otto's dismembered corpse secreted in the tunnel in suitcases. On the one hand, he appears as an agent of unchecked ego; on the other, in the eventual denial of his given role, he emerges as the combatant of the symbolic order that shapes the Cold War.

It takes a kind of innocence to presume to put personal interests above those of Western democracy; and herein lies the chief formal significance of the novel: it deploys the framework of a spy novel to produce an innovative psychological fiction in which a collapse of identity is glimpsed before being reasserted in such a way as to undermine the basis of Cold War politics.

In preparing the screenplay for the film version of the novel, McEwan made a series of interesting changes to the narrative. Most obvious is the use of the events of 1989 as a narrative frame, which sees Leonard returning to Berlin (in 1989 rather than 1987) to witness the celebrations of the bringing down of the Berlin Wall, and to meet Maria. The film ends with their embrace, she placing a flower in his hair as she had done on the night they met. A number of other changes serve to intensify the human drama. In the murder scene, for example, Otto brandishes divorce papers, which he has refused to sign (rather than papers about rights to Maria's flat): he offers to sign them if Leonard will reveal the truth about his work. This offer of Maria, in exchange for military secrets, requires Leonard to choose between private life and public life, as he eventually does in deciding to 'betray' the tunnel. It is possible to imagine the novel being adjusted to incorporate such refinements.[14]

Black Dogs

In *Black Dogs*, McEwan is exploring similar territory to *The Innocent*, continuing the process of reinvigorating the personal and the political in the context of post-war Europe. Ostensibly, *Black Dogs* is about human evil. Critics tend to baulk at using the term 'evil', often for quite understandable reasons – to some ears it will evoke a good/evil dichotomy with particular religious connotations that may be unintended. More worryingly, in political rhetoric the dichotomy forms part of the discourse of self-legitimization. In more recent times, McEwan has indicated that he does not find the term 'evil' helpful. Human behaviour may be so monstrous as to encourage us 'to reach for this numinous notion of evil', but he suggests it would be 'better to try and understand it in . . . political or psychological terms.'[15] Without denying the eminent good sense of this as a general principle, to my mind there may yet be episodes of human atrocity that are so monstrous that one still must have recourse to the term 'evil', even after the attempt to anatomize them in political or psychological terms. The Holocaust would be one such episode.

The particular force of the novel's effects emerges from memories of the Holocaust, and the reflection that the black dogs – the symbolic embodiments of Nazi terror – remain abroad in 'the mountains from where they will return to haunt us, somewhere in Europe, in another time' (*BD*, p. 174). These are the concluding words of the novel, which sound a cautionary note, and which belong to the mode of a moral and political fable. In the *Oxford English Literary History* Randall Stevenson emphasizes this dimension of the novel, highlighting its concern with Nazi crimes, in a discussion of how the Second World War 'continued to cast a shadow over fiction in the 1980s and 1990s'.[16] This seems to be especially true of McEwan, whose imaginative engagement with the legacy of the Second World War does not reach its fullest expression until the publication of *Atonement* in 2001.

In *Black Dogs*, there are two strands of particular importance. The first is, on the face of it, a straightforward thematic opposition between the rational and the spiritual life, conceived as contending ways of facing up to the terror of human history. The second strand, however, complicates all of this in crucial ways: this is the doubt concerning the motives and reliability of the narrator. Initially this seems to be a technical issue, pointing to the author's developing narrative skills, and anticipating the more extensive treatments of unreliable perceptions in *Enduring Love* and *Atonement*. Soon, however, it becomes clear that the narrator is psychologically damaged in ways that, we are encouraged to think, may affect his judgement, for all his external considerateness.

Connections are made between the larger historical evil and smaller acts of cruelty or unkindness. To a degree, this produces a satisfying whole, in the sense that the treatment of the private and the public, the personal and the political, are made to cohere, the larger historical lesson suggesting a moral code for daily life. Ultimately, however, the book is not reducible to so trite a summary: the ways in which the narrator's questionable hand is shown to shape key testimony, and the appearance of events, create a sense of unease, a technical equivalent to the idea that the black dogs remain loose in the mountains of Europe.

To give an initial sense of the novel's thematic concerns, I will put to one side the question of the narrator's role. Let us accept, for the time being, the notional conceit that our narrator is the convenient conduit, merely, for McEwan to relate the story of Bernard and June Tremaine, the narrator's parents-in-law. The story of these estranged partners, pieced together by the narrator from conversations with both, establishes a clear context for intertwining the public and the private. It is presented in its most straightforward form in Part Four of the novel. Here we learn how they meet, in 1944, and fall passionately in love, while Bernard has a desk job with the intelligence services and June is working as a linguist. They are not released from their wartime work until 1946, nearly a year after the end of the war. Then they marry – in Spring 1946 – and embark on their honeymoon, which will take the form of a tour of France and Italy.

The Tremaines, at this time, are idealistic young people, both members of the Communist Party and desirous of helping to build a new Europe. Shocked by the devastation they see, they volunteer for six weeks' tough labour at a Red Cross packing station. A fortnight before they are due to return to England, with the intention of settling down to peacetime married life, they embark on a walking tour in the Languedoc region of France. Here, on a road descending into a mountain gorge, June encounters two enormous black dogs, while amateur entomologist Bernard, out of sight on the road further back, has been distracted by the spectacle of a train of caterpillars.

As the dogs prepare to attack her, June experiences a Presence, at once *of* her and *not* of her, and finds the power to fight off the dogs, with a penknife as a sword and her rucksack as a shield (*BD*, pp. 149–52). It is her Damascene moment. They change their plans (with Bernard baffled), retrace their steps back up the gorge, and June recovers in a hotel. The local *Maire* is alerted to the episode, and he explains that the dogs are former Gestapo dogs, formerly used to intimidate the population, but which have now run wild. He tries to tell the lurid story of how the dogs had been trained to rape women, though he is interrupted furiously be Mme Auriac, the hotel owner, who dismisses the story as a salacious fantasy, designed to shame a woman attacked by the Gestapo (*BD*, pp. 155–62).

The rift between June and Bernard begins at this point: he is deeply sceptical of the story of the dogs, while she progresses into a mood of profound spirituality. As they continue their journey, Bernard has his own revelatory experience when they witness a stonemason carving fresh names in a war memorial where they are having lunch. The sight of a woman grieving for her husband and two brothers, whose names are apparently being added to the monument, brings home to Bernard the cost of the war in human terms. The consequences of the war he now sees less as a geopolitical fact, but, rather:

> a multiplicity, a near-infinity of private sorrows, as a boundless grief minutely subdivided without diminishment among individuals who covered the continent like dust, like spores whose separate identities would remain unknown, and whose totality showed more sadness than anyone could ever begin to comprehend. (BD, p. 165)

The question that formulates in Bernard's mind as a consequence is a political conundrum, filtered through this empathic response: 'what possible good could come of a Europe covered in this dust, these spores, when forgetting would be inhuman and dangerous, and remembering a constant torture?' (*BD*, p. 165).

On the evening of the same day they come by chance upon a derelict bergerie in an idyllic spot, and the berger, who sells it to the enraptured June. It is to become a holy place for her, and she goes to live in France in 1951 with her three children, beginning an existence of study and meditation. The children spend periods with Bernard in London: he leaves the Communist Party in 1956, after the Soviet invasion of Hungary (June had left it shortly after her encounter with the black dogs), and becomes an 'acceptable radical on BBC discussion programmes', and a Labour MP (*BD*, p. 171).

The story recounted in Part Four corresponds with the piecemeal account given earlier of a passionate love affair disrupted by conflicting world-views, the rational opposed to the spiritual. Both of these protagonists are presented as having formed a response to the horror of the Second World War, according to their predilections. Bernard's politics are tempered by the revelation of human suffering. June, however, feels that politics are insufficient in the face of human evil. A month before her death, June is reported as having given this account of her Damascene encounter (noted in shorthand by the narrator, who is nominally her biographer):

> 'Jeremy, that morning I came face to face with evil. I didn't quite know it at the time, but I sensed it in my fear – these animals were the creations of debased imaginations, of perverted spirits no amount of social theory could account for. The evil I'm talking about lives in us all. . . . And then, when the conditions are right, in different countries, at different times, a terrible cruelty, a viciousness against life erupts, and everyone is surprised by the depth of hatred within himself.' (*BD*, p. 172)

This explanation also tallies with Bernard's account of how June had developed Churchill's term for a depression – black dog, in the singular: 'June's idea was that if one dog was a personal depression, two dogs were a kind of cultural depression, civilisation's worst moods' (*BD*, p. 104). For June, however, the revelation of evil makes her realize that 'the human heart, the spirit, the soul, consciousness itself – call it what you like – in the end, it's all we've got to work with. . . . Without a revolution of the inner life, however slow, all our big designs are worthless' (*BD*, p. 172).

This strand of the book, the Bernard and June story taken at face value, establishes *Black Dogs* as an impressive novel of ideas, staging the conflict between two moral systems facing up to the implications of the Holocaust. For M. John Harrison, reviewing the novel in the *Times Literary Supplement*, the fourth part of the book works exactly in this way, having the quality of 'a perfect little Ian McEwan short story' that 'relieves our anxiety by shaping and ordering. What we learnt piecemeal we now appreciate as a whole.'[17] There is a good deal of insight in this, since Part Four of *Black Dogs* does carry a level of conviction by virtue of the way it orders and shapes the experiences described earlier; and part of that ordering process is to lay bare the ethical questions the narrative produces. However, there is a paradoxical counter-dynamic in the book that obliges us to question the level of credulity that is established here. This counter-dynamic concerns the other key strand that I have mentioned: the questionable role of the narrator. It is this that lends the book its truly unsettling quality.

The reader does not have to hunt for clues that question the reliability of individual testimony. Indeed, this becomes a structural motif in the book. For example, after the account of Bernard's revelation of personal suffering in Languedoc in 1946 – prompted by the sight of a grieving woman apparently witnessing the names of her husband and two brothers being carved upon a memorial – Jeremy undercuts the basis of this revelation by reporting that, in 1989: 'I found that the base of the monument was inscribed with Latin quotations. There were no names of the war dead' (*BD*, p. 165). Earlier, Bernard contradicts June's account of their first sexual encounter, placing the scene she recalls as happening two years later, in Italy (*BD*, pp. 57, 85). He goes on to bemoan the way in which 'myth' supplants 'truth', arguing that Jeremy's subject, as biographer, should be 'how people like June bend the facts to fit their ideas instead of the other way round. Why do people do that?' Jeremy finds himself 'hesitating over the obvious rejoinder' which he does not, in fact, make (*BD*, p. 86). What would the obvious rejoinder be? That Bernard is as guilty as June, in this regard? That we all do it? That as a biographer Jeremy is inevitably weaving 'myth' out of 'truth'?

All of these unspoken possible rejoinders resonate for us, most especially concerning Jeremy's role. There is no clearer signal of his need to shape events into a narrative with personal meaning than in the account of his visit to France in 1989 when he dines in the same hotel to which Bernard and June had repaired after her encounter with the dogs. Here Jeremy is prompted to challenge a brutish father who has struck his son: the pair go outside and, improbably, Jeremy instantly beats the man to the ground, receiving no blow in return. He is restrained, and brought to his senses by the words of a Parisian woman, using the words that June uses in her attempt to restrain the black dogs: 'ça suffit.'[18] It is this that makes him understand 'that the elation driving me had nothing to do with revenge and justice', that the destructive impulse embodied by the dogs has momentarily manifested itself in him (*BD*, p. 131).

There is, however, a different feel to the episode overall in which the sense of Jeremy's heroism as the boy's saviour is predominant. As the cruelty of the boy's parents intensifies through the meal, so Jeremy's empathy grows, filtered through the lens of his own memory of despair after his parents died (*BD*, p. 128). Freely projecting onto the boy, he makes this plausible but unverifiable interpretation of his mood:

> I think I understand what happened to the boy just then. As the table was readied for the next course, as the stewed rabbit was set down, he began to cry; with the coming and going of the waitress came confirmation that after his humiliation, life was to proceed as normal. His sense of isolation was complete and he could not hold back his despair. (*BD*, p. 129)

At this point the father strikes the child and, as Jeremy arrives at the table, a young waitress is already comforting the beaten boy, making 'flute-like notes of concern' that Jeremy registers as 'a lovely sound' (*BD*, p. 130). After the fight, Mme Auriac, the patronne, ministers to Jeremy, bandaging his hand and pouring him a cognac, while the boy eats an ice-cream, 'wrapped in the maternal arms of the pretty young waitress who,' reports Jeremy, 'appeared flushed and in the embrace of a great happiness' (*BD*, p. 131). The tableau is a fantasy of heroism, of tempered masculine aggression that draws a responsive maternalism. It is an episode which sets right the wrongs of Jeremy's personal past, since Jeremy stands up for the self he perceives in the boy. (He is simultaneously atoning for the abandonment of his niece Sally, a character I discuss below.) Part Three of the novel ends with this tableau, an emphatic reminder of Jeremy's central role in the casting of events immediately before we read his memoir of June and Bernard.

Another important aspect of Jeremy's psychological make-up is that, like June and Bernard, he has had a formative experience through an encounter with the legacy of the Nazis. Here, in Poland in 1981, the narrator meets and falls in love with Jenny Tremaine while both are members of a cultural delegation invited by the Polish government (*BD*, p. 105). Earlier in the text, he has expressed the view that his life was an emotional void between the ages of eight (when his parents are killed) and thirty-seven (when he marries Jenny) (*BD*, p. 18). In the recollected Poland episode, the narrator's experiences provoke a maturation of his political consciousness when he witnesses communism as 'a network of privileges and corruption' and 'the instrument of occupation by a foreign power.' He realizes that anti-communism should not be associated, merely, with 'cranky ideologues of the right' (*BD*, p. 107). The key experience, however, is the trip Jenny and the narrator undertake to the Majdanek concentration camp outside Lublin: their first love-making (and, by implication, the first stage in the narrator's emotional rehabilitation) occurs after their tour of the camp.

The revelation of evil for Jeremy and Jenny is twofold. First there is the realization of the staggering scale of the Holocaust: 'the extravagant numerical scale, the easy-to-say numbers – tens and hundreds of thousands, millions – denied the imagination its proper sympathies' (*BD*, p. 110).[19] The second aspect of the revelation anticipates the extension of the title image on the last page, where the black dogs are deemed to be at large in Europe, waiting to return 'in another time'

(*BD*, p. 174). Outside the entrance to the camp they read 'a sign which announced that so many hundreds of thousands of Poles, Lithuanians, Russians, French, British and Americans had died here.' Jenny observes that there is 'no mention of the Jews', that 'it still goes on', adding 'the black dogs', in an aside (*BD*, pp. 109–10).[20] The sign, Jeremy reports, is sufficient 'to transform Majdanek for me in an instant from a monument, an honourable civic defiance of oblivion, to a disease of the imagination and a living peril, a barely conscious connivance with evil' (*BD*, p. 110).

The flowering of love between Jenny and Jeremy in the episode containing this revelation may thus appear as a defiance of oblivion, a celebration of love in a novel about how personal goodness is necessary to defeat the black dogs. In this respect – the emphasis on the personal – the novel seems to come down slightly on June's side in the debate about the appropriate response to political events, although this emphasis is secular, divested of the mystical sheen that June gives to it. Yet, even here, as we shall see, the novel cultivates an air of ambivalence.

To the extent that we accept the memoir condensed in Part Four as a faithful reordering of the characters' key experiences, we rely on Jeremy as a faithful and reliable conduit. So much of the novel, however, invites us to question his reliability and our reliance on him. In the Preface, Jeremy self-consciously establishes himself as an emotionally damaged orphan, and a cuckoo who seeks out the company of the parents of his peers. His teenage pomposity he explains as a defence, a consequence of missing his parents 'terribly' (*BD*, p. 14).

This understatement is characteristic of the Preface, which suggests that Jeremy is emotionally scarred in ways that he has been unable to address. Crucial to this is his relationship with his small niece Sally, for whom he was an essential prop in a violent home (*BD*, p. 16). When Jeremy has gained his A Levels he makes good his escape from his sister's flat to take up a place at Oxford. On the point of departure, while trying to evade Sally's suspicious and persistent questioning ('Where are you going? When are you coming back?'), his agonized sense of abandoning Sally to a cocoon of loneliness still worse than his own overcomes him: 'when she thought to lure me back, to divert me from a History degree with the suggestion, so pertly, so optimistically put, that we play instead, Sailing to a New Place, I put down my armful of books and ran out to the van to sit in the passenger seat and weep' (*BD*, p. 17).

Although Jeremy asserts that Sally does not play a part in what follows (*BD*, p. 17), it is clear that this is a thematic prelude to the main action, where the theme of cruelty and individual suffering is magnified in the treatment of human evil and personal responsibility. When we subsequently discover that Sally's adult life has been haunted by domestic violence, and that she has been both victim and perpetrator, losing her little boy to foster parents, we understand why Jeremy feels responsible for her unhappy life (*BD*, p. 68). It may not be reasonable to wonder if it was his responsibility to care for his niece, but it is clear that he consciously abandoned her to her fate at the hands of parents he knew to be irresponsible.

Part of the function of the Preface is to draw a line under Jeremy's early life: he indicates that his emotional life begins with marriage and fatherhood. Yet he also indicates that the 'emotional void' that characterizes most of his life had 'an important intellectual consequence: I had no attachments, I believed in nothing. . . . there was simply no good cause, no enduring principle, no fundamental idea with which I could identify' (*BD*, p. 18). He discovers this through conversations with his parents-in-law. (Tellingly, his habit of acquiring other people's parents persists, to Jenny's annoyance.) This establishes Jeremy as an empty vessel, in moral terms.

While this might seem convenient in the narrator of a novel of ideas, it also complicates the novel's ethical patterning, for this assertion of moral vacuousness post-dates the union of Jenny and Jeremy, in the shadow of their revelation at Majdanek, which, when it is related later in the novel, seems to imply a moral conviction uniting private and public realms. When one remembers the Preface, one has to conclude that the episode does *not* have this lasting effect on Jeremy who remains a moral absence, the better equipped to negotiate with wonderment the competing convictions of Jenny's parents:[21] 'Rationalist and mystic, commissar and yogi, joiner and abstainer, scientist and intuitionist, Bernard and June are the extremities, the twin poles along whose slippery axis my own unbelief slithers and never comes to rest' (*BD*, p. 19). This passage is often quoted to establish the terms of the book's central opposition, rationalism versus spiritualism. What is not usually observed is how this opposition might be presented as the backdrop to a more arresting feature of the book: the slithering unbelief of the narrator.

Jeremy's interviews with June, before her death from Leukaemia in 1987, are ostensibly to gather information for her biography. He is uncomfortable, however, about being used as 'a conduit, a medium for the final fix June wanted to put on her life' (*BD*, p. 40). We might assume that the novel's fourth section is what Jeremy has produced in lieu of a conventional biography, a narrative that concentrates, without apparent favour, on June and Bernard's competing philosophies and the experience that drives them apart.

Jeremy's role in gathering his information, however, already tainted by his dubious 'cuckoo' identity, is further complicated by his failure as a go-between for June and Bernard, both of whom are keen to hear news of the other when Jeremy speaks to them. In response to their evident interest in each other, he admits that: 'I was evasive. There was nothing I could say that would have given satisfaction, and besides, they could have phoned or seen each other any time they wanted.' In denying the role of go-between, he bemoans the absurd pride of the pair (*BD*, p. 49). Yet the slight suspicion arises that Jeremy, the emotional vacuum, has no interest in trying to effect a reconciliation, but a strong vested interest in supplanting each of the lovers within the ambit of the other. It seems revealing that Jeremy makes no attempt to build a bridge until after June's death, when he finds himself 'wondering what I was about, attempting to reconcile [Bernard] to a dead wife' (*BD*, p. 92).

A crucial scene in the novel that does not figure in Jeremy's final, 'ordered' memoir is the episode related to him by Bernard on the flight to Berlin. Bernard recalls this episode as having occurred on the honeymoon a week or more before the newlyweds reached the Gorge de Vis. This is the scene on a railway platform in Provence, in which they argue about the capture of a dragonfly, and June reveals she is pregnant. Bernard hands the captured dragonfly to June to hold, cupped in her hands, while he digs in his bag for his killing bottle.

Sensing that she is about to set the insect free, Bernard tells her he will never forgive her if she does. She acquiesces, but this is merely the prelude to a row in which she berates Bernard for his cool scientific rationalism. His desire to collect insects is of a piece with his politics, both governed by abstraction and the desire for tidiness, order, she says; and his unemotional response to the world also governs his attitude to their relationship. In reply, he mounts a conventional defence of fieldwork, stressing the connection between classification and the love of nature; but, since this is a conversation about their relationship, and not entomology, he makes an angry, schoolboyish declaration of love, which prompts June's tearful declaration of her pregnancy. Her superstitious fear is that the killing of the 'beautiful dragonfly' is a 'mistake' and that 'nature would take its revenge and something terrible was going to happen to the baby.' The train they were waiting for pulls in and departs while they embrace, and Bernard attempts to comfort June with an explanation of Darwin (*BD*, pp. 75–8).

Feeling himself compelled to 'make mischief on June's behalf', Jeremy asks Bernard about the 'insect's revenge' (Jenny had been born with a sixth finger (*BD*, p. 81)). Later in the Berlin episode, Jeremy makes a more serious attempt to shake Bernard's rationalism by pointing out that a girl in whom Bernard sees traces of June is the one who returns to assist Bernard and Jeremy in the fracas with the fascist yobs. Jeremy's obstinate persistence with 'unsettling the rationalist' is a dubious attempt to rekindle Bernard's 'superstition', in his first sixth months of grief, that the dead June would try and communicate with him (*BD*, pp. 99, 83).

Still more significant, however, is the omission of the episode from Part Four. Here we are told that Bernard and June would 'surely have felt cheered about their contribution to a new Europe to have known that they had already conceived their first child, a daughter, my wife, who would one day put up a good fight for a seat in the European Parliament.' We are also told, simply, that they travelled through Provence, by bus and train (*BD*, p. 138). The couple could not know about their unborn daughter's future commitment to Europe, of course; but they *did* know about the pregnancy during this part of the journey, according to Bernard's testimony. This does not feature here, aside from Bernard's reaction to June's emotional outburst in the hotel, after her encounter with the dogs, when he momentarily wonders if he is 'about to witness a birth, a miscarriage, some spectacular feminine disaster' (*BD*, p. 154).

In a sense, narrative expediency (McEwan's) demands that the pregnancy be dealt with in an earlier episode; were this to be foregrounded in Part Four, an alternative explanation for June's experience of a Presence assisting her defeat of the black dogs would instantly suggest itself: the temptation to interpret this scene as an instance of 'superhuman' maternal strength or determination would be compelling. Yet, given the structure of the book, it is impossible entirely to disentangle McEwan's narrative expediency from Jeremy's. The character's subconscious desire to sustain the alienation of the protagonists, if such is the case, would be consistent with his suppression of Bernard's account of the dragonfly episode, with its mood of reconciliation.

Our framing suspicion of the dragonfly episode is already complex: this is Bernard's recollection of an episode forty-three years earlier, filtered through Jeremy's narrative (even if it does not register in the tidied-up memoir). Even so, this context of radical unreliability is offset by Bernard's apparently forensic recollection that doesn't present him in a particularly favourable light. There is also something irrational, or at least inadequate, in his attempts to explain the context of his own repressed feelings in a scene of heightened emotion, and in his ludicrous effort (which he appreciates, with hindsight) to allay June's superstitious concern with a lecture on biology. Moreover, June's apparent irrationality is underpinned by a kind of maternal logic that enables her to provoke a scene that will clear the decks, and oblige them to take stock of their lives (*BD*, p. 79). June's superstitious outburst has its own cool logic, while Bernard's rational veneer is a poor cover for his inadequacy. The binary poles of the book's schema are richly mingled here, as they are, in fact, elsewhere in the book.

McEwan offers clues, then, that dismantle Jeremy's binary construction. The impression builds that Jeremy's personal quest for meaning is the book's focus, rather than the war of ideas embodied in the ideological standoff of his parents-in-law, an impression reinforced by the way he appropriates their ideas alone in the bergerie. The 'argument' between the two stems from differing interpretations of why Jeremy had frozen before putting his hand on a scorpion, which he could not see, when reaching out for the switchboard cupboard (*BD*, pp. 115–16). June's 'voice' argues that Jeremy should acknowledge that he sensed her presence protecting him; Bernard's 'voice' argues for a rational explanation, that he must have recognized the scorpion subliminally, perhaps (*BD*, pp. 117–18). He hears the voices in an extended debate about science and religion, which dominates his stay. He cannot stop their 'self-cancelling argument', so tries joining in (*BD*, pp. 119–20).

The odd thing about this is that, while June is dead by this stage (1989), Bernard is still alive: Jeremy has put him on a plane back to England before continuing his trip to France. If the book cultivates a degree of credulity about the spiritual presence, there is a contradiction here that undermines it, and which locates the voices within Jeremy's imagination. At the very end of the book, Jeremy makes reference to 'Bernard's ghost' pouring scorn once more on June's Damascene experience (*BD*, p. 173). At this point we remember the reference to his ghost in the Preface, where Bernard is spoken of in the past tense (*BD*, p. 21). Yet the 'present' of the narrative frame, the time when Jeremy notionally completes the memoir, seems to be shortly after the episodes recounted in 1989 when Bernard is very much alive (partly because the novel must have been composed in the aftermath of the events of 1989). If we follow the conceit that the novel is a collection of material that stands as a memoir – finally ordered in Part Four – then Jeremy seems to be writing for posterity, for a time when both protagonists have died and the memoir can be published. The effect, however, is to dispose too suddenly of one of the narrative's key figures, and to emphasize his utility in the narrator's own search for a point where his slithering unbelief might come to rest.

The foregrounding of narrative unreliability in *Black Dogs* clearly problematizes the fictional projection of gathering material for a biographical work. The imagined process of approaching biography is the context of the narrative, and a chief source of unease – not just for the 'biographer' Jeremy, but for the author and the reader, too. In this respect, *Black Dogs* shares some of the ethical concerns that have preoccupied critics of life writing.

The particular circumstances of this biographical work are interesting, since it is, notionally, collaborative. Yet when Jeremy wonders 'ungenerously, if I was being used – as a conduit, a medium for the final fix June wanted to put on her life', a thought that makes him 'less uncomfortable about not writing the biography she wanted' (*BD*, p. 40), we are invited to think seriously about the ethics of life writing. Jeremy articulates his resistance to being used as a 'conduit' as a justification for appropriating June's life for his own ends; yet he acknowledges that the thought that he is being so used is 'ungenerous'. Ungenerous because it is not true, we may wonder? Or ungenerous because such a desire is natural in the subject of a biography, the human motivation with which any biographer must negotiate? However one interprets this, Jeremy's justification for refusing to oblige June is undermined. McEwan produces a fictionalized account of the kind of problematic collaborative (auto)biography that 'inevitably probe[s] the self's responsibility to the proximate other', where, in the words of Paul John Eakin, writing 'about the other' may be seen as 'a violation of that responsibility.'[22]

The dilemma the reader must ponder is whether Jeremy's use of June's (and Bernard's) story in his personal quest for meaning is indeed parasitic, or whether – as in actual life writing – his impetus points towards a new mode of 'relational identity' in which we may feel less concerned about the biographical subject's desire to fix meaning. The novel explores this dimension of life writing, which obliges us to extend 'our familiar literary and ethical categories', since the 'inviolate personality' enshrined in law is 'routinely violated' in this mode.[23] Is it only by establishing this relational identity, with its possible violation of the identities of June and Bernard, that Jeremy's narrative can posit more generalized meaning to their lives?

For McEwan, as for many writers of fiction, there is evidently a profound ethical dilemma in the translation of real-life encounters into fiction, a dilemma that has a bearing on the idea of biography in *Black Dogs*, and a still more central relationship to the conception of *Atonement*, where the dilemma is vividly dramatized. The pertinent questions here are those formulated by Wayne C. Booth: 'what are the author's responsibilities to those whose lives are used as "material"?'; and, more precisely: 'are there limits to the author's freedom to expose, in the service of art or self, the most delicate secrets of those whose lives provide material?' As Booth concludes, however, such a question may have minimal impact on the reception of a literary work: 'biting as it may be for a given author, it does not arise for readers except when they have more or less accidental knowledge about the author's life.'[24] That which is a pressing and public ethical dilemma for the biographer shades into a more private anxiety for the novelist.

The novelist's ethical dilemma, faced with the necessity of drawing on the raw material of personal acquaintance, is a relatively narrow matter, a question of side-stepping personal betrayals that may, in any case, have no wider impact. McEwan's fictional dramatization of the ethical paradox at the heart of life writing, in such a way as to highlight the semi-conscious manipulations of his biographer (together with the biographer's implied guilt), marks out an adjacent, but different territory. This is the territory where that which is intensely private (such as the experience of religious conversion), is necessarily transformed, by virtue of experiences that resonate beyond the personal (here, the connotation of the black dogs), into the material of public history.

Superficially, it might seem paradoxical to suggest that Jeremy is the narrative facilitator of this transformation, that his role is to allow public history to be glimpsed through the enactment of the subjective process of narrative manipulation. The resolution to the paradox lies in the way in which *Black Dogs* enlists the reader's participation. McEwan uses the technique of presenting a moral problem that is irresolvable at the simple level of narrative content; we are forced, instead, to evaluate the manner of the telling and the problem of competing perspectives. Crucially, however, the relativism is limited. Our anchor is supplied by a series of solid historical reference points: fascism, communism, the Second World War, the crumbling of the Berlin Wall. Along with narrator Jeremy, we are invited to make sense of the shape of post-war Europe and the spectre of violence done in the name of political ideology, which still haunts our fragile sense of civilization.

A question mark about the narrator's reliability is established in the very first sentence: 'ever since I lost mine in a road accident when I was eight, I have had my eye on other people's parents.' (*BD*, p. 9) Thereafter, Jeremy's identity as a self-conscious cuckoo establishes the frame that conditions our reception of the novel, and especially his appropriation of the life stories of his parents-in-law. This means that the schematic presentation of two competing world-views, or 'kind[s] of interpretation', in Jeremy's words – Bernard's rationalism, set against the intuitive mysticism of June (*BD*, p. 19) – is a calculated reduction which says as much about Jeremy's orphan mentality and the hunger for guidance as it does about the relative merits of the opposing ethical views, socialism and religion.

Most important in establishing the larger political significance of the novel *through* the problematic narrative frame is the generalized significance of Jeremy's orphan mentality: it denotes the collective hunger of the post-war generation for social and political stability in Europe, a felt lack and a historical structure of feeling that McEwan's readers will share. Thus the implied unreliability of Jeremy as a character-narrator shades into a sense of shared uncertainty generated by the character's representative role. The novel's formal framework, that is to say, elicits a dual response from the reader, simultaneously wary of, and empathic towards, the narrator's quest for meaning. Another way of putting this is to say that if there is a felt sense of impatience in Jeremy's tendency to condense debates, the reading experience makes us less troubled by the book's schematic structure than we would be if presented with it in summary: like Jeremy, we are impatient for answers.

There are no answers, of course. Even the closing account of what happened on that day in June 1946 when June encountered her black dogs is fenced in with doubts about its authenticity. Jeremy's first-person memoir has, by this point, mutated into a third-person narrative, a device that we have to assume, for the technical consistency of the book, Jeremy has adopted in order to convey the essence of the key scene. The competing testimonies of Bernard and June are combined in a fictional projection authored by a character who was not present. Of course, the reader's natural response is to embrace the immediacy afforded by this new omniscience that takes us to the heart of the novel thematically, as well as in terms of narrative suspense. Another dual response is demanded which invites us to perform, through our reading, the dialectic that orders the book: at a rational, intellectual level we have to question the way in which these second-hand memories have been dramatized; but at a more intuitive level we engage with the power of the story, the kernel of the novel which, established as another level of fiction within the fiction, acquires a mythic status.

What I have observed about the closing section of *Black Dogs* seems to me to be true of the novel as a whole, if in a less intensified way: an engaged reading of the book is also a performance of its ordering argument, requiring a simultaneous receptiveness to the rational and the intuitive.

Notes

1   On this element of political allegory in the novel, see Slay, *Ian McEwan*, pp. 136–7.
2   Malcolm Bradbury, *The Modern British Novel*, pp. 298, 425.
3   McEwan acknowledges David C. Martin's *Wilderness of Mirrors* in his 'Author's note', and one can trace the reliance on this source for particular details about Operation Gold. McEwan also borrows some less factual material, such as the anecdote about Bill Harvey, the Head of the Berlin CIA, in which Harvey worries about 'George', and his vulnerability to pillow talk, as 'the only one who's had a piece of ass lately', according to overheard gossip. (George was a dog, adopted as the warehouse mascot.) See *I*, p. 66, and *Wilderness of Mirrors* (1980; Guilford, Connecticut: The Lyons Press, 2003), p. 82.
4   Ryan, *Ian McEwan*, p. 55.
5   Rosa González, 'The Pleasure of Prose Writing vs. Pornographic Violence', *The European English Messenger*, 1: 3 (Autumn 1992), pp. 40–5 (p. 43).
6   Ibid., pp. 41–2.
7   Julia Kristeva, *Powers of Horror*, p. 4.
8   Ibid., p. 4.
9   Ibid., p. 17.
10 Ryan, *Ian McEwan*, p. 60.

11   Slay, *Ian McEwan*, pp. 136–7.

12   Joan Brandt, 'Julia Kristeva', in Julian Wolfreys, ed., *The Edinburgh Encyclopaedia of Modern Criticism and Theory* (Edinburgh University Press, 2002), pp. 382–90 (p. 386).

13   González, 'The Pleasure of Prose Writing', p. 42.

14   Other changes, rather like the reuniting of Leonard and Maria, seem to be concessions to filmic narrative: the dismemberment (necessarily) happens off camera, for example; and Maria *engineers* her relationship with Bob immediately after the killing of Otto, in order to save Leonard. See *The Innocent* (Island World, 1993), directed by John Schlesinger, starring Anthony Hopkins (Bob Glass), Isabella Rossellini (Maria) and Campbell Scott (Leonard).

15   Helen Whitney, 'Faith and Doubt at Ground Zero' (interview), *Frontline* (April 2002), available at www.pbs.org/wgbh/pages/frontline/shows/faith/interviews/mcewan.html (accessed 19 October 2005).

16   Randall Stevenson, *The Oxford English Literary History, Volume 12, 1960–2000: The Last of England?* (Oxford University Press, 2004), pp. 442, 443.

17   M. John Harrison, 'Beating the Retreat' (review of *Black Dogs*), *Times Literary Supplement*, 4655 (19 June 1992), p. 20.

18   The verbal echo of the scene in which Leonard Bast is killed in E. M. Forster's *Howard's End* (1910) – 'That's enough' says Charles Wilcox after delivering the fatal blow – might bear some analysis, since both scenes examine the self-justification of a violent act that cannot be easily defended.

19   This is the passage that Stevenson quotes from the novel, in his discussion of the historical shadow cast by the Holocaust over fiction fifty years on. See *The Oxford English Literary History, Volume 12, 1960–2000*, p. 442.

20   The official Majdanek State Museum website states the following: 'The scarcity of source materials does not allow to establish [*sic*] the exact number of camp prisoners and its victims. It is estimated that over 300,000 people of 50 different nationalities "passed through" Majdanek. The majority of prisoners were Jews /over 40%/ and Poles /about 35%/. Other major nationalities included: Belorussians, Ukrainians, Russians, Germans, Austrians, French, Italians and Dutch.' See www.majdanek.pl/en/oboz.htm (accessed 6 December 2004).

21   This point is complicated by the fact that the episode in Poland occurred in 1981, but is recollected in the narrative present of the novel, which is 1989 or soon after. However, the fact that the recollected response does not fully square with Jeremy's persisting amorality suggests that the immediate, visceral reaction to the experience has not resulted in a lasting change to his world-view.

22 Paul John Eakin, 'The Unseemly Profession: Privacy, Inviolate Personality, and the Ethics of Life Writing', in Adamson, Freadman and Parker, eds, *Renegotiating Ethics in Literature, Philosophy, and Theory*, pp. 161–80 (p. 172).

23 Ibid., pp. 175–6.

24 Wayne C. Booth, *The Company We Keep: An Ethics of Fiction* (Berkeley: University of California Press, 1988), pp. 130–1.

6

'A mess of our own unmaking': *Enduring Love*

The testing of scientific rationalism, a recurring theme in McEwan's work, receives its fullest treatment in *Enduring Love*. The relationship between Joe Rose, a science journalist, and his wife Clarissa, an academic, is threatened by the obsessive and delusional attachment of Jed Parry to Joe. Parry's condition, diagnosed by Joe and then in Appendix I as 'de Clérambault's syndrome', leads him from stalking to extreme violence. The pun in the title, signalling both the love that lasts and the love that is suffered, encapsulates the human triangle at the story's centre. Joe's narrative, at one level, is a test of how scientific rationalism can make sense of delusional behaviour. McEwan's larger project, however, is to consider the function of the novel when set against the claims of post-Darwinian science about the evolutionary basis of morality and interpretation.[1]

Enduring Love implicitly stages a contest of the relative merits of science and literature, as a careful fusion of form and content, contained within a suspense novel. The hybrid nature of *Enduring Love* is aptly caught in David Malcolm's description of it as 'a kind of epistemological thriller'.[2] More than a novel of ideas, it is a novel about ideas, about ways in which the world can be known and understood.

Malcolm observes that the 'reference to Keats's upcoming two hundredth birthday . . . sets the novel just before 1995.' However, he finds 'no reference to contemporary politics or to any historical or social forces that might have shaped characters' lives.' As a consequence, he feels the novel represents 'a return to the eerily insulated worlds of *The Cement Garden* and *The Comfort of Strangers* and a departure from the historically and socially focused worlds of *The Child in Time*, *The Innocent*, and *Black Dogs*.'[3] It may be that *Enduring Love* marks the beginning of a new phase in McEwan's career in which the value of literature is subjected to renewed scrutiny; but this may represent a different kind of social focus, rather than a return to insularity. In this novel, it is the intellectual rather than the political context that is important: McEwan turns to science for the tools with which to interrogate given social models.

The powerful opening scene, detailing the ballooning accident, introduces the book's ethical enquiry. Five men (including the novel's principal narrator, Joe Rose) run across a field, from different directions, to help a balloonist in distress: faced with forceful, gusting winds, the balloonist has become entangled in the guy ropes, while trying to anchor the helium balloon and save his grandson, who is frozen with fear inside the basket. The five bystanders grab hold of the trailing ropes and try to drag the balloon back to earth. A fresh gust takes them up into the air, and four of the five let go and fall back to the ground, leaving one man stranded. The balloon sails into the sky, and eventually his grip fails and he plummets to his death.

Joe Rose describes this event as 'the fall' (*EL*, p. 2), which has an obvious literal connotation with respect to the terrible plight of the dead man, John Logan. However, it also connotes the drop of each of the other four men, and the failure of their collective altruistic impulse. What kind of fall from grace is this? Retrospectively Joe rationalizes it as a failure of the basic principle of human co-operation. If they had all held firm, the balloon would have been tamed once the gust had passed; but, with 'no agreement to be broken', self-interest prevailed, and the men became 'a bad society' in microcosm (*EL*, p. 15). Philosophizing about the event, Joe sees it as an enactment of 'our mammalian conflict – what to give to the others, and what to keep for yourself. Treading that line, keeping the others in check, and being kept in check by them, is what we call morality' (*EL*, p. 14).

McEwan is here in debate with *The Moral Animal* by Robert Wright, a work (cited in the Acknowledgements) that attempts to correct some of the misperceptions about evolutionary psychology. Wright shows how something amounting to a paradigm shift in modern Darwinian social science has emerged in reaction to the 'standard social science model' that projects a 'view of human nature as something that barely exists and doesn't much matter'.[4]

Wright argues that 'evolutionary psychologists, contrary to common expectation, subscribe to a cardinal doctrine of twentieth-century psychology and psychiatry: the potency of early social environment in shaping the adult mind.' This particular combination of genetic inheritance and environmental conditioning leads Wright to a qualified view of morality. For him, morality is rooted in utilitarianism and the privileging of acts that produce happiness for the greatest number of people: 'belief in the goodness of happiness and the badness of suffering isn't just a basic part of moral discourse that we all share. Increasingly it seems to be the only basic part that we all share.' This utilitarian morality can be reduced to a simple assertion: 'widely practiced utilitarianism promises to make everyone better off; and so far as we can tell, that's what everyone wants.'[5]

The selfish gene, however, is a complicating factor for the evolutionary psychologist contemplating morality: 'the basic mechanism by which our genes control us is the deep, often unspoken (even unthought), conviction that our happiness is special. We are designed not to worry about anyone else's happiness, except in the sort of cases where such worrying has, during evolution, benefited our genes.' The further complication, from this perspective, is that 'morality' can be exposed as a deceptive construct: 'the feeling of moral "rightness" is something natural selection created so that people would employ it selfishly. Morality, you could almost say, was designed to be misused by its own definition.'

Wright concludes that 'we are moral' in the sense that 'we have, at least, the technical capacity for leading a truly examined life'. Self-consciousness, in the form of 'self-awareness, memory, foresight, and judgment', then becomes crucial, pointing to a form of utilitarian morality that may require us to resist our genetic or evolutionary disposition:

> Chronically subjecting ourselves to a true and bracing moral scrutiny, and adjusting our behavior accordingly, is not something we are designed for. We are potentially moral animals . . . but we aren't naturally moral animals. To be moral animals, we must realize how thoroughly we aren't.[6]

The ballooning accident might seem to engender a fictional deliberation about morality in the spirit of Wright's analysis, where the selfish gene is pitted against the collective good in a very precise confrontation of nature and nurture. Yet the novel soon pushes beyond what it might mean to play one's role in a 'good society' on these terms. This utilitarian conception of morality, of social organization, describes a contractual obligation, merely. It is bereft of an explicit notion of value, and cannot fully explain why such a stigma should attach to having been the first to let go of a rope (after which the tragedy was inevitable): each of the survivors 'claims not to have been the first' (*EL*, p. 14), and Joe is haunted by the fear of being thought of as the first to fall. When he first meets John Logan's widow, for example, he assumes (wrongly) that he is going to be accused, and summons 'an image of something, someone, dropping away in the instant before' he let go, as he prepares to get his 'own account in first' (*EL*, p. 122).

The letter from Joe's partner Clarissa, written at the point where they are still estranged towards the end of the novel, pinpoints Joe's need to 'make [his] peace' with the thought that he might have dropped before the others, and suggests that his failure to 'confront that idea' led to a mismanagement of Jed Parry's obsession, since Parry offered an 'escape' from the guilt (*EL*, p. 217).

The guilt and the trauma indicate an innate ethical sense that goes beyond Joe's presentation of the accident as a parable about social co-operation and morality as pragmatism. That reflection assumes the air of rational hindsight; but there is a much more immediate and visceral response that Joe reports to have had in the 'second or two' it takes for Logan to fall. A recurring nightmare comes back to him in which he would be witnessing a disaster – 'an earthquake, a fire in a skyscraper, a sinking ship, an erupting volcano' – and would witness the deaths of 'helpless people, reduced by distance to an undifferentiated mass':

> The horror was in the contrast between their apparent size and the enormity of their suffering. Life was revealed as cheap; thousands of screaming individuals, no bigger than ants, were about to be annihilated and I could do nothing to help. I did not think about the dream then so much as experience its emotional wash – terror, guilt and helplessness were the components – and feel the nausea of a premonition fulfilled. (*EL*, p. 18)

The terror, guilt and helplessness of this nightmare, from Joe's formative adult years, are the components of his social self – understood as an identity in which the balance between self- and communal interest is more than the product of simple pragmatism. The terror is simultaneously fear for oneself, but also horror at the (shared) sense of human frailty; and it is that sense of empathy – an emotion that precedes rational thought – that engenders the feeling of pathos, and the guilt and helplessness that go with it.

Of course, one can seek to supply a partial genetic explanation for every emotion, so this is not an issue that can be easily resolved. The essential point is that Joe, like his creator, is in debate with evolutionary psychology as a form of knowledge about the world. McEwan deploys English lecturer Clarissa, with her love of Keats that is a personal interest rather than merely a professional one, as a way of staging the competing claims of the scientific and the literary response.

It is the figure of Edward O. Wilson, however, who dominates the book's implicit comparison of science and literature as ways of knowing the world. The nature/nurture debate is one aspect of this, a debate that has itself been dominated by Wilson, since the publication of his book *Sociobiology* in 1975. In this work Wilson outlined the basis of a new discipline in which biology could be seen as the basis of all social behaviour. ('Sociobiology' was later to mutate into 'evolutionary psychology'.) In his original conception of this discipline, insofar as it relates to human behaviour, Wilson pointed to our evolutionary heritage to explain not just the division of social roles according to gender, or manifestations of violence, but also those human attributes that are more usually thought of as signs of individual intellectual development, such as religious faith or moral conviction.

Here it may be worth observing a distinction between McEwan's ongoing fascination with this branch of science, as evidenced in his non-fictional deliberations, and the undeniably ambivalent treatments found in the novels. McEwan's enduring interest in Edward O. Wilson's work eventually leads him to pursue the idea of a synthesis. In a review of Wilson's later book *Consilience: The Unity of Knowledge*, the trajectory of this thinking becomes clearer. Here McEwan pursues his reading of 'consilience' – as 'the linking of facts and theories across disciplines to create a common groundwork of explanation' – but with a clear-sighted understanding that, for Wilson, the morality that accompanies purposive human direction will be bestowed by the clarity of science:

> On the map of all knowledge, consilience among the scientific disciplines is already clear and reliably effective. The social sciences and the humanities show no such coherence. The key to consilience here, their interfacing subject, is biology. The brain is a product of biological evolution. The mind, and its vastly complex artefact, culture, are ultimately biological products.[7]

McEwan briefly acknowledges the apparent 'reductionism' of this, but he is enthused by the larger goal that Wilson has in mind: 'his conclusion . . . has lucidity and strength; a united system of knowledge is the surest means of identifying the unexplored domains of reality; in this pursuit of consilience, ethics is everything. It would be an achievement to get Homo sapiens settled down and happy before we wreck the planet, and for this we need the best decisions based upon the soundest knowledge'.[8]

Wilson's pragmatic understanding of ethics, underpinned by biology, is made plain in the concluding paragraphs of *Consilience*:

> We are learning the fundamental principle that ethics is everything. Human social existence, unlike animal sociality, is based on the genetic propensity to form long-term contracts that evolve by culture into moral precepts and law. The rules of contract formation were not given to humanity from above, nor did they emerge randomly in the mechanics of the brain. They evolved over tens or hundreds of millennia because they conferred upon the genes prescribing them survival and the opportunity to be represented in future generations. . . . We . . . have discovered which covenants are necessary for survival, and we have accepted the necessity of securing them by sacred oath.[9]

This is a more innocent interpretation of social covenants than Wright's conviction about the necessarily selfish element of moral rectitude as an inherited trait. It also lacks that self-conscious dimension that Wright prescribes in observing that 'to be moral animals, we must realize how thoroughly we aren't.'[10] Wilson's account of the evolution of social ethics seems distinctly more vulnerable, too blunt, perhaps, to distinguish malign political legislation from those social covenants that are necessary for survival.

There is a long-standing view in the humanities that runs counter to this, of course, and which views anything that smacks of social Darwinism as unethical at root. In pondering the claim that there is an evolutionary basis to human social existence, and that moral precepts and law have developed gradually for the good of all, we have to weigh other considerations in the balance. Why do civilizations collapse? Why do civilizations produce moral or religious codes that justify their expansionist designs? And how is it that constitutional changes can be swift and dramatic (as they have been in Britain in McEwan's lifetime)?

Wilson's larger aim in *Consilience* is highly laudable: he proposes an integration of 'knowledge from the natural sciences with that of the social sciences and humanities', the better to solve 'most of the issues that vex humanity daily – ethnic conflict, arms escalation, overpopulation, abortion, environment, endemic poverty, to cite several most persistently before us'.[11] It is difficult, however, to see what this might mean, practically, for the humanities in general and literary studies in particular. Pursuing this goal might produce the kind of problem that is sometimes confronted in the study of literature and environment, or literary ecocriticism: how to make a utilitarian and predetermined reading process convincing and meaningful to a community of scholars inclined to be suspicious of the partisan approach. Using a book in support of a particular world-view may, in fact, appear to be *unethical* in the way that the humanities understands ethics, as being open to the other, and willing to be surprised or even changed by the aesthetic experience of reading.

It is the section in *Consilience* on 'The Arts and Their Interpretation' that is particularly problematic for most academics working in English studies. Basing his discussion on a conviction that 'gene-culture coevolution is . . . the underlying process by which the brain evolved and the arts originated', Wilson argues that enduring works of art 'touch upon what was universally endowed by human evolution.' The emphasis is then on 'the invention of archetypes, the widely recurring abstractions and core narratives that are dominant themes in the arts.' Wilson suggests that 'in myth and fiction as few as two dozen such subjective groupings cover most of the archetypes'. He pursues the method of 'definition by specification', that method which 'works well in elementary biological classification', to suggest a list of a dozen archetypal narratives, such as 'the tribe emigrates to a promised land', 'the hero descends to hell', and 'the trickster disturbs established order'.[12]

Students of literature will find Northrop Frye (*The Anatomy of Criticism* (1957)) and Vladimir Propp (*Morphology of the Folktale* (1928)) richer sources for deliberating archetypes and narrative taxonomy. It may be churlish to condemn the non-specialist Wilson for being unsuccessful as a literary critic, given the extravagance of his overall design and the learning that underpins it. However, it is worth pointing out some potential areas of contradiction. *Consilience* begins with an explanation of how the young Wilson's intellectual journey began when he grasped that evolution had profound implications for basic biological categorization, how he 'couldn't stop thinking about the implications evolution has for classification . . . static pattern slid into fluid process.' It is wholly unsatisfactory, then, to see Wilson draw on the inadequate methods of biological classification to produce a finite list of narrative types. This merely generates a restrictive set of canonical standards, rooted in classical mythology, which artificially restricts the perception of cultural diversity. His production of a typology rooted in a celebration of 'the masters of the Western canon' seems thin when set alongside his more complex account of biology and, specifically, of how, within the process of 'genetic homogenisation', 'variation increases' and 'new forms of hereditary genius and pathology' may arise.[13]

The important aspect of this digression for the current purpose is the effect that Wilson's grand scheme of consilience – the integration of knowledge across disciplines to create a single mode of explanation and understanding – has had on McEwan's thinking. In an essay from 2001, McEwan compares literature and science and makes some interesting observations about both. On the reading 'contract, between writer and reader', McEwan suggests something timeless about literature, and the reader's ability to 'understand' and 'appreciate' literary characters, despite their 'strangeness' (when read across time or cultures, say):

> To do this, we must bring our own general understanding of what it means to be a person. We have, in the terms of cognitive psychology, a theory of mind, a more or less automatic understanding of what it means to be someone else. Without this understanding, as the psychopathology shows, we would find it virtually impossible to form and sustain relationships, read expressions or intentions, or perceive how we ourselves are understood.[14]

Where literature deals in specifics, this is held in tension with its overall pretensions to universality, since 'at its best, literature is universal, illuminating human nature at precisely the point at which it is most parochial and specific'.[15]

The essay establishes the common ground between literature and science – suggesting how deeply McEwan has been impressed by the grandeur of Wilson's project. Adopting one of Wilson's own phrases, McEwan writes approvingly of the 'gene-culture co-evolution, elaborated by E. O. Wilson among others', which 'dissolves the oppositions of nature versus nurture.' 'Literature', he asserts, 'does not define human nature so much as exemplify it.' In a passage contesting claims for sudden generational changes in human nature, including Woolf's semi-ironic assertion in her essay 'Mr Bennett and Mrs Brown', that 'in or about December 1910, human character changed', McEwan stresses the more cautious view, where literature is shoulder to shoulder with scientific thinking:

> If there are human universals that transcend culture, then it follows that they do not change, or they do not change easily. And if something does change in us historically, then by definition it is not human nature that has changed, but some characteristic special to a certain time and circumstance.[16]

The key difference between McEwan's interest in the universal continuity of human nature, and Wilson's similar vision, is that McEwan does not offer a prescription for how study in the humanities should be conducted. If we confine ourselves to the pursuit of the universal, we may be restricted to classifying each of McEwan's novels to a predetermined category, as instances, merely, of a shared cultural evolution. However, if we attend, not to evolutionary triggers, but to those cultural characteristics that seem 'special to a certain time and circumstance' instead, we find a good deal more to say to illuminate their importance, socially and historically.

If the trajectory of McEwan's later thinking about Edward O. Wilson suggests a divergence from the 'universalism' he flirts with, *Enduring Love* enacts some of the problems consequent upon evolutionary psychology rather more emphatically. It is true that subsequent discoveries in genetics supply the context that make the kind of sociobiology originally espoused by Wilson particularly persuasive to Joe Rose. On the basis of *Enduring Love*, however, McEwan remains uncommitted. There is an important early qualification of Joe's interest in this branch of science that begins a counter-movement in the book. When Logan has fallen to his death, James Gadd, the grandfather of the boy in the balloon, is (inevitably) more interested in giving pursuit than he is in Logan's fate. Joe reports the mental note he made at the time about this: 'such is his genetic investment, I remember thinking stupidly' (*EL*, p. 19). The thought is 'stupid', because it is out of place. In the single sentence, McEwan highlights the tension between a cold scientific rationalism and the actuality of lived experience, which demands another, more emotional kind of engagement.

The tension is treated at greater length a little later in the novel, specifically on the issue of the infant smile, 'one social signal', reports Joe, 'that is particularly easy to isolate and study', and so a simple demonstration that 'the way we wear our emotions on our faces is pretty much the same in all cultures':

> It appears in !Kung San babies of the Kalahari at the same time as it does in American children of Manhattan's Upper West Side, and it has the same effect. In Edward O. Wilson's cool phrase, it 'triggers a more

abundant share of parental love and affection'. Then he goes on, 'in the terminology of the zoologist, it is a social releaser, an inborn and relatively invariant signal that mediates a basic social relationship.' (*EL*, p. 70)

The passage draws on Wilson's book *On Human Nature*, from which the quote is taken.[17] Wilson's suggestion is that such simple and automatic behaviour 'may well be genetically hard-wired into the cellular units of the human brain and facial nerves', part of the preprogramming of genetically successful familial roles.[18]

Given this emphasis on how genetic inheritance mediates social relationships, it is easy to understand why Wilson's theories have attracted fierce criticism over the years. *Sociobiology*, in fact, created a storm when it first appeared, with the more extreme antagonists suggesting that sociobiology might be the product of the kind of deterministic thinking that leads to eugenics.[19] McEwan, with the skill of the novelist treating ideas, is swift to incorporate the counterpoint of Clarissa's own antagonistic response to Joe:

> She was perturbed when I read Wilson's passage to her. Everything was being stripped down, she said, and in the process some larger meaning was lost. What a zoologist had to say about a baby's smile could be of no real interest. The truth of that smile was in the eye and heart of the parent, and in the unfolding love which only had meaning through time. (*EL*, p. 70)

This emphasis on the imponderables of love and time, in the construction of a relationship, is a recurring concern for McEwan; and it indicates the author's own investment in pursuing the apparent opposition between Clarissa and Joe, and the apparent opposition between nature and nurture.

The smile of infants, and the affectionate response triggered in parents, may be a good example of the *functional* nature of emotions, from a genetic point of view. Yet, as the status and treatment of children becomes a focus for the book's exploration of morality, the tenderness of both Clarissa and Joe towards the children of others – a response without *personal* genetic investment – becomes pointed. This may not refute the idea of a functional emotional capacity that is inherited, since the foster parent may also rely on such traits; but there is a shift of emphasis in the motif of foster-parenting (Joe and Clarissa eventually adopt a child, the second appendix informs us (*EL*, p. 242)), a shift towards a cultural model of collective responsibility in which the genetic function is redeployed.

Clarissa's personal tragedy is her inability to bear children, and this opens up in her the propensity to emotional instability. The death of a friend's baby in the past had provoked 'disabling grief', revealing her 'own mourning for a phantom child' (*EL*, p. 31). The ballooning accident, according to Joe, probes this area of weakness, since, in the aftermath, she focuses on the fact that Logan is a father who wouldn't let go of the rope because of the boy in the basket: 'He was a good man', she opines, and Joe's reading of her mood is persuasive: 'the boy was not his own, but he was a father and he understood. His kind of love pierced Clarissa's defences. With that pleading note – he was a good man – she was asking her own past, her ghost child to forgive her' (*EL*, pp. 31–2).

Clarissa's positive response to her sense of loss is to be a great friend to her nieces, nephews, godchildren, as well as the children of neighbours and friends: there is a room in Joe and Clarissa's house – 'part nursery, part teenage den' – set aside for children. Joe reports that Clarissa admires the way he has with children and, although he feels he has 'never been tested in the true fires of parental self-denial' (*EL*, p. 31), her judgement is shown to be correct in the scene where he engages the Logan children in a conversation about ethics, without condescension (*EL*, pp. 119–20). It is his lack of self-confidence, however, that proves his particular strength, here. Joe explains how, when he meets a child, he sees himself from the child's perspective, remembering how adults had seemed 'a grey crew' to him as a ten-year-old, making him worry that they would detect his pity for them (*EL*, pp. 118–19). This rather complex concern for the other's view, in the child, is reformulated in the adult. This is how Joe approaches the Logan children:

> I saw myself configured in their eyes – yet one more dull stranger in the procession lately filing through their home, a large man in a creased blue linen suit, the coin of baldness on his crown visible from where they stood. His purpose here would be unintelligible, beyond consideration. Above all, he was yet another man who was not their father. (*EL*, p. 119)

There is no self-pity in this, in common with the earlier self-appraisal where Joe wonders at the miraculous fact that Clarissa should love 'a large, clumsy, balding fellow' like him (*EL*, p. 7). Joe is clear-eyed about empirical facts, as he sees them, and this extends to the recognition of his own physical ordinariness. In his acute sense of empathy with the Logan children, however, there is a desire to engage with their emotional needs. The fact that he does this through a conversation about ethics, tailored to the children's grasp of logic, reveals an important paradox, for in Joe logic and empathy, reason and emotion, are significantly combined, but also confused. In talking to the children, it is the fact of engaging their interest that counts, not the particular topic.

However, Joe's sanguine self-knowledge, like all mental states in the book, is inconstant. Under the emotional pressure of the accident and Parry's subsequent actions, fearful of losing Clarissa, his self-appraisal is refigured as 'self-loathing' when he conceives of himself as, in her eyes, 'a giant polyp of uninspired logic' (*EL*, p. 140).

There is, then, an undertow of enriching ambiguity that complicates the surface scheme to the book, and which complicates the way in which the rationality of Joe, the science writer, is pitted against the emotion of Clarissa, the academic indulging her passion for Keats through extended research.[20]

In my view, this refutes some of the aesthetic objections to McEwan's work. James Wood has probably put this kind of complaint in the most unequivocal fashion when, apropos of *Enduring Love*, he writes of 'the thematic geometry, whereby McEwan bends each fiction into intellectual enquiry'. For Wood, this is less damaging to the stories, which 'can function as symbolic code work because they are over before we have time to resent their calculatedness'. The novels, however, 'suffocate with design', he feels: 'they trap their subjects in prim webs of information and argumentation'. Lamenting this schematic tendency, Wood concludes that 'his novels are efficient fictional engines, but not true novels.'[21]

The prominence of ideas, characterized thus, is not the same issue that confronted McEwan as he prepared the ground for writing *The Child in Time*: the 'move abroad' from fiction, embodied in writing the words for the oratorio *Or Shall We Die?* and the screenplay for *The Ploughman's Lunch*, gave him an outlet for those partisan political ideas that would, he felt, have been damaging to the novel. The issue here is the simple fact of staging some kind of debate, rather than the promotion of a particular set of ideas. Michael Wood's account of this element of McEwan's work, which is more sympathetic than James Wood's, helps to clarify this category of fiction:

> Kundera distinguishes novelists from writers (who also write novels): 'The writer has original ideas and an inimitable voice . . . The novelist makes no great issue of his ideas. He is an explorer feeling his way . . .

He is fascinated not by his voice but by a form he is seeking.' . . . Certainly
Golding and McEwan are novelists in Kundera's sense, but they do make
an issue of their ideas. I'm not suggesting that they push their ideas at
us, or that there is something inartistic, insufficiently ludic, about their
asking us to think so hard. Only that they use their novels to focus quite
specific questions, rather than allowing their questions to arise, if at all,
from a world imagined for its own multifarious sake.

If there is a risk in this kind of fiction, it is less that of preaching than
that of debating, telling us too clearly what our intellectual options are,
displaying both sides of a case in an unduly judicious way, as if left and
right, hard and soft, north and south, were a universal allegory, always to
be followed, never to be believed. That's when you start feeling that play
is not only more fun but perhaps also more serious.[22]

To a degree, these comments take away with one hand what they
bestow with the other: McEwan *is* a novelist, rather than a writer of
ideas, we understand, yet he runs the risk of debating, and so diluting
the seriousness of his work. McEwan has acknowledged, implicitly, a
degree of schematic composition in the novel, and the three that
preceded it:

I think I've come to the end of a cycle of novels with *Enduring Love*, which
began with *The Child in Time*, included *Black Dogs* and *The Innocent*.
Those were novels in which *ideas* were dramatised or played out. They
are, among other things, novels of ideas.[23]

The idea of such a completed cycle should be qualified: there are some
thematic similarities between *Enduring Love* and the later *Saturday*, for
instance; but, to the extent that this is accurate, it should make us think
more positively about the 'novel of ideas' as an exploratory vehicle,
capable of delivering narrative surprises. Concerning the question of
cycles of novels in the oeuvre, *Enduring Love* marks a new phase, for
me, in which the application of ideas found in *The Child in Time* is
detached from the political anger and/or exactitude found in that novel
and the two that followed it.

A consideration of another of McEwan's scientific sources for this
novel may help further to show how ideas are integrated within
McEwan's narrative art. In outline, *Enduring Love* complicates
its 'debate' by inviting us to think beyond the old nature/culture
dichotomy. This dichotomy is mapped, broadly speaking, onto the
literature/science and emotion/reason debate embodied in: the
occupations of Clarissa and Joe; in Joe's doubts about the purity of his
work as a writer of popular science; and, of course, in the thematic

conception of the novel. McEwan cites Antonio Damasio's book *Descartes' Error* in his Acknowledgements, and it is Damasio who seems to be the key inspiration behind the dismantling of the emotion/reason dichotomy.

Damasio's fascinating hypothesis is that the traditional opposition between reason and emotion (which can be traced to Aristotle) is false. The hypothesis stems originally from the clinical observation of a patient in whom 'flawed reason and impaired feelings stood out together as the consequences of a specific brain lesion', a correlation from which Damasio deduced 'that feeling was an integral component of the machinery of reason'.[24]

Damasio is also one of those scientists who is 'sceptical of science's presumption of objectivity and definitiveness'; rather, he sees 'scientific results, especially in neurobiology', as 'provisional approximations, to be enjoyed for a while and discarded as soon as better accounts become available.' However, he still has a conviction about scientific progress: 'I do believe, more often than not, that we will come to know.'[25] This is the kind of thoughtful progression beyond the nature/nurture standoff that has come to characterize much popular science since the 1990s, and the work of those novelists inspired by it:

> The picture I am drawing for humans is that of an organism that comes to life designed with automatic survival mechanisms, and to which education and acculturation add a set of socially permissible and desirable decision-making strategies that, in turn, enhance survival, remarkably improve the quality of that survival, and serve as the basis for constructing a *person*.[26]

Still more arresting and challenging, to conventional neuroscience, is Damasio's conviction that 'the representations your brain constructs to describe a situation, and the movements formulated as response to a situation, depend on mutual brain-body interactions.' This is the conviction that leads Damasio to contest Cartesian dualism, the form of mind–body split popularly ascribed to Descartes, especially on the basis of his most famous philosophical statement, 'cogito ergo sum' ('I think therefore I am'). A literal understanding of this statement, says Damasio, 'suggests that thinking, and awareness of thinking, are the real substrates of being'; whereas the reverse emphasis is more accurate: 'we are, and then we think, and we think only inasmuch as we are, since thinking is indeed caused by the structures and operations of being.'[27]

Ultimately, Damasio's understanding of the consequences of his work is pragmatic, since 'knowing about the relevance of feelings in the processes of reason does *not* suggest that reason is less important than feelings':

> On the contrary, taking stock of the pervasive role of feelings may give us a chance of enhancing their positive effects and reducing their potential harm. Specifically, without diminishing the orienting value of normal feelings, one would want to protect reason from the weakness that abnormal feelings or the manipulation of normal feelings can introduce in the process of planning and deciding.[28]

Enduring Love will certainly support a reading that is in line with this view: insofar as the denouement reveals Joe to be accurate in his assessment of Jed, and the threat he poses, there is a recuperation or 'protection' of reason, which has faced the 'potential harm' of 'abnormal feelings'. This is by no means the only available reading, of course; but it is one that makes sense of the emplotment and the narrative resolution. The novel does not embody an assertion or a statement about the relative claims of reason and emotion: it is an enactment of these relative claims, in which the narrative doing – the fictive, the imaginary motor of the novel – is the primary element.

The influence of Damasio shows how McEwan is drawn to those writers that are already complex and whose ideas do not stage an obvious debate; it also demonstrates how McEwan uses these sources to enrich, rather than simplify, to contribute to the serious play of writing, rather than simply to delineate intellectual choices. Much of the narrative tension in the novel derives from the ways in which the characterization confounds the presentation of ideas. McEwan has said that, in Clarissa, 'I wanted someone both sympathetic and wrong', whereas 'I wanted in Joe someone who was slightly repellent, but right'.[29] This aim is fully achieved.

Outwardly, Joe seems limited by the rational world-view that Clarissa sees as childlike, a mark of innocence (*EL*, p. 33). Yet this innocence is also the sign of his 'dislocated, incomplete character', in her estimation (*EL*, p. 102). If one were to pursue the idea of a scheme in the book, one might deduce that there is a tacit concept of maturity, a state attained by those able to find a balance or compromise between reason and emotion. While acknowledging that such an idea hovers over the book, it is not treated schematically. Indeed, the impulse in the writing is exploratory, and the effects unsettling, the more so for Joe's futile attempts to pin down and identify the phenomena – both internal and external – that he observes.

The crux of Joe's self-division lies in his professional dissatisfaction as a science journalist, rather than a scientist in a purer sense. He considers himself a 'failure', whose work is 'parasitic and marginal' (*EL*, p. 99). Rather than working to produce verifiable 'truths' about Nature, he represents and popularizes new developments. His medium, in other words, is narrative, subordinated to the economic pressures of copy deadlines. The accident, and the emergence of Parry as his stalker, re-ignites his desire to do academic work 'in theoretical physics' (*EL*, p. 82), but the rapid developments in his field render his ideas redundant (*EL*, p. 106).

The notional oppositional between pure science on the one hand and parasitic science journalism on the other is apparent rather than real. At least, this is the implication that emerges from one of Joe's articles, in which he makes a historical comparison between art and science to deduce a more general principle about narrative and aesthetics that has a bearing on his own work. In this piece he traces the development from the 'culture of the amateur that nourished the anecdotal scientist' of the nineteenth century to the increasingly difficult and professionalized university science of the twentieth century, characterized by 'hard-edged theories' that have their 'own formal aesthetic', and that survive 'without experimental support'. Einstein's General Theory, 'in the textbooks from the twenties onwards', but without 'experimental verification' until the 1950s, is the prime example (*EL*, pp. 48–9).

Joe compares the development of professionalized science with the emergence of literary modernism, the 'difficult art' that celebrates 'formal, structural qualities, inner coherence and self-reference.' The premise of the article is, thus, that 'the meanderings of narrative had given way to an aesthetics of form, as in art, so in science' (*EL*, p. 49). However, Joe is soon dissatisfied with his effort. Counter-examples flood his mind – the 'brilliant theory' in Victorian physics and chemistry 'that displayed not a shred of narrative inclination.' Moreover, he reflects that 'fabulation run riot' is one way of accounting for 'scientific or pseudo-scientific' manifestations of twentieth-century thought such as anthropology and psychoanalysis. Joe concludes that his piece is not 'written in pursuit of truth', but is governed by the standard of 'readability'; and that 'a separate coherent piece' could be made from 'the counter-arguments' (*EL*, p. 50).

Joe's agnosticism with regard to systemic scientific explanations – and especially evolutionary biology – is emphatically registered late in the novel. This is the moment where Joe tries to conjure a moment of calm, drawing on his skills of scientific observation, in the episode where he has just bought his gun, has tested it in a wooded area, and finds he has to defecate. Knowing that Clarissa is being held by the apparently murderous Jed, he seeks to find a steadying 'long perspective' in 'the earthbound scale of the biological' as he scoops up a handful of earth. He observes 'the inhabitants of the microscopic realm, the parasitic fungi and the bacteria', and considers the role they play in the cycle of life:

> What I thought might calm me was the reminder that, for all our concerns, we were still part of this natural dependency – for the animals that we ate grazed the plants which, like our vegetables and fruits, were nourished by the soil formed by these organisms. But even as I squatted to enrich the forest floor, I could not believe in the primary significance of these grand cycles. Just beyond the oxygen-exhaling trees stood my poison-exuding vehicle, inside which was my gun, and thirty-five miles down teeming roads was the enormous city on whose northern side was my apartment where a madman was waiting, . . . and my threatened loved one. What, in this description, was necessary to the carbon cycle, or the fixing of nitrogen? We were no longer in the great chain. It was our own complexity that had expelled us from the Garden. We were in a mess of our own unmaking. (*EL*, pp. 206–7)

The Fall is here conceived in traditional terms, since the complexity that occasions the expulsion from the Garden is a consequence of technological and mental development, or 'knowledge' broadly defined. This is also an admission of the failure of the explanatory system that Joe inclines most towards. His revelatory moment, defecating on the woodland floor, indicates that the identification of purpose in evolutionary systems no longer has relevance to developed human societies: we are over-evolved, or 'unmade'.

The passage quoted above offers a striking parallel with the episode in chapter 22 of Thomas Hardy's *A Pair of Blue Eyes* (1873) where Henry Knight, believing he is facing death, finds himself staring – as if eyeball to eyeball – at a Trilobite fossil in the cliff face. Knight reflects on the geological layers before him and the 'immense lapses of time' they represent, indifferent to 'the dignity of man.'[30] The comparison demonstrates that McEwan is the natural heir to Hardy in his treatment of this issue. Where Hardy registers the impact of Darwin on human self-perception – specifically in the felt need to accept our animal nature, and our place in the evolutionary cycle – McEwan's Joe Rose has progressed to another stage, suited to his time. Acutely conscious of his membership of an irrational species, characterized by the propensity to pollute and by psychic disruption, he understands that the Fall is the breaking of the evolutionary cycle.

However, if McEwan's post-Darwinism represents a partial historical progression from Hardy's important registering of the implications of Darwin, there is also a sense in which Hardy is very much in tune with the angst that McEwan expresses through Joe Rose. Indeed, Hardy anticipates McEwan in that perception of human beings having over-evolved. In his Notebooks, Hardy argues 'that man has evolved too far for the imperfect environment in which he is placed. Human emotions, the capacity to feel and therefore to suffer, are "a blunder of overdoing" in the evolutionary process, "the nerves being evolved to an activity abnormal in such an environment".'[31]

Here, crucially, the basis of Joe's intellectual affiliation is unravelled. Earlier, in the spirit of Robert Wright's deliberation about the selfish employment of moral rectitude, Joe reflects on the interest of evolutionary psychologists in 'self-persuasion'. If 'persuading others of your own needs and interests' is a desirable social skill, then those who convince themselves first of the justness of their case will be better at persuading others: 'the kind of self-deluding individuals who tended to do this flourished, as did their genes' (*EL*, p. 104). The context of these reflections is the scene in which Joe rifles through Clarissa's desk, and seeks a means of justifying his actions. The self-consciousness betrays the failure of self-delusion in this instance. There is no subsequent attempt to convince Clarissa that the intrusion, which she feels to be a betrayal, was justified (*EL*, p. 132).

The same idea filters through Joe's narrative in the scene after the restaurant shooting: 'we're descended from the indignant, passionate tellers of half truths who in order to convince others, simultaneously convinced themselves', he reflects, where the impossibility of establishing objective truth is demonstrated to him (*EL*, p. 181). The relativity of perceptions, together with the failure to persuade, is another clear indication that the novel is moving in a different direction from the evolutionary psychology that partially inspires it. The delusion of Jed Parry is merely the most extreme example of a destructive subjectivity that implies humanity is no longer part of the evolutionary cycle. We have over-evolved to the point where the self-deluded insistence on our personal wants may no longer be advantageous.

These pointed reflections on the subjective view put us squarely in the realm of the literary. Roger Clark and Andy Gordon have identified a degree of postmodern relativity in the novel, most especially to the degree that science emerges as 'a form of storytelling.'[32] The tendency in theories of postmodernism to characterize science as one narrative among others, with no particular claim to truth, has been the focus of much controversy. One notorious episode was the hoax perpetrated by the physicist Alan Sokal in 1996, a flashpoint in the art and science debate that *Enduring Love* seems clearly to respond to.

In the Spring–Summer 1996 issue of *Social Text*, Sokal published a spoof article that pandered to that journal's prejudices, in his estimation. He calculated that the editors, suspicious of 'disinterested' science, would be attracted to constructions of science that sought to put it to some predetermined (and left-leaning) political end.[33] In Sokal's later reflection, he summarizes the point of his hoax, to satirize the view 'that science, in order to be "liberatory," must be subordinated to political strategies.' His other main target, he makes clear, is the 'dogma in cultural studies that there exists no external world'; or that science 'obtains no knowledge of it.'[34]

The first appendix of the novel is McEwan's own scientific spoof, a psychiatric case study which summarizes the novel's human dynamic, and which fooled some reviewers into believing that McEwan had constructed his novel around an actual case history of the obsessional mania de Clérambault's syndrome. The clue to the authorship of this bogus paper is in the surnames of the writers – 'Wenn' and 'Camia' – which comprise an anagram of Ian McEwan. The hoax would have been perpetrated more extensively had the appendix been published by the *Psychiatric Bulletin*, where McEwan sought to place it.[35]

What should we make of McEwan's hoax, in the wake of the Sokal hoax? Sokal sought to ridicule postmodern relativism in the arts and social sciences, while the impetus of McEwan's hoax is to draw parallels between fiction and psychiatry. Clearly, this is not the same gesture in reverse: Sokal's anger is underpinned by a commitment to the pursuit of truth in understanding Nature in the physical sciences, and nobody would make quite the same claim for the clinical sciences. However, the gesture does serve to underscore the importance of narrative in the pursuit of understanding, and to unsettle the higher claims of psychiatry, much as the novel unravels the putative coherence of evolutionary psychology.

Intrigued by evolutionary psychology, McEwan produces a hero still more enamoured of the latter's truth claims, but puts him in a narrative structure that tests to breaking point some of its tenets, especially: the idea that self-delusion in the prosecution of self-interest is a cultivated genetic trait; and the notion that the habit of constructing 'morality' may also be an inherited trait. The novel shows humanity to be at a stage of evolution and/or social complexity that takes us out of the evolutionary loop, and that demands of us an ethical sense that addresses the problem of self-interest with acute self-consciousness.

The phenomenon of first-person narration – and McEwan's choice of this mode here – has a significant bearing on the novel's subject. Considering the dominance of first person narration in 'literary novels' published since the 1980s, David Lodge suggests this bestows authenticity on the novel as a vehicle for rendering human experience in its particular context:

> In a world where nothing is certain, in which transcendental belief has been undermined by scientific materialism, and even the objectivity of science is qualified by relativity and uncertainty, the single human voice, telling its own story, can seem the only authentic way of rendering consciousness. Of course in fiction this is just as artful, or artificial, a method as writing about a character in the third person; but it creates an illusion of reality, it commands the willing suspension of the reader's disbelief, by modelling itself on the discourses of personal witness: the confession, the diary, autobiography, memoir, the deposition.[36]

In the case of Joe's first-person narrative, we have a mode that serves to emphasize the individual's interpretation that so much else in the novel warns us against. An interesting point to consider is how the human propensity to tell stories might be explained in that branch of science that so impresses Joe. Lodge has the answer:

> Evolutionary psychologists have suggested that the ability to imagine what another person – an enemy, for instance – might be thinking in a given situation, by running hypothetical scenarios on the brain's hardware, was a crucial survival skill for primitive man and might explain the storytelling instinct that seems to be a part of all human cultures.[37]

Of course, the cultural dependence on narrative is no longer linked to military strategy. Novel-writing, in other words, is a primary manifestation of human endeavour that is redundant in evolutionary terms (even if the impulse to narrate has an evolutionary basis), and which is thus beyond the explanatory reach of post-Darwinian science.

The paradoxical evocation of genetic inheritance, while the limits of such understanding are exposed, points to the central structural irony of *Enduring Love*, which also has a bearing on its technical effects. For example, responses to narrative that may be inherited – such as the desire for order, closure – are played off in the novel against the idea of radical uncertainty, in a performance of the book's ordering ideas.

There is certainly a loaded irony in the way in which McEwan exploits the reader's desire for closure. Thus, although much of the book raises questions about the relativity of human impressions and the difficulty of objective judgement – as well as the reliability of Joe as narrator – there is still a clear indication in the narrative of a 'correct' interpretation of the main events.[38] In the structure of the book as a whole, governed by one voice, there is a persuasive emphasis on the dominant version that is also vindicated by other means.[39]

The resolution of the narrative shows Joe to have been right about Jed Parry all along. The first appendix indicates that Joe and Clarissa are eventually reconciled, and successfully adopt a child, in the final validation of an ethical humanism that is *not* linked to a direct biological imperative (*EL*, p. 242).

The question of the relativity of perception remains at stake. Clarissa's letter to Joe (*EL*, pp. 216–19) puts the case that Joe's 'being right is not a simple matter' (*EL*, p. 216), that he might have exacerbated some of Parry's delusions in the approach he took to dealing with him. The novel closes with a letter from Parry as a second appendix, written after three years incarceration, still proclaiming his deluded love for Joe. However, the final chapter of the novel proper sees Joe painstakingly bringing the relevant parties together to prove to Jean Logan that her conclusion that her husband had been having an affair was based on a misinterpretation of the evidence. It is a significant rhetorical closure, an insistence that the effort to seek a broadly true version of these events is necessary, that this version matters, and that it must be commonly understood.

Rather than the pursuit of unassailable 'truth', the quest is for an agreed story – or, one might equally say, an agreed moral code – in the full knowledge that the story is artificial, and merely the best fiction by which to live. The novel performs the social effort required in human ethics, which now necessitates a recognition of the inherited human nature constructed by genetic science, and a self-conscious progression beyond that recognition.

Notes

1 The particular scientific focus makes the novel representative of its time. Patricia Waugh puts *Enduring Love* in the context of a decade in which novelists 'show a marked orientation towards and engagement with the biological sciences.' Waugh summarizes how biological science, in the 1990s (leading up to the publication of the Human Genome sequence), began to discern 'a scientific explanation of mind' and so to glimpse the possibility of 'a final theoretical closure which includes in its account of the material universe an account of itself.' Through such closure, the 'undecidability . . . at the heart of postmodernism' could be 'overcome'.

My reading of McEwan's novel is broadly in accord with Waugh's: 'he presents a picture of human existence which demonstrates the final inadequacy of any reductionist evolutionary account but without therefore capitulating to the postmodern evacuation of knowledge and judgement.' See Patricia Waugh, 'Science and Fiction in the 1990s', in Nick Bentley, ed., *British Fiction of the 1990s* (London: Routledge, 2005), pp. 57–77 (pp. 62, 63, 68).

2 Malcolm, *Understanding Ian McEwan*, p. 157.

3 Ibid., p. 172.

4 Robert Wright, *The Moral Animal: Why We Are the Way We Are* (1994; London: Abacus, 2004), p. 6.

5 Ibid., pp. 8, 334, 335.

6 Ibid., pp. 336, 344.

7 Ian McEwan, 'Move Over, Darwin' (review of *Consilience* by Edward O. Wilson), *The Observer*, 'Review' (20 September 1998), p. 13.

8 Ibid., p. 13.

9 Edward O. Wilson, *Consilience: The Unity of Knowledge* (1998; London: Abacus, 2003), p. 332.

10 Wright, *The Moral Animal*, p. 344.

11 Wilson, *Consilience*, p. 12.

12 Ibid., pp. 242, 243, 241, 248, 249.

13 Ibid., pp. 2, 236, 305.

14 Ian McEwan, 'The Great Odyssey', *The Guardian*, 'Saturday Review' (9 June 2001), pp. 1, 3 (p. 1).

15 Ibid., p. 1.

16 Ibid., p. 3.

17 Edward O. Wilson, *On Human Nature* (Harvard University Press, 1978), p. 62. Wilson is drawing on the work of the anthropologist Melvin J. Konner in this passage. *On Human Nature* is one of three titles by Wilson

listed by McEwan in his Acknowledgements (*EL*, p. 247). This observation about the infant smile is an example that Wilson has found compelling: it is repeated, for example, in the later *Consilience* (1998), p. 168. In the 2001 article cited above, McEwan discusses Darwin's own work on human expression, observing Darwin's argument that 'expressions of emotion are the products of evolution'. See 'The Great Odyssey', p. 3.

18   Wilson, *On Human Nature*, pp. 62–3.

19   For an account of the controversy, see Ullica Segerstråle, *Defenders of the Truth: The Sociobiology Debate* (Oxford University Press, 2000).

20   In the 2004 Pathé Pictures version of the novel, directed by Roger Michell, great emphasis is placed on the near psychological collapse of Joe (played by Daniel Craig, against Rhys Ifans's Jed). Although McEwan was Associate Producer on the project, this is an adaptation that confirms the impression left by all the other adaptations: the subtleties of McEwan's fiction do not translate well to film.

21   James Wood, 'Why It All Adds Up' (review of *Enduring Love*), *The Guardian*, 'G2' (4 September 1997), pp. 9–10 (pp. 9, 10).

22   Michael Wood, 'When the Balloon Goes Up', *London Review of Books*, 19: 17 (4 September 1997), pp. 8–9 (p. 8).

23   Jonathan Noakes, 'Interview with Ian McEwan', p. 23.

24   Antonio Damasio, *Descartes' Error*, p. xii.

25   Ibid., pp. xviii, xix.

26   Ibid., p. 126.

27   Ibid., pp. 228, 248.

28   Ibid., p. 246.

29   Noakes, 'Interview with Ian McEwan', p. 17.

30   Thomas Hardy, *A Pair of Blue Eyes* (1873; London: Macmillan, 1975), p. 240.

31   Roger Robinson, 'Hardy and Darwin', in Norman Page, ed., *Thomas Hardy: The Writer and His Background* (London: Bell and Hyman, 1980), pp. 128–50 (p. 132).

32   Roger Clark and Andy Gordon, *Ian McEwan's 'Enduring Love'* (London: Continuum, 2003), p. 42. Another blurring of the distinction between literary and scientific writing follows from McEwan's attraction to Edward O. Wilson's writing on aesthetic grounds: in his review of *Consilience*, he writes of the 'exalted brilliance' of the expression, commenting that 'there are paragraphs of his writing which you want to read aloud.' McEwan, 'Move Over, Darwin', p. 13.

33   In the words of his own article, Sokal sought to appeal to those predisposed to agree 'that the discourse of the scientific community, for all its undeniable value, cannot assert a privileged epistemological status with respect to counterhegemonic narratives emanating from dissident or marginalized communities'. Alan Sokal, 'Transgressing the Boundaries:

Toward a Transformative Hermeneutics of Quantum Gravity', *Social Text*, Spring–Summer 1996, reprinted in *The Sokal Hoax: The Sham That Shook the Academy*, edited by the editors of *Lingua Franca* (Lincoln and London: University of Nebraska Press, 2000), pp. 11–45 (p. 12).

34 Alan Sokal, 'Revelation: A Physicist Experiments with Cultural Studies', *Lingua Franca* (May–June 1996) reprinted in *The Sokal Hoax*, pp. 49–53 (pp. 51, 50). It is also worth noting that Sokal's stated real target is 'the intellectual arrogance of Theory – postmodernist *literary* theory' (p. 52).

35 For an account of the hoax, and reactions to it, see Roger Clark and Andy Gordon, *Ian McEwan's 'Enduring Love'*, pp. 68–9.

36 David Lodge, *Consciousness and the Novel*, pp. 87–8.

37 Ibid., p. 41.

38 Sean Matthews' inventive essay concentrates on the motif of unreliability, finding (in a playful literary-critical echo) seven distinct types. He ends his essay with a Foucaldean emphasis on the relation between constructions of madness and sanity, as a way of bringing the unreliability of Rose into focus. See Sean Matthews, '*Enduring Love*: Seven Types of Unreliability', in Peter Childs, ed., *Ian McEwan's 'Enduring Love'* (London: Routledge, forthcoming).

39 This aspect of the book is reminiscent of Iris Murdoch's *The Black Prince*, with its complicating postscripts that do not displace the chief version of events, and the novelist's enactment of the morally charged pursuit of order, in the face of randomness and contingency.

7

Amsterdam: McEwan's 'spoiler'

Appraisal of *Amsterdam*, McEwan's Booker Prize-winning novella, has been clouded by its perception as an inferior Booker winner: when an established writer is awarded a literary prize for a book that is not representative of his/her best work, there is the suspicion that the award is made for the author's accumulated efforts, rather than for the book in question. McEwan had previously been short-listed, in 1981, for *The Comfort of Strangers*, and again in 1992, for *Black Dogs*. *Enduring Love*, however, did not make the shortlist in 1997. *Amsterdam*, produced in quick time for the following year's Prize, raises the further suspicion that the author, hoping his time had come, produced his own 'spoiler' to defeat the ambitions of other contenders.[1]

That term 'spoiler', of course, figures prominently in the novella as an index of a professionalism that occludes the ethical view. There are two noteworthy uses of the term: first, when newspaper editor Vernon Halliday's coup is 'spoiled' – his prized front-page photograph of the foreign secretary in drag revealed for the television cameras before he can publish (*Am*, p. 124); and, second, at the dénouement of the plot. Here, the ludicrous and ultimately self-destructive tendencies of Halliday's professional standards are finely exposed when, realizing that his composer friend Linley has killed him in an act of mutual, enforced euthanasia, he acknowledges 'reverentially' this 'spoiler' (*Am*, p. 173).

That the activity of spoiling should be treated with respect underscores the notion that professional acuity has become an end in itself. Of course, this extra-textual debate may seem to be damaging to our perception of McEwan's novella: if it is viewed as a spoiler itself, does it not partake of the world of vicious professionalism that it also satirizes? For one reviewer there was 'a satisfying irony in knowing that this is exactly the kind of book that the society McEwan satirizes would pick as the best book of the year.'[2]

The irony, however, may be more complex than this suggests. It is not so much that the Booker panel were duped, seduced into awarding the Prize to a book that tacitly implicated literary prize culture in its social critique. Or, if that is partly true, the gesture of producing this accomplished novella to snatch the 1998 Prize goes beyond that simple irony. For McEwan was a worthy winner, and *Amsterdam*, though not his best, is a work of some literary merit. Yet its real significance may be as a literary *event*, where the satire bleeds out into the world of literary culture, but without the force of outright condemnation. There is an authorial self-critique in *Amsterdam*, too, and this is another equivocal factor that makes it a highly unstable piece, 'unsettling' in new and various senses.

The context for this equivocal and unsettling literary event is crucial to understanding it. McEwan responds deeply to the apparent paradox that the Thatcher–Major era, systematically vilified in much of the literature it provoked, seems with hindsight to have ushered in a period of renaissance in English fiction. Thatcherism, as a political phenomenon, was perceived generally by writers and artists as radical and divisive. Novelists very often found their broadly liberal sensibilities deeply offended by the attack on traditional collective values. The apparent paradox, then, is merely one which confirms that valuable literature often feeds on a sense of moral outrage. Yet it is true that by the end of an extensive period of Conservative rule, some of the Tories' most articulate opponents had established themselves in such a way as to make them the beneficiaries of the very policies they had decried.[3]

As a direct response to this paradox, *Amsterdam* offers a satirical portrait of those who 'had flourished under a government they had despised for almost seventeen years' (*Am*, p. 12). In a sense, this is a deliberation on compromise, on left-intellectual achievement in an (apparently) hostile political context; but McEwan's real interest is in the point where compromise becomes capitulation, where self-interest finally ousts the shreds of social conviction that remain.

The author's impression of this stratum of the intelligentsia is conveyed through a detached narrative voice that vacillates between an ironic mood and one that is less implicitly critical. This makes the dissection of amorality in the two principals more complex than a casual reading suggests.

These two, Vernon Halliday and Clive Linley, each face an ethical dilemma, which will expose a fatal lack of substance in their professional conduct. For Halliday, the key moment involves his decision to publish compromising photographs of the xenophobic foreign secretary, Julian Garmony. His paper, *The Judge* (modelled on 'modernizing' broadsheets like *The Guardian*, *The Observer* and *The Times*), faces its own internal struggle over editorial policy. Halliday hopes his scoop will boost circulation and help take *The Judge* downmarket in accordance with his policy of modernization. However, when he chooses to publish his photographs of the cross-dressing Garmony – a decision in any case tainted by personal motivation – he is out-manoeuvred, and the 'scoop' explodes in his face. Halliday fills an entire front page with an image of Garmony, sporting a three-quarter-length dress, false breasts and make-up. The 'highest professional standards' discernible in this 'classic' front page are those of a professional elite operating without an ethical code (*Am*, p. 116). Halliday – 'once an apologist for the sexual revolution' – now tries to cash in on a reactionary moral conservatism (*Am*, p. 73).

For Linley, the key moment of decision is more clear-cut. Linley considers himself to be 'Vaughan Williams' heir' (*Am*, p. 21), and his conservative musical style has secured him the commission to write 'The Millennium Symphony' for the celebrations in 2000. Unable to find the decisive variation that will bring the finale together, Linley goes walking in the Lake District for inspiration. Here he begins to discern the motif for his finale in the call of a bird, only to be disturbed by a disputing couple. (It transpires that the woman is actually in the clutches of a serial rapist.) Linley leaves her to her fate in order to preserve his creative spark, and departs hastily from the Lakes in a state of agitated self-justification, concentrating on his new-found 'sublime sequence of notes' (*Am*, p. 89).

The symphony, it transpires, is flawed by its final movement when completed. In fact, the performance is cancelled: the work is pronounced 'a dud', containing 'a tune at the end' derivative of Beethoven (*Am*, p. 176). McEwan, in the portraits of his two principals, exposes the vacuity of an enclosed professionalism, unresponsive to the contradictions and complexities of social life. Linley turns his back on a woman in distress, refusing to interpret the scene before him, much as Halliday allows his obsession with ends to uncover the crudeness of his professional means.

A target, here, is the decontextualized Grand Gesture, powerfully symbolized in Linley's ruined Millennium Symphony. (Hindsight inevitably brings the ill-conceived Millennium Dome to mind.) This consummately realized novella – a sonata rather than a symphony – concludes with an elegantly counterpointed dispensing of just desserts. Linley and Halliday have a pact, so that if either of them were to develop a condition such as rapid-onset Alzheimer's disease, the other would arrange a trip to Amsterdam, with its relaxed euthanasia laws, to curtail the suffering and indignity.[4] In a mutual vendetta inspired by their pact, and justified by their respective moral failures, they prove each other's nemesis, poisoning each other at a drinks party. A novella can bear the neatness of this plot device, which in any case carries the more substantial point that it may be in the nature of unselfconscious professionalism to dispense with any ethical roots. Such a state, satirized in this portrait of the 'humane' achievers of McEwan's own generation, is presented as a kind of dementia, best expunged.

One of the assumed codes of fiction is that discussion of a character's artistic endeavour is often a channel for creative self-reflection by the author. This is another complicating factor in *Amsterdam*, where there is an invitation to see in Linley's compositional efforts a parallel to McEwan's. As Frank Kermode observes, 'the failure of the composer's final symphony, after we have heard so much about the process of composition, might uncharitably be seen as an allegory of the novel it occurs in.'[5]

Where the parallel breaks down, however, is in the limited ambitions of McEwan's novella, for in *Amsterdam* he quite clearly lowers his sights, aiming for a modest work that is of an entirely different order to Linley's celebratory, millennial gesture. There may still be a revealing paradox in McEwan's treatment of the musical theme, and especially in the drawing of Linley's character. The *Salon* reviewer, Craig Seligman, suggested that 'McEwan wants to despise Clive', yet 'he devotes the novel's loveliest and most fascinating pages to the creation of that symphony.' Seligman finds a direct (and inventive) parallel between the treatment of Linley's score and the ultimate failure of the novella, as he reads it. Linley's crucial compositional mistake – aside from the plagiarism of Beethoven – is to insist on reintroducing an earlier theme into his finale, as his deadline overtakes him, without finding the necessary 'significant variation' (*Am*, p. 142). For Seligman, it is the creative inflexibility that undermines the composer and the work:

It never occurs to him that one solution is to not reintroduce the melody. And it doesn't occur to McEwan, either. He returns, at the end of the book, to the broad, troubling theme from which the novel takes its title; his carefully wrought structure demands it. McEwan is an aesthete like Clive, seduced by the beauties of symmetry, and he is undone, in the end, by his own exquisite craftsmanship: instead of betraying his structure, he betrays his book.[6]

This is a persuasive critique, as far as it goes; but what is not addressed in this account is the author's evident consciousness of the parallel. As Linley reflects on the orchestral rehearsal of his flawed symphony, he makes a significant connection:

The absence of the variation had wrecked his masterpiece, and he was clearer than ever now, if such a thing was possible, about the plans he had made. It was no longer fury that drove him, or hatred or disgust, or the necessity of honouring his word. What he was about to do was contractually right, it had the amoral inevitability of pure geometry, and he didn't feel a thing. (*Am*, p. 161)

The 'amoral inevitability of pure geometry' is that which undermines the symphony. It is also Linley's anticipation of the killing of Halliday (under the guise of 'euthanasia'); and a signal of McEwan's plot contrivance that will see Halliday reciprocate. In other words, the neatness of his symmetrically constructed novella is linked, by the author, to the 'amoral inevitability' of mutual destruction; and that mutual destruction is a consequence of the collapse of personality under the sign of enclosed professionalism.

The chief significance of this chain of association, however, has more to do with the book as a literary event – and specifically as a spoiler prepared for the Booker panel – than it does with an evaluation of McEwan as a stylist. The self-consciousness, here, cannot be taken as a built-in criticism of plot-driven writing, since novellas – good as well as bad – often *do* betray greater narrative rigidity than novels. Further, the question of 'morality' in relation to *Amsterdam*, with McEwan implicitly drawing himself into the debate about professionalism, concerns the work as a wider literary event.

Before arriving at a final evaluation of this crucially unsettling aspect of the work, I wish to consider in more detail the related ambivalences within it; and the most important of these elements is the treatment of Linley.

In the opening scene, at Molly's funeral, Linley's compositional habits, rendered in free indirect discourse, make his talent seem workmanlike, rather than inspirational:

> He watched his own vaporised breath float off into the grey air. The temperature in central London was said to be minus eleven today. Minus eleven. There was something seriously wrong with the world for which neither God nor his absence could be blamed. Man's first disobedience, the Fall, a falling figure, an oboe, nine notes, ten notes. Clive had the gift of perfect pitch and heard them descending from the G. There was no need to write them down. (*Am*, p. 4)

The easy passage from the rumination about freak weather and the damage done to the planet – and the implication that the Fall of Man, the acquisition of knowledge, is to blame for global destruction – is ludicrously pat. The musical phrase denoting this reflection, instantly composed, is obviously bathetic. The final two sentences then humorously puncture the pretensions of Linley, with the kind of satirical edge that the reviewers generally felt to be absent from the book.[7]

When another mourner informs Clive that her eleven-year-old granddaughter had studied one of his pieces for a violin grade exam, he feels 'faintly depressed' (*Am*, pp. 9–10); and when Garmony tells him 'my wife knows a few of your piano pieces by heart', he wonders: 'was he as domesticated and tame a talent as some of his younger critics claimed, the thinking man's Gorecki?' (*Am*. p. 13).

This kind of writing evokes, faintly, the satirical style of Evelyn Waugh or early Anthony Powell, but without the comic exuberance;[8] and before the reader settles into this mode, exposing Linley's pompous self-importance, McEwan confuses the signal. Garmony goes on to make an extravagant claim for his wife's talent: 'She was brilliant. Goldsmith's, then the Guildhall. A fabulous career ahead of her . . .' (*Am*, p. 14). This forms part of an anecdote, so its veracity is in question; but it raises the possibility that only an accomplished musician can play Linley's music, leaving us uncertain about his self-estimation as 'Vaughan Williams' heir' (*Am* p. 21).

It is unclear whether this is simply an arrogant claim; or whether it denotes the camp into which he naturally falls, as a composer of some note, at least, opposed to 'the whole modernist project', as embodied in 'tonal and aleatoric music, tone rows, electronics, the disintegration of pitch into sound' (*Am*, p. 21). It is hard not to see a parallel between Linley and McEwan here. Linley laments the fact that 'the old guard of modernism had imprisoned music in the academy where it was jealously professionalised, isolated and rendered sterile, its vital covenant with a general public arrogantly broken' (*Am*. pp. 21–2). McEwan's consistent production of page-turning bestsellers, also deemed to be 'literary', is the equivalent to Linley's conviction that traditional artistic virtues remain significant; or, in the specific case of music, that 'melody, harmony and rhythm were not incompatible with innovation.' (*Am*, p. 22)

One should also set against those bathetic moments of pat musical inspiration the more reverential accounts of the effects of music (e.g. *Am*, p. 135), or the sheer difficulty of orchestral composition. In the passage concerning the complex mechanics of orchestral scoring, McEwan betrays a fascinated respect for the intellectual effort that is involved, which anticipates his celebratory descriptions of neuro-surgery in *Saturday* (*Am*, pp. 23–4). Just as those passages were inspired by the process of shadowing a surgeon, so one can assume that, in *Amsterdam*, McEwan drew on his memories of his collabora-tive work with the composer Michael Berkeley.[9]

There is a felt anxiety in the arch parallels between the writer's own political and intellectual context and the creative exhaustion of Linley. The anxiety, however, points towards a general cultural mood, rather than McEwan's own career; and this is evoked through the psychological deterioration of the combatants, Halliday and Linley, in respect of which the book is less ambivalent.

After Molly's funeral, both men appear to succumb to hypochon-driac fears about their own mortality. For Linley, overwork, pressure and a mood of morbidity after the funeral combine to produce an effect of poor circulation that he begins to interpret as a progressive systemic condition (*Am*, p. 25). Lying in bed, 'resonating from mental effort, he saw jagged rods of primary colour streak across his retina, then fold and writhe into sunbursts' (*Am*, p. 25). The condition, pointedly, suggests the artistic immediacy of an abstract colourist, far removed from the ponderous and more literal creative impulses of Linley. It is a condition, in short, that highlights his artistic inadequacy when it first manifests itself, by suggesting the vitality of something that has been repressed.

Halliday's parallel scare provokes in him the thought that 'his right hemisphere had died' (*Am*, p. 31); but this 'sense of absence' (*Am*, p. 30) stems from the apparent futility of his professional existence, slowly impinging on his consciousness. Two hours of exercising editorial power have the strange effect of generating this inner lack: 'it seemed to Vernon that he was infinitely diluted; he was simply the sum of all the people who had listened to him, and when he was alone, he was nothing at all' (*Am*, p. 29).

Christina Byrnes suggests that the two men may be betraying the signs of syphilis, contracted from Molly Lane. Byrnes observes that Molly dies from 'a disease of the central nervous system which may have been tertiary syphilis', and that Linley and Halliday display symptoms – 'loss of judgement' and 'delusions of grandeur' – that are 'typical of neuro-syphilis'. In Byrnes' reading this is a hint that still leaves 'Molly's diagnosis open to speculation.'[10]

This is an interesting observation, but the uncertainty about it is important: any explicit suggestion that the principals are suffering the consequences of sexual promiscuity would suggest a morality tale with a puritanical streak. Such a mood is absent from *Amsterdam*. However, the hint that a disease may have been transmitted contributes, at a metaphorical level, to the idea of a social malaise.

In relation to Linley and Halliday, the idea of illness is clearly metaphorical. The pair's reflections on mortality, in the wake of Molly's rapid-onset brain disease, produce symptoms that highlight their inadequacy. For Linley, it is the lack of creative spontaneity that is exposed, and which, by implication, is not necessarily required in a successful composer. For Halliday, it is the lack of gravitas as a writer – he is a journalist without convictions – that is signalled by his sense of absence. As a broadsheet editor, he is the instrument of corporate command, merely. The personal deficiencies, thrown into relief by the self-regarding psychosomatic symptoms each experiences – a clear instance of the irruption of subconscious fears – concentrate the satirical point. No meritocracy, this, but rather a highly professional world in which talent is not the chief ingredient of success.

McEwan's accounts of editorial meetings are the highpoint of the satirical comedy in *Amsterdam*. The most memorable such scene is the one in which Halliday, seeking to drag his more principled colleagues along with him in his efforts to modernize and popularize *The Judge*, is enthused by the story of Siamese twins who have fallen out. Discovering that the twins have bite marks on their faces – the outward sign of their antagonism, he presumes – his instinct to run the story with a picture is reinforced (*Am*, p. 37). When the Machiavellian Frank Dibben takes over as editor, the switch from news to entertainment is flagged in cartoon-style satire: the new editor announces the policy of hiring a regular columnist, 'someone of low to medium intelligence, possibly female, to write about, well, nothing much.' The senior staff chip in helpfully with possible topics: 'Can't work her video recorder. Is my bum too big? . . . Always gets the supermarket trolley with the wobbly wheel' (*Am*, p. 129).

There are, then, conflicting moods in the novella, which vacillates between an uncomfortable self-consciousness at one extreme, and direct, knock-about satire at the other. This makes the book elusive of interpretation, most especially concerning the treatment of its central moral dilemmas. Apropos of *Amsterdam*, Brooke Allen evokes that tradition of the modern novel 'from James to Conrad to Forster', in which 'the loaded and fateful moral choice has always been the centrepiece.'[11] While this is generally true of McEwan's fiction, his particular contribution to this tradition is to simultaneously problematize the grounds from which the novelist presumes to moralize. *Amsterdam* partakes of the same ambivalent moral purview, but takes it to an extreme where the treatment of the moral dilemma verges on parody.

Linley's 'familiar misanthropy' (*Am*, p. 63) makes his failure to intervene at the rape scene predictable. His ignoble, self-justifying thoughts – 'they might both turn on him for presuming to interfere' (*Am*, p. 87) – reveal him to be motivated by self-interest, but vaguely conscious of his failure as a social being. Despite the internal debate he rehearses about whether or not to intervene, 'he understood that his hesitation had been a sham' (*Am*, p. 88). In his anxiety to leave the Lake District immediately, the guilt is barely concealed, as the narrative voice renders the self-justifying inner dialogue: 'surely it was creative excitement that made him pace up and down the cramped hotel bar waiting for his taxi' (*Am*, p. 89).

In the debate between Halliday and Linley about the compromising photographs of Garmony, Linley assumes the moral high ground. Halliday's argument is utilitarian: by humiliating Garmony, he believes he will prevent him from becoming Prime Minister. As a consequence, he speculates, the country will be spared from five years of socially disastrous policy-making (*Am*, p. 74). Yet this can only be achieved by pandering to (and reinforcing) public prejudice against cross-dressing. It is an ugly utilitarianism, in which putatively noble ends must justify squalid means. Here, Linley's moral argument has greater clarity: 'If it's OK to be a transvestite, then it's OK for a racist to be one. What's not OK is to be a racist' (*Am*, p. 73).

Ultimately, neither character is on sound ethical ground; however, Linley's parting shot to Halliday reveals that he really objects to the proposed publication of the photograph 'because of Molly', whose mischievous spirit will be betrayed (*Am*, p. 75), rather than because of a moral abhorrence of illiberal motives. Halliday's motives are additionally tainted, of course, by the possibility of a personal vendetta against Garmony, a hated love rival. Most important, however, is the impossibility of either character achieving a position of moral disinterestedness in relation to the photographs: the very act of putting a case is ethically flawed for both of them.

In Halliday's self-justification, the vein of satirical humour resurfaces. As a consequence of publication, Halliday reflects,

> hypocrisy would be exposed, the country would stay in Europe, capital punishment and compulsory conscription would remain a crank's dream, social welfare would survive in some form or other, the global environment would get a decent chance, and Vernon was on the point of breaking into song. (*Am*, p. 111)

The anticipation of professional success and personal vengeance combined is articulated as the dawning of a golden political age. Self-deception conceals the personal motivation; or, perhaps, the personal is elided with the political in an egregious act of egotistical projection.

It is, of course, a peculiarly male world that is satirized in *Amsterdam*. For Alain de Botton, it is 'a pitiless study of the darker aspects of male psychology, of male paranoia, emotional frigidity, sexual jealousy, professional rivalry and performance anxiety.'[12] McEwan underscores this dimension of the book at the conclusion, where George Lane reflects with satisfaction on the despatch of his late wife's former lovers, and anticipates taking Halliday's widow out for dinner (*Am*, p. 178). The genuinely successful combatant emerges from the shadows to round off the novella's playful ironic ending.

This playfulness suggests that this is not a work of great seriousness, as reviewers like Phil Baker intimated. (Baker suggested that 'if, like Graham Greene, McEwan divided his books into "novels" and "entertainments", then there is no doubt into which category this one would fall.'[13]) This also suggests banality in the treatment of moral concerns: Stuart Burrows, for instance, acknowledged that 'ethical dilemmas, specifically the question of the relationship between art and morality, are also at the heart of *Amsterdam*'; but he felt that 'any interest they might hold is brutally swept away by McEwan's weakness for melodrama.'[14]

My reading of *Amsterdam* as a spoiler is in partial but limited agreement with these characterizations of the work; for they do not address the full gesture the book came to embody. By making the satire an aspect of the book as a literary event – inviting reflection on literary prize culture and the celebrity status of the author – McEwan ensures that its 'patness' carries a loaded moral critique. *Amsterdam* projects its debate about morality and professional standards outwards, inviting us to think more seriously about them.

Notes

1 Also on the shortlist were three established authors – Beryl Bainbridge, Julian Barnes and Patrick McCabe – who had not won the Booker Prize, and who had also been short-listed before. For Bainbridge, 1998 was the fifth time she had been in contention for the Prize. The apparent injustice of McEwan's success caused Will Self, on the live TV Booker broadcast, 'to do his nut', in the words of Nicholas Lezard. The Prize, Lezard argued, 'really is meant to go to novels, not five-finger exercises.' See Nicholas Lezard, 'Morality Bites', *The Guardian*, 'Saturday Review' (24 April 1999), p. 11.

2 Juliet Waters, 'The Little Chill: Has the Booker Prize Chosen the Noveau Beaujolais of Fiction?'. See www.montrealmirror.com/ARCHIVES/1998/ 120398/book.html (accessed 13 July 2005).

3 The extent to which the book is clearly of its times provoked speculation about its *roman-à-clef* elements among the reviewers: for Stuart Burrows, the foreign secretary appeared to be 'a dead ringer for Michael Portillo'; while John Sutherland saw, in the Garmony plot, an invocation of 'scurrilous (and unfounded) rumours about certain cross-dressing ministers in John Major's last cabinet.' For Robert Hanks, it was 'obvious' that 'the unpleasant right-wing foreign secretary Julian Garmony borrows his CV and aspects of his public persona (though not, I should point out for the lawyers, his complex sexuality) from Michael Howard.' In depicting Garmony, Hanks argues, 'McEwan's one concern was to minimise any resemblance to Douglas Hurd, who occupied the post at the time of writing. With Hurd chair of this year's Booker panel, that looks suspiciously like foresight.' See Stuart Burrows, review of *Amsterdam*, *New Statesman*, 127: 4402 (11 September 1998), pp. 47–8 (p. 48); John Sutherland, 'What's It All About?' (review of *Amsterdam*), *Sunday Times*, 'Books' (13 September 1998), p. 12; and Robert Hanks, 'Flashes of Inspiration' (interview), *The Independent*, 'Weekend Review' (12 September 1998), p. 14.

4 The author, apparently, had made a similar joke-pact with a psychiatrist friend, which inspired this theme (and the novel's title): 'Amsterdam!' then

became a grimly jocular rebuke for absent-mindedness, between the two. See Hanks, 'Flashes of Inspiration', p. 14.

5 Frank Kermode, 'Point of View' (review of *Atonement*), *London Review of Books*, 23: 19 (4 October 2001), pp. 8–9 (p. 8).

6 Craig Seligman, review of *Amsterdam*, Salon.com (9 December 1998), http://dir.salon.com/books/sneaks/1998/12/09sneaks.html (accessed 12 June 2005).

7 Adam Mars-Jones, for example, wrote: 'McEwan's literary personality is too cool to allow for actual satire – even when he is pushing his book to its extreme conclusion he can't bring himself to let go. In *Amsterdam* he can at least boast the satirist's disaffection with his creatures, but perhaps he lacks the mysterious enzyme by which rage is metabolised as relish.' See 'Have a Heart' (review of *Amsterdam*), *The Observer*, 'The Review' (6 September 1998), p. 16.

8 In interview, McEwan remarked that *Amsterdam*, as a social satire, was a 'departure' for him, 'heavily influenced by the early novels of Evelyn Waugh'. 'An Interview with Ian McEwan', *boldtype* (Random House) 1998, www.randomhouse.com/boldtype/1298/mcewan/interview.html (accessed 7 November 2005).

9 McEwan's libretto for Berkeley's oratorio, *Or Shall We Die?*, is discussed in chapter 4 above. In his Acknowledgements to *Saturday*, McEwan records his gratitude to Neil Kitchen – a Consultant Neurosurgeon at The National Hospital for Neurology and Neurosurgery, Queens Square, London – whose work he observed over a two-year period.

10 Christina Byrnes, *The Work of Ian McEwan*, p. 146.

11 Brooke Allen, 'Illustrations of Inertia and Compromise', *New Criterion*, 17: 8 (April 1999), pp. 60–4, www.newcriterion.com/archive/17/apr99/brooke.htm (accessed 12 June 2005).

12 Alain de Botton, 'Another Study in Emotional Frigidity' (review of *Amsterdam*), *Independent on Sunday*, 'Culture' (13 September 1998), p. 12.

13 Phil Baker, 'Comfy Conspiracies', *Times Literary Supplement*, 4979 (4 September 1998), p. 9.

14 Stuart Burrows, review of *Amsterdam*, p. 47.

8

'The wild and inward journey of writing': *Atonement*

Prior to *Atonement*, *The Child in Time* was McEwan's most ambitious and, in one sense, most satisfying or perfectly formed novel; and his first work to present a positive view of human potential. *Atonement* is a still more ambitious work, and his greatest achievement to date. It was also very well received by reviewers. In the British press, there was high praise from Hermione Lee, Geoff Dyer, Robert Macfarlane and Frank Kermode who, in an important review, rated it 'easily his finest'.[1] It is also the author's most extended deliberation on the form of the novel, and the inherited tradition of modern (especially English) fiction and criticism. Austen, James, Forster, Woolf, Lawrence, Rosamund Lehmann, Elizabeth Bowen and F. R. Leavis are some of the touchstones in a treatment that is sometimes ironic, but serious in its intention. Thus, the theme of guilt and atonement is inextricably linked to an investigation of the writer's authority, a process of self-critique conducted through the creation of the writing persona Briony Tallis.

This central theme is also related to a public theme, and here the familiar private–public link that runs through the oeuvre is explored with reference to a longer historical process (as in *The Ploughman's Lunch*): McEwan's portrayal of the retreat to Dunkirk as a hellish ordeal puts a different perspective on a historical event usually viewed, through a patriotic lens, as a rescue of heroic proportions. It is not exactly that the heroism is denied (though some inhumanity within the ranks of the allies in retreat is depicted);[2] but, rather, the horror of death and mutilation is foregrounded. The interrogation of history, then, has a dual focus: McEwan is concerned with how national myths are inscribed, but also with the construction of a literary tradition.

As Hermione Lee observed in her review, all through the novel 'historical layers of English fiction are invoked and rewritten.'[3] Perhaps the most astute comment on this aspect of the novel is the following from Geoff Dyer's review:

> On the one hand, McEwan seems to be retrospectively inserting his name into the pantheon of British novelists of the 1930s and 1940s. But he is also, of course, doing more than this, demonstrating and exploring what the mature Briony comes to see as a larger 'transformation . . . being worked in human nature itself'. The novels of Woolf and Lawrence did not just record this transformation; they were instrumental in bringing it about. McEwan uses his novel to show how this subjective or interior transformation can now be seen to have interacted with the larger march of twentieth-century history. . . . It is less about a novelist harking nostalgically back to the consoling uncertainties of the past than it is about creatively extending and hauling a defining part of the British literary tradition up to and into the twenty-first century.[4]

The locus of this theme is the long letter Briony receives from Cyril Connolly (or so we surmise from the signature, 'CC' (*At*, p. 315)), who offers advice to the budding writer. We must conclude that she has taken this advice to heart, if we take Part One of the novel to be – after a protracted process of redrafting – based on 'Two Figures by a Fountain', the story that Briony had originally submitted to *Horizon* (*At*, p. 281). Frank Kermode observes how we can assume that particular details have been altered following the fictional Connolly's counsel: the vase should *not* be Ming (it is Meissen porcelain in the novel (*At*, p. 24)); the Bernini fountain is in the Piazza Barberini, not the Piazza Navona (the detail is duly corrected (*At*, p. 18)).[5]

The most important aspect of Connolly's advice, however, concerns the kind of novel he feels is most valuable. The editorial opinion at *Horizon*, Connolly reports, had been to wonder if Briony's story 'owed a little too much to the techniques of Mrs Woolf.' He acknowledges that 'the crystalline present moment' is 'a worthy subject in itself', a valuable 'experimentation' that enables the writer to explore 'the vagaries . . . of the private self'. However, he also suggests that 'such writing can become precious' without a sense of 'forward movement'. It is clear from the finished novel that Briony has come to appreciate 'the underlying pull of simple narrative' that Connolly advocates (*At*, p. 312).

McEwan's fictional letter convinces because it enunciates the kind of position that is recognizably Connolly's. In *Enemies of Promise*, for example, Connolly seeks to establish the ingredients of the kind of novel that might achieve longevity, by combining the best elements of two competing styles. On the one hand there is what Connolly terms the 'Mandarin' style, associated with subtle 'inflections of sensibility and meaning', but which can entrap its practitioners, committing them to 'a tyranny of euphonious nothings.'[6] From the Mandarins – Woolf is cited as a key Mandarin – the writer must 'borrow art and patience, the striving for perfection, the horror of clichés', while avoiding 'indolence', 'egotism' and 'exhibitionism'. The opposing style is characterized by Connolly as 'the realist, or vernacular, the style of rebels, journalists, common-sense addicts, and unromantic observers of human destiny'. In Connolly's recipe for the ideal novel, the realist mode teaches, above all, 'construction', the essential 'discipline in the conception and execution of a book'; yet, the writer must avoid the realists' 'flatness of style', their 'homogeneity of outlook' and their 'distrust of beauty'.[7]

It is in the letter from Connolly that a specific point of stylistic comparison is made. Elizabeth Bowen, he reports, picked up the manuscript by chance; before becoming 'hooked for a while', and eventually feeling moved to make some notes to assist with a revision of the piece, Bowen had initially 'thought the prose "too full, too cloying" but with "redeeming shades of *Dusty Answer*"' (*At*, p. 314). Jonathan Coe suggests that the experience provided by Rosamund Lehmann's *Dusty Answer*, 'a thickly concentrated mixture of embarrassment and pleasure . . . is typical of adolescence'. In Coe's perceptive reading, this is a novel that evokes the enchantment of childhood, but which is also 'a powerful study of that later, more complex period when nostalgia for childhood momentarily overlaps with the dawning of adult sensibilities.' The parallels with *Atonement* are clear.[8] The real Connolly, in *Enemies of Promise*, felt *Dusty Answer* to be easily categorizable, an 'extreme example' of the Mandarin style in 1927, alongside Bowen's own *The Hotel*, and in contrast to the extreme vernacular style of Hemingway's *The Sun Also Rises*, from the same year.[9]

Interestingly, Brian Finney finds the shorter, simpler sentences of Part Two of *Atonement* to be reminiscent of Hemingway, which, following the pastiche of Lehmann (and others) in Part One, suggests that McEwan is conducting an experiment in competing styles.[10] Yet the whole novel, like all of McEwan's writing, represents a more complex fusion of these 'competing' styles, broadly defined – the interior style with complex methods of focalization, embedded within well-wrought plots, skilfully and periphrastically narrated through flashback and anticipation, analepsis and prolepsis.

There are innumerable discussions of twentieth-century fiction that investigate terrain similar to Connolly's opposition of Mandarin and vernacular styles. In these discussions, as for Connolly, it is modernist-inspired interior narrative that establishes a new pole to set against the exterior and plot-driven forms of fiction consolidated in the nineteenth century.

In my introduction, I suggested that Iris Murdoch's formulation of this opposition is instructive to an understanding of McEwan's writing. In her pursuit of a synthesis of opposing philosophical views – a unifying theory which perceives the individual to be free and separate, but at the same time involved with the social world as 'a moral being' – Murdoch saw the form of the novel as the essential vehicle. She defined two types of twentieth-century novel, neither of which is able to generate the desired philosophical synthesis. First, there is the 'crystalline' or 'quasi-allegorical' novel, in which character is inadequately drawn (when compared with the superior models of the nineteenth century); second, there is the 'journalistic' or 'quasi-documentary' novel, which Murdoch felt to be a 'degenerate descendant' of the superior form of the previous century.[11] ('Crystalline' is a term McEwan assigns to Connolly in the letter to Briony.)

While acknowledging that the better novels are those written in the 'crystalline' mode, Murdoch emphasizes its real danger, which is the failure to grapple with 'reality', while tending to console readers with myths or stories. The form of the novel becomes loaded with social significance in this account because, for Murdoch, the solution to this formal problem involves the recuperation of a moral world with a structure more complex than that defined by liberal democratic society.

In this view, freedom hinges upon a more complex form of attention than that encouraged by a Welfare State, and must be advanced by literature, which has taken over some of philosophy's own tasks. Of course, this is a manifesto for Murdoch's own style of fiction, geared to demonstrating that 'reality is not a given whole', by encouraging 'a respect for the contingent', and which privileges 'imagination' over 'fantasy'. In passing, it is worth noting that Briony's lie – and 'moral failure', so to speak – stems from an inadequate respect for the contingent; from, that is, a desire to impose order on that which she cannot fully imagine. For Murdoch, the failure associated with an impoverished world-view is reconfigured as a problem of literary form, in which the desire for consolation can be overcome by a broader concept of form that embraces contingency, and does so, particularly, through the naturalistic deployment of character.[12]

This is, perhaps, more a case for regenerating the exterior form of narration than it is an argument for a synthesis; but it does acknowledge the need to combine some elements perceived to be separated in the crystalline/journalistic dichotomy. McEwan's self-conscious evocation of this kind of distinction, in the fictional letter that reaches back to the real Cyril Connolly's own division between Mandarin and vernacular, is an implicit statement about his own achievements as a novelist in general, and in the creation of *Atonement* in particular: as in all of McEwan's best fiction, the novel combines a complex narrative structure – in which the interior revelations are minutely detailed – with a compelling storyline. The Mandarin style is combined with the vernacular, the crystalline with the journalistic, to produce a synthesis that is peculiarly rich. The novel also embodies McEwan's most emphatic refusal of consolation.

Yet there is no evident certainty for McEwan, in marked contrast to Murdoch's convictions about the novel, concerning its moral efficacy. It is clear that *Atonement* presents narrative fiction as having centrally *to do* with moral questions, without necessarily being able to *resolve* them. Indeed, *Atonement* provokes reflection on moral responsibility that is *tortuous*, rather than efficacious. As a point of literary-historical interest, it may be relevant to observe the difference, not just between McEwan and Murdoch on this point, but between McEwan and Connolly as well. In *Enemies of Promise*, for example, Connolly made this startling claim, which anticipates the more philosophical formulations of Murdoch:

> Within his talent it is the duty of a writer to devote his energy to the search for truth, the truth that is always being clouded over by romantic words and ideas or obscured by actions and motives dictated by interest and fear. In the love of truth which leads to a knowledge of it lies not only the hope of humanity but its safety.[13]

In one sense, *Atonement* is a rehearsal of why such a search is doomed to fail, while remaining both laudable and necessary. Indeed, the novel is radically ambivalent about establishing a model of desirable ethical behaviour and responsibility. Its chief effect, in fact, is to question the morality of the author figure seeking to establish truth.

Another – and, perhaps, surprising – perspective on this cultivated uncertainty is suggested by the context of the book's publication, in

September 2001. The first reviews of the novel appeared in the immediate aftermath of the attack on America on 11 September, at which time McEwan's own published responses to the attack suggested a straightforward understanding of authorial ethics. Inevitably, this has had an effect on popular understanding of the novel. It is clear from the pieces that McEwan wrote in the week following the attack, most obviously in his front-page article for *The Guardian*, that he willingly took on the role of a kind of global moralist. In this article, McEwan movingly articulates the horrified response to the four days of news about the attack that most people would share. He focuses on the final mobile phone calls made by the victims, trapped in the World Trade Center, replayed on TV: 'I love you . . . is what they were all saying'. These words, he argues, 'compel us to imagine ourselves into that moment. What would we say? Now we know.'

Simply, and movingly, McEwan establishes the 'nature of empathy' and the 'mechanics of compassion' that 9/11 calls forth. He imagines the plight of a passenger on one of the hijacked planes – to demonstrate the connection between imaginative projection and compassion – before arguing that among the hijackers' crimes was 'a failure of the imagination', because 'imagining what it is like to be someone other than yourself is at the core of our humanity. It is the essence of compassion, and it is the beginning of morality.'[14] The argument of the article, together with the brief demonstration of imaginative projection, also hints at a privileged place for the capacities of the novelist in the process of moral thinking.

Three days earlier, in an instant response, McEwan had described how he and his son had 'surfed' TV news channels, 'hungrily, ghoulishly' and 'in a state of sickened wonderment'. Revealingly, he also wrote: 'there was barely time to contemplate the cruelty of the human hearts that could unleash this. Were they watching with us now, equally hungry to know the worst? The thought covered me in shame.'[15] This article, written without the luxury of an additional few days contemplation, is more ambivalent about the author's position: the global media village establishes unwanted connections between the terrorist and the average viewer, a shared appetite for disaster that is shaming. Beyond this, we might ponder what interests are involved in creating these appetites, and the extent to which the average news surfer is implicated in these interests. There is no unequivocal moral position to be established on the basis of such a generalized shame.

The ambivalence about the moral response to 9/11 can be summarized in this way: it is abundantly clear that a principle of common humanity can be established that, rightly, demonizes acts of terror; yet establishing an unsullied vantage point for moral pronouncement is impossible in the era of globalization. Published in the same month as 9/11 (and, obviously, written prior to the attack), *Atonement* is an exploration of this kind of paradox, oriented towards the ghoulish and shameful aspects of the novelist's vocation that must emerge, even while a form of atonement for these faults is sought.

These questions of paradox surrounding the morality of fiction and authorial responsibility find a pointed expression through the implicit debate about 'character' conducted in the novel. Through its design, and its preoccupation with the authorial persona, the novel raises questions about character in fiction. Ultimately, however, *Atonement* relies on a traditional form of character function. Consequently, it betrays the work of a writer who is, in the final analysis, untroubled by critical notions that might call into question the very enterprise of portraying character in the novel, the representation of an imagined individual whose fictional fate invites an effort of empathy on the part of a reader. Of course, Ian McEwan's characters – and this applies to all of his novels – are psychologically complex, and invariably inconsistent, creations. This may imply an openness or fluidity in the author's exploration of personal identity, but the same basic principle applies: however unpredictable or inconsistent, a McEwan character is a bounded zone, an imagined individual in which McEwan's readers are invited to invest the belief and, often, the emotional identification required of the realist reading contract.

In the introduction to this book, I observed a significant consonance between McEwan's extended fictional project, with its ongoing and often deeply troubled investigation of morality, and recent critical work in narrative ethics, which covers roughly the same historical period as McEwan's writing. McEwan's developing treatment of the relationship between character and moral exploration demonstrates how he partakes of, and responds to, this intellectual moment. *Atonement* is the creative equivalent or counterpart of this critical position. It evokes a strong sense of lived experience that is morally moving; and yet insists on the constructed nature of fiction, and the morally dubious authority wielded by the writer.

The novel form is used in *Atonement* to raise questions about morality and authorship in a highly self-conscious way, while simultaneously and paradoxically casting doubt on the novel as an inherently moral medium. The novel's ambivalence appears to signal a point of departure, in fact, from narrative ethics. The larger claim, within this branch of criticism, is that the novel has the capacity to achieve a unique form of moral philosophy, and particularly through its investigation of character, dilemma and moral agency; and that this capacity can and should be put to social uses. *Atonement* seems to raise this possibility, only to dash it.

The book's narrative design illustrates McEwan's moral ambivalence. Addressing the question of whether or not Briony's narrative may be inaccurate, or even a fantasy, McEwan clearly signals his view, which steers us away from a postmodern 'hall of mirrors' reading in which nothing is stable. McEwan speaks of 'Briony's sense that her atonement has consisted of a lifetime of writing this novel. She's condemned to write it over and over again.' He goes on to give a significant account of the ambiguous ending:

> Now she's a dying woman, she has vascular dementia, her mind is emptying, and finally she writes a draft which is different from all the others. She fails, as she sees it, to have the courage of her pessimism, and rewrites the love story so that the lovers survive.

McEwan's further comment, in this revealing response, establishes a clear sense of the novel's narrative ethics: 'I wanted to play with the notion of storytelling as a form of self-justification, of how much courage is involved in telling the truth to oneself.' Briony is a creation designed to 'go a step further' than Catherine Morland in Austen's *Northanger Abbey* (1818), to extend the notion of the crime of deluded perception producing damaging consequences for others. The 'step further' demands an examination of – rather than the crime – 'the process of atonement' conducted through storytelling.[16]

Part Three of the novel ends with Briony's initials, 'BT', and the date, London 1999. We are instructed to accept the novel up to this point as Briony's 'new draft', her 'atonement' for her crime, finally completed sixty-four years on.[17] This, however, may also oblige us to adjust our understanding of the foregoing narrative, and its operations, in a technical sense. A very attentive reader, as I shall argue below, may have begun to piece the correct picture together on a first reading; but there will still be a process of confirmation, which means that a full comprehension of the narrative technique is inevitably retrospective. We now realize that Briony is implicated in the narrative stance; indeed, we realize that we can plausibly take her to be the narrator. In Part One we thus have an older version of Briony (seventy-seven, in fact), seeking to make sense of her actions as a thirteen-year-old.

Hindsight suggests that we should classify Briony alongside Pip in *Great Expectations* (1860–61): as narrator she occupies a position outside the story – an extradiegetic level in Gérard Genette's terms – but is also a participant in the action, and so occupies a homodiegetic relationship to the story. Now we can see instances of internal focalization within the external narration: a record of things the young girl saw and felt (as far as she can now make sense of them), rendered through the adult's vocabulary. This combination of elements in Briony's relationship to the story – extra-homodiegetic in narratological terms – now seems appropriate to Part Three of the novel. It is only the signature 'BT', however, that enables us to make this technical re-evaluation. Until the fourth section of the novel ('London, 1999'), however, which functions as a form of coda, there is no first-person narrator to signal unequivocally the homodiegetic status, which we may hitherto have recorded mentally as heterodiegetic.[18]

In the early stages of the novel, however, an omniscient, external narrator registers the discrepancy between the perceptions of the young Briony and the later personal re-evaluation that maturity brings:

> At the age of eleven she wrote her first story – a foolish affair, imitative of half a dozen folk tales and lacking, she realised later, that vital knowingness about the ways of the world which compels a reader's respect. (*At*, p. 6)

This does not necessarily imply the connection between the narrative voice and the later Briony that the frame of the novel finally makes. However, as the first section develops, that connection is strongly hinted at. By the end of the third chapter, the attentive reader will detect something more complex than a simple omniscient vantage point in the narrative voice:

> And only in a story could you enter these different minds and show how they had an equal value. That was the only moral a story need have.
>
> Six decades later she would describe how at the age of thirteen she had written her way through a whole history of literature, beginning with stories derived from the European tradition of folk tales, through drama with simple moral intent, to arrive at an impartial psychological realism which she had discovered for herself, one special morning during a heat wave in 1935. She would be well aware of the extent of her

> self-mythologizing, and she gave her account a self-mocking, or mock-heroic tone. . . . She knew . . . that it was not the long-ago morning she was recalling so much as her subsequent accounts of it. It was possible that the contemplation of a crooked finger, the unbearable idea of other minds and the superiority of stories over plays were thoughts she had had on other days. She also knew that whatever actually happened drew its significance from her published work and would not have been remembered without it. (*At*, p. 41)

The points of reflection mentioned here – the literary ruminations, the self-mocking tone, the contemplation of a finger – are all reflections that have been encountered earlier in the narrative. At this point, the narrator of the first section is implicated in the fictional authorial self-reflexiveness, and in such a way as to invite an equation between Briony and the narrator, revealed as her older self.

The implication can escape readers – or, indeed, reviewers – on a first reading.[19] There are other clues, however. For example, repeated references to Briony's juvenile perception of writing become abrasive, or defensive, a kind of self-justification by virtue of their attempt to highlight the impercipience of childhood, and so the *inevitability* of Briony's misperceptions.

A fully attentive reading of the novel – which may be a rereading – must continually register a high degree of narratorial guilt and complicity, whether or not the conceit of the novel is fully grasped at once. The elderly writer Briony, if we accept the conceit that she is the organizing influence of the narrative, deploys quite subtle literary devices as part of the process of self-laceration. For example, in the opening scene, just before Briony commits her crime, she catches sight of 'a disembodied human leg' as she peers into the drawing room from outside. Then, as 'she grasped the perspectives', she perceives it is attached to her mother (*At*, p. 161). If Briony's status as unreliable witness is economically signalled here, in the prelude to her false accusation, the extent of the self-critique takes on a new dimension when a different disembodied leg appears a few pages later, to become a minor leitmotif. Now, in Part Two, with Briony imagining the experiences of Robbie on the retreat to Dunkirk, she has him observe an actual disembodied leg, lodged in the fork of a tree. As he pieces the evidence together in his mind – the leg, the burnt shreds of pyjama-like cloth, the bombers overhead – Robbie presumes the leg to have belonged to a French boy, blown to bits while sleeping (*At*, pp. 192, 194).

The technical reassessment is still more troubling in Part Two. Again, the signature obliges us to accept the third-person narration as Briony's, but as we know she is narrating events to which she could not have been privy, the artifice of the construction becomes a necessary focus. This is offset to a degree in the novel's coda, where it is implied that Briony had relied on the lovers' letters, held in the archives of the Imperial War Museum (*At*, p. 371). Equally important is 'the bundle of letters Mr Nettle wrote' to Briony 'about Dunkirk' (*At*, p. 359): since Corporal Nettle is one of Robbie's companions on the trek to Dunkirk, we are invited to assume that Part Two is not pure invention, but is a fictionalized account based on the testimony of Nettle. This is an important detail that is easily missed.

While reading the novel, readers probably continue to invest their belief in Briony as a creation, so that, within the fictional frame, questions of perspective and narrative artifice centre on the version she gives of her past and the lovers' plight. Questions of 'guilt' and 'atonement', as we read, may then chiefly concern the tension between self-exculpation and self-laceration in her rendition.

Simultaneously, however, readers will be aware that Briony's guilt, and the issue of the need for atonement, raise questions about the authorial role with regard to the state of modern morals. A much larger problem emerges from this questioning, a concern that the actions of the novelist might *always* be morally dubious. If the young Briony's disastrous construction of events leads to personal disaster for others, might there be, in a less dramatic way, something ethically unsound about the way in which the novelist takes inspiration from the lives and accounts of other individuals?

McEwan's acknowledged sources for this novel reveal some borrowing that is pertinent here. Gregory Blaxland's *Destination Dunkirk* (1973) is a source for logistical detail about the evacuation; but it is the other two published sources cited by McEwan – Walter Lord's *The Miracle of Dunkirk* (1982) and Lucilla Andrews' autobiography, *No Time For Romance* (1977) – both rich in anecdote and personal testimony, which reveal particular points of inspiration. One of the most tense, and important, scenes in the Dunkirk episode is the near-lynching of a RAF man – 'a wiry little fellow with thick, unclean lenses in his glasses' who 'looked like a filing clerk, or a telephone operator' (*At*, p. 250) – who is blamed by a mob in a seafront bar for the absence of RAF cover during the retreat. McEwan gives the episode a particular moral edge: Robbie Turner, with the two corporals, Mace and Nettle, contrive to save the man, and in doing so, the three remain a co-operative unit, upholding principles of respect and human dignity, resisting the temptations of the mob mentality (to which Robbie is vulnerable, as he approaches his state of delirium (*At*, pp. 251–2)). It is interesting to find the germ of this episode in Walter Lord's book:

> 'Where is the RAF?' The familiar cry went up again and again. In their exasperation one column turned on a hapless stray wearing airforce blue . . . He was no pilot – just a clerk from some disbanded headquarters – but that didn't help him. The enraged troops pushed and threatened him – the symbol of all their pent-up bitterness.

A fresh Stuka attack, rather than the noble intervention that McEwan devises, gives the clerk the cover he needs to vanish.[20]

The most arresting borrowing, however, comes from Lucilla Andrews' autobiography, *No Time For Romance*. Andrews is renowned as an author of 'hospital fiction'; but in the autobiography she gives her account of nursing the Dunkirk wounded. Like Briony, Andrews attended the Nightingale Training School at St Thomas's Hospital (though not until 1941). It is her prior experience, however, as a voluntary nurse at a military hospital near Salisbury Plain in 1940 that supplies material for *Atonement*.[21]

It is hardly surprising that McEwan should turn to a first-hand account for the depiction of war injuries and their treatment. He relies on Andrews' account of removing shrapnel, in one instance: her trick of counting up the number of embedded pieces with the patient is ascribed to Briony; and the reaction of the soldier in pain – clinging to the bedhead – is imported into the novel. McEwan has his soldier scream an obscenity (where Andrews' patient is stoically silent), but both are consoled with brandy; and, in a spirit of verisimilitude, McEwan is careful to ensure that the largest piece of shrapnel that Briony removes (four and a half inches long) corresponds to the first-hand account.[22]

Andrews is sent by a Sister to sit and talk with a dying soldier, with half of his face missing. He soon descends into a discourse of nonsense. He also requests that his bandage be loosened: Andrews obliges, but nearly faints at what is revealed, and attempts to retie the bow. When he dies, he lurches forwards into her arms, leaving a smear of blood on her face, which the returning Sister instructs her to wash off, for fear of upsetting the patients.[23]

McEwan relies entirely on this account for his description of Briony being asked by Sister Drummond to go and speak to the dying Luc Cornet (*At*, pp. 305–10). Aside from the grim details, however, what McEwan draws on, as so often in his borrowing from other sources, is the narrative situation: like the Sister instructing Lucilla Andrews, Drummond tells Briony that there is no need to wear a mask, but she fails to pick up the clue that he is near death. Both Andrews and Briony, in their naivety, are concerned with the propriety that their training requires, but which is irrelevant here. Both reveal their Christian names, in an instinctive empathic understanding of the emotional charge of the moment, even though it is expressly forbidden for a nurse to do this.

When one delves into some of McEwan's sources, then, it is clear that he has relied on acute personal experiences, ranging from feelings of embarrassment or inadequacy at one end of the spectrum, to death at the other. Evidently, there are ethical problems that must arise in the use of such material. Most problematic is the fictionalizing of an actual death caused by severe head injuries. It is clear that the novel's debate about the propriety of the author's role, recasting first-hand testimony into fiction, has a direct bearing on the composition of the novel.

I will return to this; but it is necessary, first, to examine this as a fictional theme. The important issue in this connection is the invitation to consider the propriety of Briony's use of other character's lives in her lifelong project to compose her fiction of atonement. This is a theoretical debate insofar as it relates to Briony and to McEwan's other fictional creations in the novel; but it is a debate with wider ramifications, pertinent to the novelistic impulse.

The young Briony's 'wish for a harmonious, organised world' (*At*, p. 5) is a mark of her immature inability to accept contingency and the randomness of experience. This is also the source of her 'crime', of course, since it is her compulsion for order and control that leads to her false accusation against Robbie. The weakness is also an authorial weakness, however. Briony finds that the play rehearsals 'offended her sense of order' as she senses the 'self-contained' world produced in solitary composition 'dribbling uncontrollably away' (*At*, pp. 36–7).

Her first impulse is to wish she had written a story for her brother Leon – rather than the play written in honour of his return – in the simplistic belief that 'a story was direct and simple'. The principal impact of the novel, of course, serves to problematize her view that fiction is a 'neat, limited and controllable form' (*At*, p. 37). As the young

Briony contemplates her narrative construction of Robbie, after reading the obscene note he has sent to Cecilia in error, she conceives of a disinterested narrative point of view, 'some lofty, god-like place from which all people could be judged alike, not pitted against each other, as in some lifelong hockey match, but seen noisily jostling together in all their glorious imperfection.' The young Briony concludes, because of her disgust at the aspect of Robbie's character lately revealed to her: 'if such a place existed, she was not worthy of it' (*At*, p. 115).

One of the chief tasks in reading the novel – and certainly in rereading it – is to assess the degree to which the older Briony, as the writing persona, achieves a position of disinterestedness in her narrative perspective, and, by that token, to assess what this might contribute to the idea of atonement. This can be a fairly complicated metafictional investigation, especially where we perceive a re-evaluation of her motives as a thirteen-year-old. Briony-as-narrator informs us that the accusation was 'honest', 'passionate', 'founded in common sense', suggesting a mood of self-justification; but on the next page, this is tempered with the self-accusation of having 'marched into the labyrinth of her own construction' (*At*, pp. 169–70).

Another moment of dissonant perspectives follows from the passage in Part Two of the novel where Robbie, brooding on the past, remembers an episode when Briony revealed a schoolgirl crush on him, three years before the fateful night of her false accusation. In this episode, with Robbie as focalizer, Briony jumps into the pool where they have gone for a swimming lesson in order to make Robbie save her life. When he does so, she counters his anger at her dangerous experiment by declaring her love for him (*At*, pp. 229–32). Although he had thought the matter soon forgotten, with hindsight Robbie puts a different construction on it, deciding that 'she must have nurtured a feeling for him', and, discovering that he favoured her sister Cecilia on the fateful night in 1935, she took the 'extraordinary opportunity . . . to avenge herself' (*At*, p. 233). In Part Three, where we are given the older Briony's narrative reconstruction of this 'real crush that had lasted for days', we are told 'she confessed it to him one morning in the garden and immediately forgot about it' (*At*, p. 342).

The governing narrative conceit, however, obliges us to reassess the thoughts given to Robbie as Briony's later reconstruction (even if we imagine that she picks up hints about Robbie's internal state from the letters of Corporal Nettles). Such moments of reconstruction, part of the complex 'atonement' that we are asked to imagine Briony engaging in, invite readers to ponder the pursuit of veracity. An element of self-righteousness might seem to emerge when we compare the different recollections of the pool episode: if Briony really forgot about the crush immediately, then Robbie is unjustified in assigning a vengeful motive to her on account of it. Yet it is Briony's narrative construction – this final version of the story that comprises the first three parts of the novel – in which the comparison emerges. Is this an instance of elaborate narrative self-justification? Or is it to be taken as an acceptable, even laudable, attempt to engage with the thoughts and feelings of another, since Robbie's brooding is quite understandable, and his attempt to assign a motive to Briony perfectly reasonable?

The projection of different interpretations can be fairly anodyne. In Part One, for example, the imagined tetchiness between the lovers, before they have recognized their feelings, is dramatized through simple means, as in the account of Robbie entering the house and removing his boots and socks. In the reflections attributed to Cecilia this is interpreted as a gesture 'designed to distance her', an instance of Robbie 'play-acting the cleaning lady's son come to the house on an errand.' (At, p. 27) Later, in reflections attributed to Robbie, the motive for the removal of the socks is embarrassment: discovering them 'holed at toe and heel and, for all he knew, odorous' he removes them on impulse (At, p. 84). The differing interpretations suit the emotional state of the two characters in Briony's version, with Robbie recognizing his attraction to Cecilia, but not knowing how to proceed; and Cecilia, in denial, losing patience with him.

More troubling, on rereading the novel, are the future projections attributed to Robbie and Cecilia. In Part One, as he is making his way to the fateful dinner party, Robbie imagines himself at fifty, in 1962, a 'weathered, knowing doctor' surrounded by 'the trophies of a lifetime's travel and thought' (At, p. 92). A few pages later, the future projection attributed to Cecilia is self-critical, when she dons a black crêpe de Chine dress and sees in the mirror 'her future self, at eighty-five, in widow's weeds.' (At, p. 97) This is the thought of an instant, which sends her back to her room to change; but there is a terrible irony in the habit of thinking ahead, attributed to both characters in quick succession, given the revelation of their deaths in the last few paragraphs of the book (At, p. 370).

Perhaps the most questionable narrative invention by Briony, from an ethical point of view, is the writing of Robbie's delirium before his rescue from Dunkirk, even though he 'really' died there from septicaemia (*At*, p. 370). Convincingly, the larger trauma of the war merges in his mind with the personal disaster of Briony's false accusation, and the legal procedures that might be necessary to make it right:

> Everyone was guilty, and no one was. No one would be redeemed by a change of evidence, for there weren't enough people, enough paper and pens, enough patience and peace, to take down the statements of all the witnesses and gather in the facts. The witnesses were guilty too. (*At*, p. 261)

It is a forceful version of the larger 'crime' of war, rendered in that idiom where sanity emerges from the condition of insanity. McEwan's effective device, however, is also the novelist Briony's rhetorical trick, which appropriates the episode of Robbie's death for the larger theme, and which simultaneously allows Briony's crime to be subsumed in – and overshadowed by – the larger movements of twentieth-century history. This is also an attribute of the narrative design as a whole.

Kermode comments on the book's title, with its suggestion 'that Briony will do something by way of atonement', but finds that 'nothing quite fitting that description seems to occur.'[24] The lifetime task of rewriting the novel, as a substitute atonement for that which cannot be undone (as the lovers are 'really' dead), finally reveals the authority of writing to be incompatible with atonement on a personal level. As Briony summarizes the conundrum: 'how can a novelist achieve atonement when, with her absolute power of deciding outcomes, she is also God?' (*At*, p. 371).

The young Briony's reflection on the ethical paradox of narrative fiction is the paradox that resonates throughout the novel: 'she wondered whether having final responsibility for someone, even a creature like a horse or a dog, was fundamentally opposed to the wild and inward journey of writing' (*At*, p. 159). Her final position, having spent fifty-nine fruitless years rewriting an impossible fictional atonement, surviving the only individuals who could pardon her, and suffering a progressive form of dementia, is as perfect a form of torment for a novelist as one could imagine. At the same time it is entirely apposite, if we see Briony's situation as a metaphor for the novelist's predicament per se. Like Briony, the novelist always exercises a responsibility to his or her art that must overshadow personal or individual ethical questions.

As I discussed in chapter 5, for many novelists there may be an ethical dilemma in the translation of real-life encounters into fiction.

This dilemma has a bearing on the idea of biography in *Black Dogs*; but it has a more central relationship to the conception of *Atonement*, where the dilemma is dramatized to the point where it becomes the main structural principle. More particularly, Briony's situation is McEwan's: like his creation, he has researched his fiction in the Department of Documents in the Imperial War Museum, drawing on 'unpublished letters, journals and reminiscences of soldiers and nurses serving in 1940' (*At*, Acknowledgements), as well as on those published sources that reveal him fictionalizing first-hand accounts that are often traumatic. The self-accusations of Briony, which emerge either explicitly, or implicitly through the process of composition, are a form of confession that relates both to the production of *Atonement*, and to the particular kind of authority that novelists always garner to themselves.

To illustrate this dilemma, with an instance specific to the kind of material *Atonement* requires, but with a more general resonance too, let us return to the episode of the soldier with half his head blown away. The narrative situation of Lucilla Andrews' first-hand account inspires McEwan, particularly the contrast between the naivety of the volunteer nurse and the sudden intrusion into her consciousness of the brutality of war, for which no training can offer adequate preparation. The brilliant adaptation of the emotion implicit in Andrews' account fits superbly the idea of Briony's learning curve, in which she comes to recognize the egotistical element of her self-sacrifice, and, eventually, the hopelessness of self-abnegation and, by contrast, the need for a form of agency. But McEwan knows that he is also borrowing from an actual death *scene*, and that this has troubling ethical implications: the fictionalizing of a death – whether or not any friend or relative of the dead man reads the novel and recognizes the source – crosses a *symbolic* line, and privileges fiction over life. The example is extreme; but it is emblematic of the novelist's situation, the situation that *Atonement* dramatizes so thoughtfully. The author's responsibility, and principal duty, is to 'the wild and inward journey of writing', however discomfiting it may be.

The degree of self-consciousness about writing in *Atonement* suggests a crisis about the novel as a vehicle for moral ideas, and the function of the author in terms of any ethical dimension beyond the responsibility to writing. Indeed, there is a paradox in this metafictional process of making us uneasy about the business of novel reading and writing, given that it occurs in this extended deliberation on the inherited tradition of English fiction and criticism. *Atonement* has the air of an author writing himself, albeit problematically, into a literary tradition, a gesture that seems a world away from the 'shock-lit' of his early works. Brian Finney comments on this 'extraordinary . . . distance' between *First Love, Last Rites* and *Atonement*, in which 'the closed claustrophobic inner world' of the early protagonists has been replaced by a complex narrative form and a new 'degree of self-consciousness'. Finney argues, in effect, that in 'a work of fiction that is from beginning to end concerned with the making of fiction', the metafictionality produces an aesthetic structure that reflects 'the complexity and horror of life' in the second half of the twentieth century, after the Holocaust, the development of nuclear weapons, and the Cold War.[25]

What is most unsettling about *Atonement*, however, is the manner in which its own aesthetic structure, and the inherited literary tradition on which it feeds, is implicitly undermined. The greatest paradox about McEwan's career is that, while his early works functioned to extend the category of the literary, *Atonement* serves, if not to diminish the literary, then to hedge it in with many damaging reservations.

In Mrs Tallis's impatient account, Cecilia 'had lolled about for three years at Girton with the kind of books she could equally have read at home – Jane Austen, Dickens, Conrad', imbibing a sense of cultural superiority, or 'modern . . . snobbery' (*At*, p. 152). Leavis's Great Tradition, and the idea of literature as an ennobling force, seems to have a more urgent impact upon Robbie, informing his internal debate about his vocation. He has listened to Leavis's lectures at Cambridge, and, in settling on medicine, he has decided that 'reading books and having opinions about them' is 'not the core', just 'the desirable adjunct to a civilized existence.' Instead, 'he would have skills far more elaborate than the ones he had acquired in practical criticism' (*At*, p. 91).

His ambitions are thwarted by Briony's wielding of a banal literary imagination, and the intervention of the war, both of which underscore the need for a more urgent re-evaluation of cultural work than Leavis can offer. *Atonement* is one such re-evaluation, the effect of which is to loosen the link between 'literature' and 'vocation' (just as Briony's lifetime of writing, *for her*, is conducted in a spirit of exploratory personal atonement, rather than material achievement), and to suggest that literature can offer no more than a form of consolation.

This is not a new idea about the novel, of course; but the fact that it is conveyed in a consummately realized, and aesthetically admirable, form adds a further paradox. This highly inventive metafiction seems to be an emphatic instance of consolation: it enacts the lifelong consolation of Briony (consolation as theme and form), and offers a form of consolation for the reader, through formal intellectual stimulus. However, this is surely undermined by the shocking disappointment of the revelation of the lovers' deaths, that moment where our investment in the codes of realism is betrayed.

It is true that this anti-literary gesture is itself overtaken by Briony's faith in the consoling power of fiction: 'to let my lovers live and to unite them at the end' is not 'weakness or evasion', she insists, 'but a final act of kindness, a stand against oblivion and despair' (*At*, p. 372). Indeed, the empathetic creativity of complex fiction-making, underpinned by atonement and kindness, and signalled through metafictional device, is what *Atonement* pits against the horrors of the twentieth century.

Yet a significant lacuna is identified in this ending. In an author profile, Kate Kellaway observed that atonement is 'a difficult concept for an atheist such as McEwan', a concept that is 'about a "reconciliation with self".' Looking at the word one day, 'he saw, suddenly, how it came apart: at-one-ment.'[26] The self that Briony is 'at-one' with, in her lifetime of rewriting, is also the self whose desire for order produces her crime – and the life sentence of rewriting.[27] The circularity of this guilt–atonement reveals a general observation about the equivocation of novel-writing, shown to be in an uneasy and shifting relationship to any construction of morality.

One can see this as liberatory: if morality can be variously constructed, the writer must take responsibility for how it is treated. Briony's stand against oblivion and despair, while the practical vocation of Robbie is swept aside, may be insufficient; or, perhaps, a grand, one-off gesture. *Saturday* develops a comparable formal paradox: it projects the competing claims of literature and medicine in a more thoroughgoing form, in which still more extravagant claims for the literary are pressed more urgently, and exposed more emphatically. Yet a more concrete explanatory system for human behaviour is glimpsed; and this allows McEwan the luxury of composing his most consoling fiction yet.

Notes

1   Frank Kermode, 'Point of View' (review of *Atonement*), *London Review of Books*, 23: 19 (4 October 2001), pp. 8–9 (p. 8). Geoff Dyer marvelled at

'the scope, ambition and complexity' of the novel; while Robert Macfarlane emphasized 'its richness of detail, its gravitas and its length'. Hermione Lee found it an 'impressive, engrossing, deep and surprising novel'. See Geoff Dyer, 'Who's Afraid of Influence?' (review of *Atonement*), *The Guardian*, 'Saturday Review' (22 September 2001), p. 8; Robert Macfarlane, 'A Version of Events' (review of *Atonement*), *Times Literary Supplement*, 5139 (28 September 2001), p. 23; and Hermione Lee, 'If Your Memories Serve You Well' (review of *Atonement*), *The Observer*, 'Review' (23 September 2001), p. 16. Reviewers in the US were still more emphatic in their praise. See Brian Finney, 'Briony's Stand Against Oblivion: The Making of Fiction in Ian McEwan's *Atonement*', *Journal of Modern Literature*, 27: 3 (2004), pp. 68–82 (p. 69).

2 Hermione Lee suggests that 'the bloody, chaotic shambles of the retreat sabotages one common national fantasy, of Dunkirk as a heroic rescue'. See 'If Your Memories Serve You Well', p. 16.

3 Ibid., p. 16.

4 Dyer, 'Who's Afraid of Influence?', p. 8.

5 Kermode, 'Point of View', p. 9.

6 Cyril Connolly, *Enemies of Promise* (1938), Parts One and Two reprinted in *The Selected Works, Volume One: The Modern Movement*, ed. Matthew Connolly (London: Picador, 2002), pp. 18–141 (p. 31).

7 Ibid., pp. 90, 56, 91.

8 See Jonathan Coe, 'Introduction' to Rosamund Lehmann, *Dusty Answer* (1927; London: Virago, 2000), [no pagination]. In his children's book *The Daydreamer* (1994), which I discuss in the conclusion, McEwan takes his central character to the realization that childhood will one day be overtaken by adult sensibilities.

9 Connolly, *Enemies of Promise*, pp. 72–3.

10 Finney, 'Briony's Stand Against Oblivion', p. 74.

11 Iris Murdoch, 'Against Dryness', pp. 16, 17, 19, 20.

12 Ibid., pp. 20, 21, 22, 23.

13 Connolly, *Enemies of Promise*, p. 141.

14 McEwan, 'Only Love and Then Oblivion. Love Was All They Had to Set Against Their Murderers', front-page article, *The Guardian* (15 September 2001).

15 McEwan, 'Beyond Belief', *The Guardian*, 'G2' (12 September 2001), p. 2.

16 Jonathan Noakes, 'Interview with Ian McEwan', pp. 19, 20.

17 This kind of metafictional frame is not new in the novel, of course. As John Mullan reminds us, Samuel Richardson's *Clarissa* also 'tells the story of its own existence' by revealing, at its conclusion, 'that the "letters" that comprise the book are Clarissa's "legacy" after her death.' See John Mullan, 'Elements of Fiction', *The Guardian*, 'Review' (29 March 2003), p. 32. What is peculiar to *Atonement* is the degree of anxiety about the worth of fiction-making that is revealed by the metafictional frame.

18 See Gérard Genette, *Narrative Discourse*, trans. Jane E. Lewin (Oxford: Blackwell, 1980), chapter 5; and Shlomith Rimmon-Kenan, *Narrative Fiction: Contemporary Poetics* (London: Methuen, 1983), pp. 94–6. Applying another of Genette's terms, Brian Finney shows how McEwan uses 'variable internal focalization' to move from one focal character to another – Briony, Robbie, Cecilia – without changing the narrative voice. See 'Briony's Stand Against Oblivion', pp. 74–5.

19 William Sutcliffe, for example, suggests that it is only 'at the last gasp' that we discover that 'the entire enterprise is an act of ventriloquism'. See Sutcliffe's review of *Atonement*, *Independent on Sunday*, 'LifeEtc.' (16 September 2001), p. 15.

20 Walter Lord, *The Miracle of Dunkirk* (1982; Ware: Wordsworth Editions, 1998), p. 56.

21 Briony's admission that she merged descriptions of different hospitals – 'a convenient distortion and the least of my offences against veracity' (*At*, p. 356) – is also McEwan's admission.

22 The largest piece of shrapnel removed by Andrews in this procedure is 'just under five inches'. For the episode described in *Atonement* (pp. 298–301), McEwan's source is Lucilla Andrews, *No Time For Romance: An Autobiographical Account of a Few Moments in British and Personal History* (London: Harrap, 1977), pp. 81–2.

23 Ibid., pp. 98–101.

24 Kermode, 'Point of View', p. 9.

25 See Finney, 'Briony's Stand Against Oblivion', pp. 68–9, 81.

26 Kate Kellaway, 'At Home With His Worries' (author profile), *The Observer* (16 September 2001), http://books.guardian.co.uk/print/0,3858,4257898–99930,00.html (accessed 17 November 2005).

27 For Claudia Schemberg, the 'tacit ideal of "at-one-ment"' implies 'the feeling that our various choices and convictions should be tailored as far as possible to our individual needs, should indeed be "at one" with what we perceive of as our unique *self*.' For Schemberg, this has a broader relationship to the trajectory of McEwan's oeuvre, and 'the quest for the good life' that defines all of his later protagonists. See *Achieving 'At-one-ment'*, pp. 8, 97. For me, this locates the lacuna that *Atonement* addresses, the absence of that objective measure which defines goodness or morality: notionally, one can be 'at-one' with oneself when finding satisfaction in deceiving others, or offering them violence.

9

'Accidents of character and circumstance': *Saturday*

Saturday gives a fresh perspective on what makes McEwan's work unnerving or unsettling. There is always the temptation – fraught with risk – to construct a narrative about a writer's oeuvre, in the light of each fresh addition. *Saturday*, however, serves to confirm a dynamic that is already clear with the publication of his previous novel, *Atonement*, a dynamic of giving offence that has changed its hue in an intriguing way. In 1983, McEwan suggested that the 'unsettling' nature of his work is not conscious: 'it is all after the event. It turns out that what I've written is unsettling, but I don't sit down to think about what will unsettle people next.' In the context of this interview, McEwan is, partly, addressing his reputation as the author of macabre or shocking short stories: 'My friends, most of whom had had a literary education, seemed to take for granted the field of play in the stories; they had read Burroughs, Céline, Genet and Kafka, so that lurid physical detail and a sense of cold dissociation did not stun them.'[1]

The argument that, to the literary imagination, the short stories should be unsurprising seems slightly disingenuous. With hindsight, it is hard not to see something anarchic in the early stories, the literary wing of 'punk' culture shaking up the literary establishment, widely perceived as moribund in the 1970s.[2] That perception of 1970s literature may be questionable, less convincing with hindsight; but it certainly had a bearing on the perceived 'shock' element of McEwan's early work. Yet this may also be to clinch McEwan's point: there are proven models to show that literature can render extreme experiences in startling ways. It is a misperception – and a force for suppression – to suppose that this capacity should not be explored.

Paradoxically, then, the shock value of early McEwan serves as a reminder of the range of the literary effect: it is a value that stands *for* literariness, giving offence particularly to those who take a narrower view of literature. In a further paradox, the more overtly 'literary' McEwan's work has become, the more uncertain it has been about the role of literature. Eventually, what we see in *Atonement* is a complex exploration of the equivocal nature of literature, in an ethical sense, which is also a partial but compromised celebration of its consoling features.

A similar paradox orders *Saturday*, but here the rejection of the idea of the literary becomes a bald topic, openly presented in Henry Perowne's consciousness of his 'philistinism' vis à vis literary matters. The celebration of neurosurgeon Perowne, however, seems partly to depend on this 'philistinism'. The offence that McEwan gives here is to the idea that literature matters, in a social or cultural sense: more explicitly than in his other novels, scientific discovery is lauded as having a far greater social significance. Yet the notion of an ethical role for the novel is retained in the most obvious way – and without the uncertainty evident in *Atonement* – through the plotting of *Saturday*, and its treatment of how individuals situate themselves in relation to current ideas. This is especially topical in the era of twenty-four hour news, where readers will identify with Perowne's compulsive habit, which has 'grown stronger these past two years' (i.e. since 9/11), to tune into the news, and be 'joined to the generality, to a community of anxiety'. In this false community of the consumer as voyeur, the possibility that 'monstrous and spectacular scenes' might recur is 'one thread that binds the days.' (*S*, p. 176)[3]

Saturday gained the plaudits of reviewers in the British press, and in a way that often occasioned a broader account of his standing: Theo Tait, writing in the *Times Literary Supplement*, observed that he is 'the most admired English writer of his generation'; Ruth Scurr, in *The Times*, suggested that 'Ian McEwan may now be the best novelist in Britain – and is certainly operating at the height of his formidable powers'; while, for Peter Kemp in the *Sunday Times*, the novel 'reinforces his status as the supreme novelist of his generation'.[4]

In the spirit of this celebratory mood, Robert McCrum was moved, in a profile of the author, to make a startling claim about the likelihood of McEwan's enduring importance:

> Whatever the critical reception, there is no doubt that the international voice of contemporary English fiction is McEwan's. In 2105, readers will turn to his work to understand Britain's painful years of post-imperial transition.[5]

The reason why McCrum chooses 2105 – 100 years on from the date of publication – has a particular significance: he is responding to Perowne's pessimism about the consequences of the war in Iraq, arising from Fred Halliday's view that the attack on America in 2001 had 'precipitated a global crisis that would, if we were lucky, take a hundred years to resolve.' (*S*, pp. 32–3) (McEwan is quoting Halliday verbatim.[6])

McEwan seems broadly in tune with Halliday, who doubts if the consequences of 9/11 will be contained easily or whether lessons will be learnt quickly; yet Halliday does identify 'the root cause of this crisis' as 'intellectual'; as revealing, that is, 'the lack of realistic education and democratic culture in a range of countries, such that irrational hatred and conspiracy theory prevail over reasoned critique':

> The world will be lucky to have worked through the impact of these events and dealt with their causes in a hundred years. This is not, of course, a very long time in the span of human history, but it does suggest that a strong dose of resolve, clarity and courage will be needed, in the West as in the East, in the years to come. Above all, reason and insistence on universal values and criteria of evaluation will, more than ever, be essential. The centre has to hold.[7]

The nature of that 'centre' partly concerns redeeming the beneficent elements of American influence. Halliday stresses 'the need for a more measured political assessment of the USA'. He points out that, globally, 'more and more people . . . look to the USA as a model society and as a source of benevolent influence'. The question that then arises is: 'in what ways, small or large, [can] that influence . . . be put to better rather than worse use'?[8]

Those 'universal values and criteria of evaluation' are far from neutral: what is posited, here, is a projection of 'universality' based on the principles of capitalist democracy, as the best that can be hoped for in the global situation Halliday addresses. I suspect that many people, previously predisposed to dispute this, might accept it after 9/11, in a spirit of grim pragmatism. However, a wide spectrum of dissenting voices, from Islamists to environmentalists, will remain. More pertinent, here, are McEwan's own published views. In one of his newspaper columns in the aftermath of 9/11 McEwan made his own appeal to universal human values, arguing that the hijackers 'would have been unable to proceed' if they had been able 'to imagine themselves into' the passengers' 'thoughts and feelings'. What flows from this is a particular conception of moral sense:

Imagining what it is like to be someone other than yourself is at the core of our humanity. It is the essence of compassion, and it is the beginning of morality. The hijackers used fanatical certainty, misplaced religious faith, and dehumanising hatred to purge themselves of the human instinct for empathy. Among their crimes was a failure of the imagination.[9]

This is ostensibly an attack on religious fundamentalism, rather than an attack on religion per se. However, it does have the effect of valorizing the secular love that McEwan evokes earlier in the article (many victims tried to phone those closest to them with the message 'I love you' before being killed), and a brand of morality that is distinctly humanist. As I have discussed in relation to *Atonement*, this might seem to validate the business of the novelist, or, at least, the germ of novel-writing – 'imagining what it is like to be someone other than yourself' – as an intrinsically moral activity, even though such a notion is radically undermined by the overall conception of *Atonement*.

In *Saturday*, this humanism is eventually given a philosophical hue that takes it beyond the immediate political context. At the end, Perowne looks out once more over London from his bedroom window. His train of thought progresses from the inevitability of a terrorist attack to a more philosophical view of history. He wonders on the similar reflections of an 'Edwardian gent', looking out of the same window a hundred years previously, unable to anticipate the carnage of the twentieth century, and particularly the 'body count' generated by its famous dictators, 'Hitler, Stalin, Mao'. Al Qaeda then seems to comprise 'totalitarians in different form', and the thought of a hundred years' war then begins to seem 'an indulgence, an idle, overblown fantasy, a night-thought about a passing disturbance that time and good sense will settle and rearrange' (*S*, pp. 276–7).

The issue that then arises is the extent to which *Saturday* is a novel of its moment. In 1989, contemplating the difference between writing drama and fiction, McEwan expressed the view that the directness with which playwrights can engage their times is unavailable to the novelist, since 'the novel is not best suited to topical issues, or catching on the wing a changing social mood.' 'Novels', he wrote, 'take longer to cook.'[10] In *Saturday*, however, McEwan treats, not an evanescent social mood, but a global political context that will surely endure.

The logic of Theo Tait's review in the *Times Literary Supplement* is to suggest that the novel is very much of its wider political moment, or, rather, that the political moment has caught up with McEwan. Tait observes how his earlier novels treat 'sinister, chaotic, violent forces' and 'domestic contentment' with equal facility; but that, while the irruption of the nightmare is always impressive – the child abduction, the ballooning accident, and so on – McEwan 'struggles to make sense of the private nightmares, to give them a wider significance.' After 9/11, Tait suggests, that struggle is no longer necessary:

> His constant preoccupation – in a word, security – has become the great obsession. The prevailing public mood has come to resemble closely that of an Ian McEwan novel. Constant menace, punctuated with nightmarish atrocities; the insult of the world's continuing normality: these are things we all understand very well.[11]

Because the attack on America and the 'war on terror' provide the backdrop to *Saturday*, McEwan does not need to explain the nightmare, in Tait's view.

Tait may be right that a particular consonance between *Saturday* and the prevailing public mood conditions its reception at the time of publication. If this is so, the threat to the security of the Perownes parallels the broader insecurity of the West in the face of Islamic extremism, and in respect of those states seeking to foment anti-Western sentiment. This does not mean, of course, that the mood of insecurity to which the novel responds is relevant only to the West, even if that is the chief connotation: the predicament of the Perownes might also evoke a situation in which domestic harmony per se is threatened by global insecurity. In pursuing the allegorical dimension, however, readers may inevitably detect a process of demonization conducted from a Western perspective, most especially in the parallel between Baxter and Saddam Hussein. We may wonder if there is an invitation to speculate on the possibility of a common psychological disorder.

The psychological make-up of dictators is always a focus of political attention and speculation; it is also a consideration in the planning of foreign policy. However, any attempt to establish the psychological state of Saddam Hussein, in the run up to both the Gulf War of 1990 and the invasion of Iraq in 2003, was clearly fraught with problems: he could not be interviewed, the information available about his childhood and background was patchy, and the efforts of Western psychologists to assess his state of mind were complicated by the further interference of cultural difference, which must surely make any conclusions problematic. Nevertheless, the political and military machinery often depends upon such incomplete psychological profiles.

One such profile was delivered to the US House Armed Services Committee in December 1990, on the brink of war, by Jerrold M. Post, and it is interesting to compare Post's conclusions about Saddam with McEwan's portrayal of Baxter. Post summarizes Saddam's 'political personality constellation' as comprising: 'messianic ambition for unlimited power, absence of conscience, unconstrained aggression, and a paranoid outlook'. These are the things that make Saddam dangerous, in Post's analysis, and which lead to his diagnosis of 'malignant narcissism', which he describes as 'the personality configuration of the destructive charismatic who unifies and rallies his downtrodden supporters by blaming outside enemies'. The immediate purpose of the war was to force Saddam to withdraw from Kuwait, and, to achieve this end, Post advised: 'it is important not to insist on total capitulation and humiliation, for this could drive Saddam into a corner and make it impossible for him to reverse his course.'[12]

The Huntingdon's disease from which Baxter suffers produces some patterns of behaviour that are similar to this, most especially the dangerous response to the humiliating experience of the morning, which leads to his assault on the Perownes, with a sidekick in tow, an attempt, apparently, 'to rescue his reputation in front of a witness' (*S*, p. 210). The plan is an attempt 'to assert his dignity, and perhaps even shape the way he'll be remembered', in Perowne's view (rendered here, as elsewhere, in free indirect discourse) (*S*, p. 211).

This is not a parallel that is fully developed, however; indeed, had it been, it would surely have impoverished the book's engagement with global politics. There is a richness in Perowne's vacillation and uncertainty about how the West should respond to Saddam, which is evidently not matched by the resolution to the dramatic scene of threatened violence: with Baxter isolated and off-guard, Theo and Perowne contrive to throw him down the stairs, without a qualm.[13]

Even though it is steeped in its political moment, this is not a novel that is replete with specific political references, or satirical instances.[14] However much *Saturday* captures the mood of post-9/11 anxiety, its central ideas are drawn from other sources. Matthew Arnold is one of the book's central reference points, and this is most obvious in section four when Daisy recites Arnold's much-anthologized poem 'Dover Beach', as we shall see. Arnold's *Culture and Anarchy* is a less obvious point of reference, but one that offers an interesting counterpoint to McEwan's treatment of the mass demonstration. Reflecting on the passing of 'the strong feudal habits of subordination and deference' that formerly affected the working class, Arnold worries about 'the modern spirit' that 'has now almost entirely dissolved those habits, and the anarchical tendency of our worship of freedom in and for itself, of our superstitious faith . . . in machinery'. Here, for Arnold, is the source of anarchy:

> More and more, because of this our blind faith in machinery, because of our want of light to enable us to look beyond machinery to the end for which machinery is valuable, this and that man, and this and that body of men, all over the country, are beginning to assert and put in practice an Englishman's right to do what he likes; his right to march where he likes, meet where he likes, enter where he likes, hoot as he likes, threaten as he likes, smash as he likes. All this, I say, tends to anarchy.[15]

In an editorial note, Stefan Collini observes that these sentences 'chiefly refer to the so-called "Hyde Park riots" of July 1866 when a large crowd attending a meeting of the Reform League got out of hand and broke down the iron railings surrounding Hyde Park.'[16] Perowne's response to the anti-war demonstrators, making their way to Hyde Park in 2003, makes for an intriguing comparison.[17] He responds to 'the seduction and excitement' of 'tens of thousands of strangers converging with a single purpose conveying an intimation of revolutionary joy' (*S*, p. 72). At the same time, however, he understands that his own view is coloured by one of his patients, an Iraqi academic who had suffered at the hands of Saddam Hussein's regime. Consequently, Perowne's view is ambivalent, and he 'can't feel, as the marchers themselves probably can, that they have an exclusive hold on moral discernment' (*S*, p. 73). His meeting with Professor Taleb is a matter of chance, he realizes, suggesting that 'opinions are a roll of the dice' (*S*, p. 73).

Later, in his discussion with Daisy, his judgement of the demonstrators hardens. He asks why the demonstrators betray no sign of criticizing Saddam. Daisy argues that this is 'a given', to which Perowne makes the following response:

> No it's not. It's a forgotten. Why else are you all singing and dancing in the park? The genocide and torture, the mass graves, the security apparatus, the criminal totalitarian state – the iPod generation doesn't want to know. Let nothing come between them and their ecstasy clubbing and cheap flights and reality TV. (*S*, p. 191)

There is some affinity between this outburst and Arnold's lament at the uncultured anarchic response, insofar as this response is associated with the 'worship of freedom' and a 'blind faith in machinery'. It is a pale echo, however; partly because the class consciousness that colours Arnold's view no longer applies; but also because the view that accrues to Perowne through the novel is less judgemental than this outburst, inspired by a father–daughter argument, in which other things are at stake.

Moreover, the 'cultured' view for which Perowne is made to stand is justified by the freedoms of the machine age. Technological enhancements of domestic life, as well as those that facilitate surgery, are openly celebrated. In the account of transsphenoidal hypophysectomy (discussed in more detail below), McEwan betrays consciousness of the technological advances that make such a procedure possible, for example (*S*, p. 44).[18]

More generally, the machine age is a matter of celebration in *Saturday*. It is not simply that machines make individual labour less onerous: it is technology that makes the city 'a brilliant invention', as indicated by Perowne's reflection on his own small part of it, 'bathed and embraced by modernity, by street light from above, and from below by fibre-optic cables, and cool fresh water coursing down pipes, and sewage borne away in an instant of forgetting' (*S*, p. 5).

At the same time, however, there is a clear consciousness, shared by McEwan and Perowne, that current comforts are precarious, sustained by activities that are complicitous in wider processes of despoliation or degradation. McEwan gives to Perowne a recipe of his own for a fish stew (*S*, pp. 176–9);[19] yet, at the fishmonger's earlier in the day, Perowne reflects on the evident 'abundance from the emptying seas', in a passage that also registers new scientific awareness 'that even fish feel pain'. The consequence is 'the growing complication of the modern condition, the expanding circle of moral sympathy' (*S*, p. 127). The culture to which Perowne contributes, and to which a novel like *Saturday* belongs, embodies consolations that, it seems, outweigh the doubts occasioned by such ethical paradoxes.

In all of this, however, there is an undeveloped contradiction. The culture of Western scientific advancement, after all, is also the culture that is widely perceived to generate global environmental degradation (even if the consumerist demands of the wealthiest nations are increasingly being emulated in developing countries); and this is the culture that is identified as the enemy by Islamic militants.

Here, the counterpoint with Arnold is illuminating, once again. The passage from *Culture and Anarchy*, quoted above, suggested to Raymond Williams a crucial flaw in Arnold's thought:

Calm, Arnold rightly argued, was necessary. But now the Hyde Park railings were down, and it was not Arnold's best self which rose at the sight of them. Certainly he feared a general breakdown, into violence and anarchy, but the most remarkable facts about the British working-class movement, since its origin in the Industrial Revolution, are its conscious and deliberate abstention from general violence, and its firm faith in other methods of advance.[20]

Where Arnold, in Williams's view, is clouded by a misperception of class, we might wonder if Perowne is clouded by a misperception of a different 'other'. For him, this is not represented by the demonstrators – he realizes he could have been one of them – but, implicitly, by the shadowy perpetrators of terror and the alternative cultural forces to which they are affiliated. We have seen that Fred Halliday's pragmatic solution is endorsed by Perowne, a solution premised on a question-able faith in the benign aspects of US influence and the global extension of capitalist democracy. In this, there is an appeal to a universal set of values that might transcend the new global ideological stand-off. This view may seem to be arrived at rather too easily.

The sketchiness (and inconclusiveness) of this political strand is less of a problem in the novel than it might be, however, chiefly because the ethical debate that emerges from the novel has another, more promi-nent, resonance: ultimately, it is the 'two cultures' debate in the book that assumes central significance. Through Perowne, the terms of this debate are established in ways that are obvious enough. In outline, this can seem more schematic than it is: a neurosurgeon, with a daughter who is a poet, and who berates him for his lack of responsiveness to literature, sticks by his own literal, scientific rationale for wonder, and is finally hailed as the champion of moral stability. It is important to recognize, however, that there is a deeply personal (rather than straightforwardly rational) basis to his intellectual affiliation.

In flashback we discover how Perowne met and fell in love with his wife, when he had been a Senior House Officer for four months, and she received an urgent operation to remove a tumour on her pituitary gland that was pressing on her optic nerve and impairing her vision. The account of the surgical procedure to remove the tumour and save her sight – transsphenoidal hypophysectomy – is partly drawn from the book cited in the Acknowledgements, Frank T. Vertosick's *When the Air Hits Your Brain: Tales of Neurosurgery*. The arresting point that emerges from a comparison between the episode in Vertosick's book and the remembered event in *Saturday* inspired by it is the extent to which McEwan has borrowed from the *narrative situation* Vertosick describes, in similar fashion to the borrowing evident in earlier novels.[21] As a trainee, sent to London for three months, Vertosick assists in the treatment of an attractive young woman, like Rosalind, referred by a casualty department, and still in her street clothes; like Perowne, he is sent to find the hospital specialist, whose diagnosis addressed to the patient bears a close resemblance to Mr Whaley's address to Rosalind in *Saturday*.

The surgical procedure in the novel is more involved than the account given by Vertosick. McEwan shadowed a neurosurgeon as part of his research for the novel, and it is clear that he had other resources to draw on.[22] Yet there are still noticeable echoes. Vertosick's surgeon exposes his patient's 'blue and taut' pituitary gland 'in less than an hour', to remove a 'purulent yellow tumour';[23] while, in the procedure witnessed by Perowne, the 'swollen purplish gland' is revealed 'in less than forty-five minutes', allowing the removal of an 'ochre tumour' (*S*, p. 44).

Most arresting, however, is the way in which the situation of Vertosick supplies a basis for this formative experience of Perowne's. Like Vertosick, Perowne is a trainee, affected by the plight of a woman with no immediate familial support: the patient's father is dead, in Vertosick's memoir, while her mother has a heart condition and cannot be contacted.[24] (Rosalind's mother is dead, and her father is abroad (*S*, p. 42).) The tone of the two books is certainly very different: where McEwan produces an internalized sense of personal development (as one might expect in a novel), Vertosick reveals the heartiness, and the raw humour commonly associated with trainees in the medical profession.[25] Yet he also implies a sense of vocation behind the blunt exterior, and it is this feeling that McEwan extends. For Perowne, the experience of witnessing the transsphenoidal hypophysectomy is life-altering, on both personal and professional levels: he has 'yet to learn clinical detachment' and is falling in love with Rosalind (*S*, p. 43); but, simultaneously, the majesty of neurosurgery is brought home to him by a procedure that is a 'miracle of human ingenuity', and that is 'humane and daring', embodying 'the spirit of benevolence enlivened by the boldness of a high-wire circus act.' (*S*, pp. 44–5) Perowne's desire to become a neurosurgeon now becomes more than 'theoretical', 'a matter of deep desire':

> As the closing up began and the face, this particular, beautiful face, was reassembled without a single disfiguring mark, he felt excitement about

the future and impatient to acquire the skills. He was falling in love with a life. He was also, of course, falling in love. The two were inseparable. (*S*, p. 45)

It is a significant divergence from the detachment usually held to be the requisite norm in the medical profession, governed by the Hippocratic oath, which obliges reverence of life, in a uniform and impersonal sense. Such impersonality is also at odds with the mood of Frank Vertosick's memoir. Recalling an episode as a trainee, he wonders at the callousness of a surgeon nearing the end of his training, able to shut out of his mind a deadly slip of the knife, and apparently to absolve himself of guilt: Vertosick wonders if 'psychopathy' is part of the necessary identity of the neurosurgeon, and if his own 'compassion [will] start to slip away.'[26] One of the functions of *When the Air Hits Your Brain* is to advertise the fact that this is not so, that the fully qualified Vertosick is deeply fulfilled, at the level of personal interaction, by his ability to heal, and to utilize his acquired skills to bring happiness to others. In *Saturday*, McEwan responds deeply to this brand of humanism, rooted in scientific advancement.

As the privileging of scientific progress in the novel becomes more pronounced, so does the paradox deepen that this view is being conveyed in the form of a novel, written by a writer widely held to be at the height of his powers. Of course, McEwan makes the paradox a central element of the book by linking Perowne's (frankly) heroic status to his failure of imaginative response in a narrow, literary sense. Mark Lawson suggests one way of accounting for this: in his view, *Saturday* is 'one of the most oblique but also most serious contributions to the post-9/11, post-Iraq war literature', and, consequently, 'it succeeds in ridiculing on every page the view of its hero that fiction is useless to the modern world.'[27] Certainly, the consummate achievement of the novel would seem to refute the view that fiction is useless; but this may not be Perowne's view, exactly.

His attitude to literature is expressed through an extended reflection on his daughter's attempts to educate his literary sensibility. In Tolstoy and Flaubert (he read *Anna Karenin* and *Madame Bovary* at Daisy's behest) he found authors who display 'the virtue, at least, of representing a recognisable physical reality', though he was 'unmoved' by Daisy's claim that 'the genius was in the detail'. These novels, he feels, 'were the products of steady, workmanlike accumulation' (*S*, pp. 66–7).

If he finds some minimal value in classic nineteenth-century novels, he has an express distaste for 'the so-called magical realists', writers of 'irksome confections' in his view. McEwan is having some fun with his character, and his readers, here: Perowne has read, it seems, Rushdie, Carter and Grass, among others, and also a novel in which 'one visionary saw through a pub window his parents as they had been some weeks after his conception, discussing the possibility of aborting him' (S, p. 67). The novel in question, of course, is *The Child in Time*, which stands as the odd-one-out in this roll-call of magic realism. The timeslip in that novel (to which Perowne refers here) is actually embedded in a series of references to theoretical physics, giving it the kind of quasi-plausibility that is never attempted in magic realism proper. This moment of self-referential play may contain within it an implicit complaint about the way in which *The Child in Time* is sometimes wrongly categorized.

Rather than a simple refutation of Perowne's evaluations, it is hard not to see some affinity between McEwan and Perowne. In a public interview with Vic Sage at the University of East Anglia, McEwan made a comment that is germane here. Discussing an early draft of *Atonement*, he explained that Robbie was initially conceived as a character with brain implants, making him the product of scientific rather than social engineering. In explaining why he rejected this early whimsical idea, McEwan was moved to make a general point about science-fiction, a mode where, 'because anything can happen, nothing is very interesting'. This, of course, is almost identical to Perowne's conclusion about magic realism in *Saturday*: 'when anything can happen', he writes to Daisy, 'nothing much matters' (S, p. 68). We should not set too much store by such extra-textual correspondences, of course; more pertinent is the way in which all of McEwan's fiction follows Perowne's predilection for 'the actual, not the magical', and focuses on 'the difficulties and wonders of the real' and the 'demanding re-enactment of the plausible' (S, pp. 67–8).

The agreement between McEwan and Perowne on this point suggests an exploratory dimension to *Saturday* rather than an assertion of a given definition of literary value. If advancing understanding of the brain is the occasion for a new form of wonder, how might the novel respond to this evolving discipline, with huge ramification for our understanding of consciousness? The novel situates its response to this question in a broader historical evocation of the 'two cultures' debate.

To get a sense of this, we need to consider the climactic scene in some detail. Here, Baxter, holding Rosalind at knife-point, insists that

Daisy reads aloud from the proof copy of her poetry collection, *My Saucy Bark*: he has made her strip naked, and her evident pregnancy has stalled the march of the intruders' sexual violence. Her grandfather, who had encouraged her to rote-learn poetry as a child, says 'do one you used to say for me', in an apparent effort to give her some fortitude, and to protect her, at least, from the additional humiliation of exposing her own writing to the intruders (*S*, p. 220). The piece she chooses to recite, pretending to read from her own book, is Matthew Arnold's 'Dover Beach'. Baxter's ecstatic response to the poem effects a dramatic mood swing, and fills him with the positive desire to go on the trial treatment for his condition that Perowne had invented earlier in the scene. The poem tips the balance in favour of the Perownes: Baxter is diverted from his scheme of revenge; his sidekick, Nigel, leaves the house in disgust; and Theo and Henry are able to overpower Baxter.

This is not, of course, a simple celebration of the 'power' of poetry, though the emotional impact of poetry is strongly registered. The scene also emphasizes the unpredictability and subjectivity of the aesthetic response, as well as the contingency of life. As Daisy reads, 'Dover Beach' takes shape through Perowne's untutored responses to a poem he doesn't recognize. On the first recitation (she is forced to recite it again), Perowne 'feels himself slipping through the words into the things they describe'. This interpretation is coloured by his preconception that Daisy is the author, his discovery that she is expecting a baby, and the day's events concerning the impending war in Iraq. He imagines she is describing a scene that involves her lover, and 'he sees a smooth-skinned young man, naked to the waist, standing at Daisy's side'. Perowne feels the poem expresses Daisy's nostalgic reflection on a time 'when the earth was new and the sea consoling, and nothing came between man and God.' Faced with the 'sadness and loss' heard in the breaking and retreating waves, Daisy turns to her lover to tell him 'that they must love each other and be faithful, especially now they're having a child, and when there's no peace or certainty, and when desert armies stand ready to fight' (*S*, pp. 220–1).

When he hears the poem again, he realizes that he missed 'the mention of the cliffs of England' (his reception was coloured by the preconception that the poem is about Daisy and her lover in France); this second hearing is coloured by his anticipation of how Baxter is receiving it: instead of the young man, Perowne now sees 'Baxter standing alone, elbows propped against the sill, listening to the waves "bring the eternal note of sadness in".' Hearing 'through Baxter's ears' the melancholy becomes more emphatic for Perowne, and 'the plea to be true to another sounds hopeless in the absence of joy or love or light or peace or "help for pain".' This reading is filtered through Perowne's attempt to inhabit Baxter's illness: he hears 'no mention of a desert' this time. In conclusion, he feels that 'the poem's melodiousness . . . is at odds with its pessimism', a not unperceptive response (*S*, pp. 221–2).

The haphazard forces of chance are at play in Daisy's decision to recite a poem that will jolt Baxter out of his vengeful mode. Her father's revised interpretation of the poem, as the suspense builds, suggests it may tip Baxter over into despair rather than euphoric hopefulness; and she could certainly have chosen other poems committed to memory, in response to her grandfather's broad suggestion. Yet in the novel, the choice of 'Dover Beach' is artful. It is ideal in several respects in relation to the novel's development, particularly given the historical context of the poem and the circumstances of its composition.

A crucial element of the poem, which McEwan underscores through Perowne's reception of it, is the speaker's loss of religious faith. What is left, instead, is the love between individuals to pit against a world compared to 'a darkling plain/ Swept with confused alarms of struggle and flight,/ Where ignorant armies clash by night.' This closing image, which Perowne initially links with the forthcoming conflict in Iraq, is a reference to Thucydides' account, in his history of the Peloponnesian War, of the night-time battle at Epipolae: in the confusion, Athenian soldiers were unable to distinguish friend from foe, and found themselves killing both indiscriminately.[28] The emphasis on love at a personal level and, by extension, the need for individual responsibility – as a counter to indiscriminate (and ultimately self-destructive) conflict, and in the absence of divine intervention – chimes entirely with the novel's simple moral strand.

The 'love' that the world lacks, in Arnold's conception, is sometimes associated with imagination more broadly, rather than with the nuptial love the poet might seem to have in mind, on the basis of his immediate inspiration. ('Dover Beach' was inspired by Arnold's visits to Dover with his new wife in 1851.) Following this association, Perowne's rapid lesson in poetic interpretation, hearing his daughter's recitation of the poem and then urgently revising his sense of its connotations, might be said to constitute an object lesson in the need for rationalism to be tempered with imagination.

However, there is another sense in which 'Dover Beach' functions as a way of sanctioning the world of the rationalist – or rather, the rationalist with Perowne's credentials – in a secular world. This is so because the poem straddles the moment of the great Darwinian paradigm shift. It is thought to have been composed between 1851 and 1852, but was not published until 1867. The significant cultural event, occurring midway between the composition and publication of the poem, is the publication of Charles Darwin's *The Origin of Species* (1859). The poem registers – and laments – a wider loss of religious faith, implying that 'love', the only 'light' or 'help for pain', perhaps, on the 'darkling plain', is going to be severely tested. This pessimism is melodiously conveyed, in the contradiction between form and content that Perowne dismissively notes.

His dismissiveness need not attract our disapproval, for in the time between the conception and publication of the poem, Darwin produces the clinching work in a new science, sweeping away Biblical explanations of creation and establishing a new way of infusing creation with wonder. In a sense, Darwin establishes a new form of 'love' or imagination. Indeed, this is his claim in the phrase from the final paragraph from *The Origin of Species* that echoes in Perowne's mind in *Saturday*: 'There is grandeur in this view of life'.[29] For Perowne (and McEwan) the grandeur arises 'from physical laws, from war of nature, famine and death' to produce 'a bracing kind of consolation in the brief privilege of consciousness' (*S*, p. 56). For Perowne, the grandeur is rooted in the rapidly advancing scientific understanding of consciousness, which might one day explain 'how matter becomes conscious'. Although he 'can't begin to imagine a satisfactory account', he believes 'the secret will be revealed – over decades', and this is 'the only kind of faith he has. There's grandeur in this view of life' (*S*, p. 255).

Here, in his reverence for consciousness, Perowne is very close to McEwan who, in an article on science and belief, stated: 'what I believe but cannot prove is that no part of my consciousness will survive my death.' While acknowledging that 'many will take this premise as a given', McEwan points out that 'it divides the world crucially', separating the rationalists from those who have done great damage by virtue of the conviction 'that there is a life, a better, more important life, elsewhere'. The premise leads McEwan to the world-view enshrined in *Saturday*:

> That this span is brief, that consciousness is an accidental gift of blind processes, makes our existence all the more precious and our responsibilities for it all the more profound.[30]

The impulse behind the ethical imperative here, our responsibility for the precious gift of consciousness, is partly generated by wonder at the biological marvel that science has revealed. In the absence of any other moral system, cognition of the science of mind, as well as that branch of science itself, becomes, in an ethical sense, the superior form of imagination. In that sense, the kind of knowledge acquired by the neurosurgeon is somehow primary, where other mental activities – writing a poem or a novel, say – might be deemed secondary, mere consequences of the consciousness that they cannot comprehend or preserve.

This suggests a new kind of territory for the novel that treats the issue of consciousness. From a technical point of view, *Saturday* reveals literary parallels, of course, the most pertinent of which is the modernist stream-of-consciousness especially as enacted in novels that span a day, like *Ulysses* and *Mrs Dalloway*. Woolf's novel, indeed, prompted a number of comparisons in the reviews.[31] McEwan is also moving in a new direction, however, trying to produce, perhaps, a diagnostic 'slice-of-mind' novel – working towards the literary equivalent of a CT scan – rather than a modernist 'slice-of-life' novel. *Saturday* is not always successful in this respect, perhaps – it is stilted in some ways, for example, especially in those tense, dramatic scenes with Baxter where Perowne's diagnostic habits seem to crowd out less rational thought processes.

Stylistically, however, the novel makes a bold attempt to engage with the immediacy of human consciousness, and it is in this way that *Saturday* finally stakes a claim to a share of the ethical high ground on behalf of the literary intervention. The most striking stylistic feature of the novel is that McEwan writes an extended fiction in the present tense for the first time, in a manner slightly reminiscent of J. M. Coetzee and the deceptive simplicity of that writer's novels.[32] McEwan achieves several things by adopting this method. There is, first, the advantage of a style that contributes to the suspense of the novel. In Section Four, for example, McEwan teases his readers with a series of arrivals to the Perownes' house before the intruders arrive. We know they are coming, because Theo's warning to his father about Baxter (*S*, p. 152) (which only partially impinges (*S*, p. 175)) prepares us; but it is only with the *fourth* arrival at the front door that the menace finally materializes. This would surely have been intolerable rendered in the past tense; but the use of the present ameliorates the teasing because there is no signal, at the level of grammar, of recapitulation by the narrator:

nothing is being withheld, so the stylistic conceit implies, all is happening *now*.

What follows from this is that McEwan has adopted a style that gets very close to the experience of reading novels. Literary critics are in the habit of discussing novels in the present tense – that is, they concern themselves with what *happens* in a novel – and they do this because the substance of a novel, the experiences described, as well as the plot, comprise events and experiences in a sequence that *happen* each time a novel is produced through reading. In this sense, a novel captures a recurring present. Of course the is nothing new in the use of the historic present tense as a vehicle for narrative fiction; but it might be said to be a stylistic attribute that comes closest to the experience of novel reading, a feature that McEwan exploits in *Saturday*.

The vitality of the present is given an additional dimension in the closing pages when Perowne, at the end of his eventful Saturday, is called into the hospital to operate on Baxter, and, at work in the operating theatre, finds himself 'in a dream of absorption that has dissolved all sense of time, and all awareness of the other parts of his life. Even his awareness of his own existence has vanished. He's been delivered into a pure present, free of the weight of the past or any anxieties about the future' (*S*, p. 258). Here McEwan allows his character to occupy the mental space that Stephen Lewis hankers after in *The Child in Time*, when he reflects that if he could replicate in his daily life the 'intensity and abandonment' of building a sandcastle with his daughter, 'he would be a happy man of extraordinary powers' (*CT*, p. 107).

The contentment that flows from inhabiting this pure present, for Perowne, is selfless, since ego is entirely suppressed. If we are tempted to draw a parallel between the activities of the neurosurgeon and the business of writing – and, surely, we are invited to do this – McEwan also makes an implicit distinction by indicating that one aspect of Perowne's contentment derives from 'working with others'.[33] The partial parallel remains in the circumstances of this 'benevolent dissociation', which requires 'difficulty, prolonged demands on concentration and skills, pressure, problems to be solved, even danger'. We probably acknowledge the parallel between the business of neurosurgery and the art of the novelist seeking to trace psychological motivation; yet we also realize that the level of difficulty, concentration and danger are of entirely different orders in each case. The result of the parallel, once more, is to privilege the skill of the surgeon, whose 'clarified emptiness' and 'muted joy' are hard won. Despite Perowne's concern that there must 'be something wrong with him' to be at his happiest on his day off when back at work, readers may be more inclined to concur that the experience renders Perowne 'fully qualified to exist' (*S*, p. 258).

The 'only kind of faith' Perowne has is in scientific progress; or, at least, in his own branch of medical science, a conviction that one day 'a satisfactory account' will be arrived at of 'how matter becomes conscious' (*S*, p. 255).[34] However, this unprovable faith is part of his inhabitation of the present moment, the secular professional's equivalent of meditation. This, however, is merely an interlude: it does not, in itself, signal a special claim for Perowne's profession, or the prioritizing of science over literature, in the book's scheme, that might enshrine Perowne's higher moral standing.

In the construction of the novel, it is not neurosurgery in general that is the focus of the episode, but this *particular* operation, for it is this procedure that delivers the satisfying sense of completion at the same time that the impression of Perowne's moral stature is confirmed. McEwan engineers a situation, in a work of unabashed symmetry, in which Perowne can make atonement, first for the abuse (as he sees it) of his professional skills in his first encounter with Baxter (where his detection of Baxter's Huntingdon's disease enabled him to humiliate him and to escape a beating); and also for his social position, and the roll of the genetic dice that distinguishes a Perowne from a Baxter.[35]

The theme of chance forms the arresting counterpoint to the aesthetic perfection, in a structural sense, of McEwan's novel. At one point we discover Daisy's reverence for *The Golden Bowl* (1904) (Henry James is one of those writers Perowne does not get on with), and we should detect, in this allusion, a hint of the consolation offered by carefully crafted fiction in the face of life's imperfections. That consolation, however, serves to underscore rather than obscure the moral problem. In *Saturday*, chance is repeatedly shown to have a determining effect on life. Perowne reflects on: 'the accidents of character and circumstance' that set Daisy apart from the drug addict he has seen out of his window (*S*, p. 65); on the chance encounter that fashions his view of the Iraq situation (*S*, pp. 72–3); and on the 'axis' that binds his life to that of a street sweeper, and that 'could tip them into each other's life' (*S*, p. 74).

The Aberfan disaster of 1966 (where 116 children were tragically killed when their school was swamped by a landslide), we discover, was a defining experience for the young Perowne, steering him away from a belief in fate or providence, or divine intervention: 'the pickiness of pure chance and physical laws seemed like freedom from the scheming of a gloomy god' (*S*, pp. 31–2, 128).

The novelist, of course, imposes order on the random material on which he or she draws. In alerting us to this facet of the novelist's art, McEwan again reveals an affinity with Iris Murdoch, whose theory of the novel was based on this paradox. For her, there was a necessary tension between form and contingency, the need for a 'unified aesthetic whole' set against the requirement to evoke the 'disunity and randomness' of 'ordinary life'.[36] In Murdoch's conception, this involved a moral dilemma for the artist, since formal unity can conceal 'truth', tipping the balance away from contingency and towards a sense of gratification or consolation for the reader.

In *Saturday*, this dilemma becomes the central point, but in a new context. For Perowne, it is genetics that determines who will have a miserable life, on the margins of society, since such a fate is 'down to invisible folds and kinks of character, written in code, at the level of molecules' (*S*, p. 272). This randomness then generates a different kind of order, a predictability about behaviour and opportunity that could not previously have been tied down so exactly. Contingency, in the sense of a roll of the genetic dice, then points to a new kind of social patterning, not discernible in the social 'chaos' that writers previously sought to draw on. This implies a different sense of social responsibility, demonstrated in the duty Perowne feels to treat Baxter in the final section of the novel.

It is worth noting that his decision to operate on Baxter is implausible, according to the narrow definition of professional ethics to which he is subordinate. But that is very much the point: Perowne is advancing to another plane of ethical care, based on an understanding of genetic predetermination, and the new form of social responsibility this must usher in.

The gesture of writing *Saturday*, a novel premised on this perception of new forms of inequality, might be said to parallel Perowne's new duty of care. There are ways in which the order imposed makes Perowne seem the author's moral agent, enacting his own desire for intervention. The inevitability of the reckoning between Baxter and Perowne and the perfection, in a moral sense, of having Perowne treat his adversary in a spirit of atonement for his own genetic privilege, are satisfying fusions of form and content.

Saturday represents a significant risk for McEwan in that it opts for consolation in the face of contemporary uncertainty. His earlier novels create the necessary tension established in Iris Murdoch's poetics of the novel, between 'the consolations of form' and 'a respect for the contingent', in the knowledge that 'only the very greatest art invigorates without consoling.'[37] Here, the tension collapses into consolation. Picking up on this, John Banville's excoriating review of the novel observes that previously McEwan 'has been the least consoling chronicler of life's perils and difficulties'; in contrast, he finds *Saturday* to be 'self-satisfied', characterized by 'arrogance', and well received by Western readers who are reassured at a time when they are shaken in their sense of themselves and their culture.[38] If one takes Perowne to epitomize Western culture, such a reading is understandable; however, his philistinism in connection with literary culture is one very significant way in which the 'arrogance' that Banville describes is shaken up. (Banville is himself offended by Perowne's ignorance of literature, which he thinks is implausible.) More significant is the treatment of medical science: if Perowne is another high achiever of the privileged West (like Halliday and Linley in *Amsterdam*), the discoveries that make his work possible issue in an understanding of human nature that transcends cultural difference; and this is what legitimizes the novel's mood of consolation.

If the novel, as a form, always plays order off against chaos, form against contingency, this dynamic in *Saturday* generates aesthetic consolations that point to a new perception of society. A crucial aspect of life's contingency, the genetic lottery, is now being deciphered, and the possibility of intervention through medical science is glimpsed. If the social consequences of this are enormous – and not necessarily benign – they are also profound for the novel. If medical science opens the door to greater human agency to address what was previously put down to chance, so might the novel begin to reflect a new kind of social order. How might the novel begin to encompass new models of agency and responsibility? This is the question that *Saturday* tacitly poses, through the 'heroism' of Perowne, reinventing his ethical code in order to save Baxter. McEwan emerges as the neurosurgeon of the cultural sphere in this novel, daring to console his readers, in an extravagant performance that celebrates the developing human capacity to know the self, in both literature and science.

Notes

1 From the interview with John Haffenden, in Haffenden, *Novelists in Interview* (London: Methuen, 1985), pp. 168–90 (p. 169).

2 This is discussed in chapter 2.

3 This brings to mind McEwan's article, in the aftermath of 9/11 (discussed in the previous chapter), in which he describes how he 'surfed' TV news channels 'hungrily, ghoulishly'. See 'Beyond Belief', *The Guardian*, 'G2' (12 September 2001), p. 2.

4 Theo Tait, 'A Rational Diagnosis' (review of *Saturday*), *Times Literary Supplement*, 5315 (11 February 2005), pp. 21–2 (p. 22); Ruth Scurr, 'Happiness on a Knife-edge' (review of *Saturday*), *The Times*, 'Weekend Review' (29 January 2005), p. 13; Peter Kemp, 'Master of the Mind Game' (review of *Saturday*), *Sunday Times*, 'Culture' (30 January 2005), pp. 41–2 (p. 42).

5 Robert McCrum, 'The Story of His Life' (author profile), *The Observer*, 'Review' (23 January 2005), p. 5.

6 See Fred Halliday, *Two Hours That Shook the World, September 11, 2001: Causes and Consequences* (London: Saqi Books, 2002), p. 24.

7 Ibid., p. 216.

8 Ibid., pp. 172–3.

9 From McEwan's front-page article, 'Only Love and Then Oblivion'.

10 McEwan, Preface to *A Move Abroad*, p. xxv.

11 Tait, 'A Rational Diagnosis', p. 21.

12 Jerrold M. Post, 'Explaining Saddam', www.pbs.org/wgbh/pages/frontline/shows/unscom/readings/post.html (accessed 9 February 2005).

13 Some readers will certainly feel that the parallel between Baxter and Saddam is invited. Christopher Tayler feels that the 'grand correspondence between the political musings and the Baxter plot never quite emerges', and that this is 'perhaps . . . for the best'. However, he does feel that this correspondence is 'expected'. See 'A Knife at the Throat' (review of *Saturday*), *London Review of Books*, 27: 5 (3 March 2005), pp. 31–3 (p. 33).

14 One notable exception is the episode at the opening of Tate Modern, where Tony Blair mistakes Perowne for a painter (*S*, pp. 143–4). This is based on personal experience – it was McEwan that Tony Blair mistook for a painter, insisting that 'he had McEwans on the wall', even when he was corrected. See Jasper Gerard, 'The Conversion of Mr Macabre' (interview with McEwan), *Sunday Times*, 'News Review' (23 January 2005), p. 5.

15 Matthew Arnold, *'Culture and Anarchy' and Other Writings*, ed. Stefan Collini (Cambridge University Press, 1993), pp. 84–5.

16 Ibid., p. 85.

17 I am grateful to my colleague Sean Matthews for bringing this parallel to my attention. A number of points addressed in this chapter were clarified for me through discussion with colleagues at the contemporary fiction

reading group in the School of English Studies at the University of Nottingham.

18 McEwan is drawing, partly, on the account of this procedure given by Frank T. Vertosick in *When the Air Hits Your Brain: Tales of Neurosurgery* (New York: W. W. Norton, 1996), p. 186, where the technological advances that made it possible are revealed.

19 In suggesting that *Saturday* is one of his most autobiographical books, McEwan has revealed that 'Henry is probably closer to me than any of my (characters). I've given him my squash game. I gave him my recipe for fish stew, which is probably a big mistake.' See Peter Fray, 'The Enduring Talent of Ian McEwan' (29 January 2005), www.theage.com.au/articles/ 2005/01/28/1106850082840.html?oneclick=true (accessed 15 November 2005).

20 Raymond Williams, *Culture and Society, 1780–1950* (1958; Harmondsworth: Penguin, 1982), p. 133.

21 The relevant episode can be found in Frank T. Vertosick's *When the Air Hits Your Brain*, pp. 183–7; the flashback in *Saturday* occurs on pp. 40–5.

22 In his Acknowledgements, McEwan thanks Neil Kitchen, Consultant Neurosurgeon and Associate Clinical Director at The National Hospital for Neurology and Neurosurgery, Queens Square, London, who he observed at work over a two-year period.

23 Vertosick, *When the Air Hits Your Brain*, p. 186.

24 Ibid., p. 185.

25 In one episode a nearly qualified trainee neurosurgeon vents his anger at a presumptuous colleague by engraving 'Fred sucks' on the inside of a bone flap, an insult that becomes public when an infection leads to the removal of the flap. Vertosick, *When the Air Hits Your Brain*, p. 147.

26 Ibid., p. 143.

27 Mark Lawson, 'Against the Flow' (review of *Saturday*), *The Guardian*, 'Review' (22 January 2005), p. 9.

28 See, for example, the notes on the poem at: http://eir.library.utoronto. ca/rpo/display/poem89.html (accessed 22 February 2005).

29 Charles Darwin, *The Origin of Species* (1859; Oxford University Press, 1996), p. 396.

30 McEwan, 'Faith v Fact', *The Guardian*, 'G2' (7 January 2005), p. 6.

31 Peter Kemp suggested that 'sanity shadowed by unreason is the theme of another novel about a day in London: Virginia Woolf's *Mrs Dalloway*.' He went on to observe that '*Saturday* shares other concerns with it, too: preparations for a party, the allure of the city, intimations of ageing and mortality, medical matters and the reverberations of war. These affinities don't seem accidental.' See 'Master of the Mind Game', p. 42. For Theo Tait, 'the real model for *Saturday*, . . . is *Mrs Dalloway*, also set over one London day. As in Virginia Woolf's novel, the juxtaposition of a wealthy

insider and a desperate outsider creates a nasty and violent climax'. See Tait, 'A Rational Diagnosis', p. 22.

32 The 'Rabbit' novels of John Updike are also written in the present tense, and may have served as a model for McEwan.

33 At the prompting of Zadie Smith, McEwan has discussed this description of surgery which is 'really . . . about writing, about making art.' See 'Zadie Smith Talks with Ian McEwan', in Vendela Vida, ed., *The Believer Book of Writers Talking to Writers* (San Francisco: Believer Books, 2005), pp. 207–39 (p. 224).

34 In this, Perowne resembles Antonio Damasio, who, though 'sceptical of science's presumption of objectivity and definitiveness', is, on balance, committed to scientific progress: 'I do believe, more often than not, that we will come to know.' See Antonio Damasio, *Descartes' Error*, pp. xviii, xix.

35 Perowne's guilt is a running theme. See pp. 102, 111, 210, 227–8, 278.

36 Iris Murdoch, *Metaphysics as a Guide to Morals* (1992; Harmondsworth, Penguin, 1993), p. 93.

37 Murdoch, 'Against Dryness', pp. 22, 23, 24. Murdoch's own novels, of course, enact this tension between form and contingency, while refusing to offer easy consolations to the reader.

38 John Banville, 'A Day in the Life' (review of *Saturday*), *New York Review of Books*, 52:9 (26 May 2005), www.nybooks.com/articles/17993 (accessed 20 October 2005).

10

Conclusion: McEwan and the 'third culture'

If *Saturday* grapples with new models of agency and responsibility, it still takes its place in a long-standing tradition in the English novel in which new discoveries in society at large are brought to bear upon experience. Moreover, this is a principle that characterizes all of McEwan's work.

Judith Seaboyer has argued that as early as *The Comfort of Strangers* McEwan 'begins a transition towards a traditional realism in which the private sphere is . . . mirrored in that of the public', and which is a way of addressing broader social and political issues.'[1] A central aspect of this realism is its continuity with Victorian realism's preoccupation with the role of science in society. This allows us to see (for example) *The Child in Time* as 'as closely allied to the literary history of realism as it is to that of speculative fiction.' Yet there is a key difference, argues Seaboyer, because the kind of interdisciplinarity implied in the literary treatment of scientific topics was 'more readily accepted' at a time when science 'was entered into by lay people as well as scientists and informed every aspect of society.' There is, then, a particular edge, a particular challenge in McEwan's project to work in the spirit of Edward O. Wilson's project of finding consilience between the arts and the sciences.[2]

After the preceding chapters of this study were written, McEwan's *Guardian* article, inspired by the republication of Darwin's book *The Expression of the Emotions in Man and Animals* (1872), was published in a longer form in a collection of essays with a very clear agenda: to advance the claims of an emerging field, that of evolutionary literary analysis.[3] Lamenting the closed 'constructivist' mind that holds sway in English departments, the editors of the volume look to intellectual trends beyond academia, to the fact that scientists writing about evolutionary matters had won Pulitzer Prizes, and that 'evolutionary themes appeared on best-seller lists and were avidly discussed in intellectual circles, including literary forums such as the *New York Review of Books*.' They point to the 'flamboyant literary agent John Brockman' and his 'stable of evolutionary authors'; and to the fact that 'a major novel influenced by evolutionary thinking had even appeared': *Enduring Love*.[4] Brockman is an important player in this trend, the advocator of a 'third culture', not the space in which 'literary intellectuals would be on speaking terms with the scientists' (as C. P. Snow envisaged when he revisited the 'two cultures' debate), but, rather, a culture in which 'scientists are communicating directly with the general public', given that 'literary intellectuals are not communicating with scientists.' For Brockman, 'the achievements of the third culture are not the marginal disputes of a quarrelsome mandarin class: they will affect the lives of everybody on the planet.'[5]

Even if this view should be tempered by our consciousness of the literary agent's advocacy, it chimes with the cultural importance accorded to popular science in McEwan's work. Reading Brockman's complaint that 'a 1950s education in Freud, Marx, and modernism is not a sufficient qualification for a thinking person in the 1990s', we find an echo of Thelma's attack, in *The Child in Time*, on 'arts' culture in the twentieth century, defined (for her) by its ignorance of revolutionary scientific thinking, and its unwarranted tendency to privilege modernism (*CT*, pp. 44–5).[6]

How far, though, should we see McEwan as being at the creative forefront of these new trends, as the pioneering literary figure of the 'third culture'? He is, after all, the sole novelist co-opted by the champions of evolutionary literary analysis in *The Literary Animal*. *The Child in Time* is usually seen as pivotal in McEwan's career because it announces an enlarged political vision. Yet I am prepared to see it as pivotal in another sense, too – and with implications for the novel in general, not just for McEwan – in the way that it imports revolutionary scientific ideas that might, theoretically, shake up the relationship between time and space for writers and readers of narrative fiction; but the shake up, perhaps, is theoretical rather than fully delivered, and may have a minimal impact on a critical reading. The treatment of evolutionary science is still more equivocal, as my discussion of *Enduring Love* suggests.

The article that McEwan reprints in the collection of evolutionary literary analyses makes a number of cogent points, beginning with the observation that human continuity is clearly indicated in our ability to engage with the literary representations of character from earlier historical periods: for this to happen, 'we must bring our own general understanding of what it means to be a person.' We rely on our 'theory of mind', our 'more-or-less automatic understanding of what it means to be someone else.' This is the kind of observation that marries with the principles of narrative ethics, as discussed elsewhere in this book, and which implies a necessary recalibration of poststructuralist critical reading. Beyond this, McEwan's effort to read this capacity through the lens of evolutionary theory has a benign, even utopian impulse: if we have all 'descended from a common stock of anatomically modern humans who migrated out of East Africa perhaps as recently as two hundred thousand years ago', then the recovery of a common human nature through the response to literature implicitly challenges the 'variations in the species that are in many cases literally skin deep', and which 'we have fetishized' in order 'to rationalize conquest and subjugation.'[7]

This seems to me to be both plausible and laudable, but without, necessarily, having a significant bearing on what the literary critic can, or ought to, do. Neither is McEwan really advocating a new way of reading (though his appearance in *The Literary Animal* might be taken to imply this): yes, he is interested in a notional 'universal human nature' that lies behind 'a commonly held stock of emotion'; but he is also conscious that emotions are 'shaped by culture', that 'our ways of managing our emotions, our attitudes to them, and the ways we describe them are learned and differ from culture to culture.'[8] The principal business of the novelist, perhaps, is to describe the ways in which emotions are viewed, managed and learned in particular circumstances: this is the art of the cultural variation rather than the universal norm. In *Enduring Love*, when Joe Rose relinquishes his evolutionary convictions and realizes 'we were no longer in the great chain . . . we were in a mess of our own unmaking' (*EL*, p. 207), he begins the process of relearning an emotional context that is peculiar to him, and which, itself, stages the persisting tension between objectivity and relativity.

In short, one can be persuaded by the idea of the 'gene-culture co-evolution' advocated by Edward O. Wilson, as 'the underlying process by which the brain evolved and the arts originated', without agreeing that this encourages a critic to find anything interesting to say about a particular literary text. Certainly, Wilson's own list of recurring literary themes and archetypes, as I discussed in chapter 6 above, is particularly reductive and discouraging.[9] Yet, in arguing that a critical reading of McEwan should focus on questions of cultural variation rather than indices of evolution, I do not mean to reaffirm a familiar nature–nurture opposition. Indeed, the *experience* of reading McEwan (or any author we may deem worthy of study) should take us beyond a reading in which *context* is brought to bear mechanistically on a literary work. The process of sympathetic reading – that is, the process of reading partially with the grain, outlined in the introduction – allows for an interaction between the work and its context: the work is *contextualized*, but that process should also involve bringing the work to bear on that context.

This is a simple enough historicist principle; a more interesting question is whether or not such a critical approach (which is not uncommon now in contemporary literary studies) has a particular relevance to McEwan, and whether or not that relevance can be explained in terms of the arts/sciences debate that McEwan obliges us to reconsider. Another way of putting the question is this: in rejecting Wilson's own sketch of a 'consilient' reading of literature, is it possible to take up the challenge he has thrown down, and sketch an alternative form of consilient reading?

In fact, I hope to have produced a few relevant sketches of my own in the preceding chapters; but I wish now to treat this issue more explicitly. In order to do so, I want to reconfigure the nature–nurture opposition in terms of the debate about the degree to which objective knowledge might be qualified by cultural relativity; and I am going to draw on a collection of essays, *The Arts and Sciences of Criticism* edited by David Fuller and Patricia Waugh, which contains some highly pertinent reflections. Indeed, the editors have assembled a series of essays that eschew the standoff between those who deny 'the possibility of any genuinely transcendental experience or disinterested epistemological criticism', and those who would defend the idea of authoritative and objectively verifiable knowledge of external reality:

> Pervasive throughout these essays is the influence of a more tempered hermeneutic tradition concerned less with the political or epistemological deconstruction of scientific truth-claims than with the effort to respect scientific models of knowledge whilst disabling their encroachment on or subversion of a humanistic understanding of consciousness. Purpose, belief, aesthetic delight, self-reflexive awareness – none, in this view, can be reduced either to a mechanistic scientific model or to an ideologically determined play of signification.[10]

A consensus view emerges from the collection, a view that 'advocates a return to meditation on the particularity of the experience of art, and on the kind of knowledge that is made available through it.' Yet one essay in particular – by Michael Bell – suggests a way in which the 'apparently conflicting demands' of knowledge and experience might be reconciled.

The idea of mythic perception is crucial to this process. In terms of cultural history, 'myth is usually regarded as a pre-conceptual awareness in which knowledge and experience exist as aspects of each other and there is no distinction between the experiencing subject and the experienced world.' Then, through modernity, humankind experiences 'a fall into consciousness' whereby mythic awareness is 'sacrificed to the theoretical and self-conscious knowledge associated with the sciences.' Modernity brings with it a form of 'self-reflexive knowing' that displaces 'unselfconscious being.' There may be an 'ideal relation to art' which allows us, momentarily, to experience our 'mythic consciousness', but critical thinking, characterized by 'detachment and objectivity', cannot capture this experience.[11] With specific reference to modernist myth, Michael Bell complicates and enriches the opposition: he claims, as the editors of the volume observe, that:

> in this particular mythic mode, criticism is part of the participatory experience, that the logical contradiction of being self-conscious and unselfconscious at the same moment is thereby undone or transvalued. To appreciate modernism in this way may provide us with an alternative model of critical practice, one in which the aesthetic, cognitive, and ethical remain separate but are not estranged from each other.

The argument flows from the conviction that 'the modernist literary work' is 'uniquely able to express the vital habitation of a world whilst simultaneously conveying awareness of living in a particular world-view.' In short, 'being and knowing are reconciled.'[12]

Bell's account of modernism traces a line back to late eighteenth- and early nineteenth-century philosophy and the quest for a new mythology in which the dichotomies between world and mind, objective and subjective, would be dissolved in poetry. The modernists, in Bell's account, were the later generation who produced this kind of mythic perception. For Bell, 'modernist myth is not a project so much as a way of being.' Modernist mythopoeia is 'a mode of apprehending the world' rather than 'a content' or 'a literary structure'. Consequently, 'myth is modernity's form of philosophical self-knowledge.' Following

Heidegger, Bell suggests that 'a defining feature of modernity' is the consciousness that 'a distinctively modern world picture' exists, together with the awareness of the 'relativity' by which this consciousness of a 'world picture' distinguishes the modernist period from earlier periods of world history. This produces a curious 'double consciousness of actually living a world-view as a world-view.'[13]

Finally, in pursuit of a complex ethical perspective, Bell calls for 'a more self-inclusive form of critical responsibility' in which the aesthetic would not be seen as separate, available for the attentions of 'ideological critique' in its 'self-fulfilling' varieties: 'the world represented in the work is not just to be judged *by* an ideology, it is itself a means of *judging* the ideology.'[14] The self-conscious historicist process of reading in context, outlined above, may be usefully supplemented by this responsiveness to the aesthetic, to the literary effect.

McEwan's work reveals the legacy of modernism to the extent that it vividly enacts a form of double consciousness in which knowledge and experience co-exist. This principle can be illustrated simply with reference to his two children's books, *Rose Blanche* (1985) and *The Daydreamer* (1994). Both books reveal affinities with his adult fiction, most especially on the topic of innocence and responsibility. *Rose Blanche* is a picture book (illustrations by Roberto Innocenti), with McEwan's text, based on a story by Christophe Gallaz. Rose Blanche, growing up in wartime Germany, discovers a concentration camp on the outskirts of her town, and gathers whatever food she can to take secretly to the incarcerated children. In the process, she becomes a kind of saintly figure, wasting away as she attends to the suffering of others. As German defeat looms and the Red Army is on its way, she is apparently shot and killed by nervous troops as she makes a final journey to the camp.

This is a brief, yet intriguing tale of how historical forces simultaneously defeat innocence and generate responsibility; and there is a moral imperative to secure the historical record, a consciousness of a located world-view. Yet the internal mood is driven by the perspective of a child identifying with other children, so that the aesthetic response to the book is premised on how the world-view (consciousness of Nazism) is experienced.

Further examples of double consciousness are to be found in the linked stories that comprise *The Daydreamer*. These trace significant imagined experiences for daydreamer Peter Fortune, beginning when he is ten, and culminating in the summer of his twelfth year. His imaginative powers produce a series of transformative experiences which see him exchange bodies with a broken doll, the family cat, his baby cousin and, finally, an adult. The running moral theme is one of discovering empathic engagement through an imaginative projection that reverses a child's unpleasant impulses. Thus the scene in which he imagines being forced to change places with the 'Bad Doll', which is missing an arm and an leg, reverses the childish urge to demonize the disfigured other (D, pp. 23–4). At such moments, McEwan runs the risk of explicit moralizing, in a familiar tradition of children's literature. Yet he avoids the drift towards an external adult sentimentality (a detached and self-conscious world-view) by ensuring that the moralizing is offset by a more sinister narrative layer rooted in the boy's experience. Thus, in the story of the dolls, Peter is mobbed by all his sister's dolls, who pull out two of his own limbs as replacements for the 'Bad Doll': this is a 'lesson' against demonizing the other; but it is convincingly rendered through the boy's excessive and sinister imagination, which unleashes inchoate personal insecurities.

The act of daydreaming is thus figured as a productive process of redefining relations through a form of double consciousness in which the boy's amoral impulses are convincingly rendered, but are partially recontained by a governing adult vision. There are moments where the writer's self-consciousness becomes pronounced. In 'The Bully', for instance, Peter demolishes the school bully with words, when he realizes that the idea of the bully has been 'dreamed up' by the other children (D, p. 56); and this introduces a simple anti-bullying theme. More usually, however, the collection allows the rendering of a boy's experience – or at least the author's attempt to render this authentically – to produce effects that exceed the adult view. The most powerful aspect of Peter's psychological growth, as in so much children's literature, is the fact that he is progressing towards adolescence. This transition is anticipated in the final story, in a holiday setting, where Peter progresses from contempt for adult behaviour to the realization that 'one day he would leave the group that ran wild up and down the beach, and he would join the group that sat and talked' (D, 89). Here the double consciousness turns in on itself, as the experience of the protagonist is elided with the adult awareness that frames the book.

The process of writing in which the double consciousness of modernity is enacted – living a world-view as a world-view – is still more relevant to McEwan's adult fiction. Indeed, one might argue that the McEwan hallmark 'set piece' is a form of mythic consciousness that conjoins experience and knowledge, and does so in such a way as to encourage the judging of an ideology. Read this way, the ballooning accident in *Enduring Love*, vividly recreated so that the reader can imagine him/herself in the predicament, produces behaviour (letting go, as altruism is defeated by self-preservation) that appears to conform to Joe Rose's self-conscious understanding of the biological basis (and limits) of morality. Yet this precept gives way, through the book, to a more complex understanding of the contingent forces operating on the self. This process ultimately exposes the inadequacy of the evolutionary perspective, as an ideology that should be judged and found wanting as a guide to the ethical life.

It may be that this form of double consciousness, which connects experience and knowledge, lies behind some of the key literary effects in McEwan's oeuvre. Indeed, one can detect it as a contributory factor to the unsettling effects of both his complex and his more straightforward works. At the simpler end of the spectrum, one can find a form of telling double consciousness in *Amsterdam*, a work that betrays the writer's consciousness of being embroiled in the world of vicious professionalism that is also satirized. At the complex end, there is the self-consciousness about the novelist's responsibility in *Atonement*. The ambivalent and disconcerting duty to 'the wild and inward journey of writing' orders the novel's structure, which must be recognized and interpreted by the reader. The double movement of *Atonement* brings the moral function of the novel to crisis point, even while the author writes himself into an inherited tradition of English fiction and criticism.

Yet if McEwan's contribution to the 'third culture' reveals structural affinities with the double consciousness of modernism, it also embodies an intensification of this impulse. In McEwan, the quest for knowledge that might be brought to bear upon experience is an extreme compulsion. It does not produce a reconciliation of the two, but rather a dynamic through which experience is constantly *transformed* in the thirst for knowledge. To the extent that post-modern art has been thought of as an intensification of modernist self-consciousness, this may be one way of articulating McEwan's contribution to it. His unsettling art upsets the equilibrium of knowledge and experience that modernism held out as a fleeting possibility.

Notes

1 Judith Seaboyer, 'Ian McEwan: Contemporary Realism and the Novel of
   Ideas', in James Acheson and Sarah C. E. Ross, eds, *The Contemporary
   British Novel* (Edinburgh University Press, 2005), pp. 23–34 (p. 24).
2 Seaboyer, 'Ian McEwan: Contemporary Realism and the Novel of Ideas',
   pp. 25–7.
3 The article 'The Great Odyssey', *The Guardian*, 'Saturday Review' (9 June
   2001), pp. 1, 3, was an edited version of a talk given at Hay-on-Wye.
4 Jonathan Gottschall and David Sloan Wilson, 'Introduction: Literature –
   A Last Frontier in Human Evolutionary Studies', in Gottschall and Wilson,
   eds, *The Literary Animal: Evolution and the Nature of Narrative* (Evanston:
   Northwestern University Press, 2005), pp. xvii–xxvi (p. xxi).
5 John Brockman, 'Introduction: The Emerging Third Culture', in
   Brockman, ed., *The Third Culture: Beyond the Scientific Revolution* (New
   York: Simon and Schuster, 1995), pp. 17–31 (pp. 18, 19). Snow considered
   the idea of a 'third culture' in the essay he added to the second edition of
   The Two Cultures, 'The Two Cultures: A Second Look'. See C. P. Snow,
   The Two Cultures, ed. Stefan Collini (1959, 1964; Cambridge University
   Press, 1998).
6 Brockman, 'Introduction', p. 17.
7 Ian McEwan, 'Literature, Science, and Human Nature', in Gottschall and
   Wilson, eds, *The Literary Animal*, pp. 5–19 (pp. 5, 10).
8 Ibid., p. 10.
9 Edward O. Wilson, *Consilience*, pp. 242, 248–9.
10 David Fuller and Patricia Waugh, 'Introduction' to Fuller and Waugh, eds,
   The Arts and Sciences of Criticism (Oxford University Press, 1999),
   pp. 1–29 (p. 5).
11 Ibid., pp. 27–8.
12 Ibid., p. 28.
13 Michael Bell, 'The Metaphysics of Modernism: Aesthetic Myth and the
   Myth of the Aesthetic', in Fuller and Waugh, eds, *The Arts and Sciences
   of Criticism*, pp. 238–56 (pp. 239, 240, 241, 242).
14 Ibid., pp. 256, 254.

Select bibliography

Works by McEwan

First Love, Last Rites (1975; London: Picador, 1976)

In Between the Sheets (1978; London: Vintage, 1997)

The Cement Garden (1978; London: Picador, 1980)

'The State of Fiction: A Symposium' (contribution), *New Review*, 5: 1 (Summer 1978), pp. 14–76

The Comfort of Strangers (1981; London: Vintage, 1997)

The Imitation Game: Three Plays for Television (1981; London: Picador, 1982)

Rose Blanche, illustrations by Roberto Innocenti, based on a story by Christophe Gallaz (1985; London: Red Fox, 2004)

A Move Abroad: 'Or Shall We Die?' and 'The Ploughman's Lunch' (London: Picador, 1989)

The Innocent (1990; London: Picador, 1990)

The Child in Time (London: Jonathan Cape, 1987)

Black Dogs (1992; London: Picador, 1993)

The Daydreamer, illustrations by Anthony Browne (1994; London: Red Fox, 1995)

Enduring Love (London: Jonathan Cape, 1997)

Amsterdam (London: Jonathan Cape, 1998)

'Wild Man of Literature (c. 1976): A Memoir', *The Observer*, 'Review' (7 June 1998), p. 16. (A memoir for inclusion in a festschrift for Ian Hamilton)

'Move Over, Darwin', review of *Consilience* by Edward O. Wilson, *The Observer*, 'Review' (20 September 1998), 13

Atonement (London: Jonathan Cape, 2001)

'The Great Odyssey', *The Guardian*, 'Saturday Review' (9 June 2001), pp. 1, 3. Reproduced, in extended form, as 'Literature, Science, and Human Nature', in Gottschall and Wilson, eds, *The Literary Animal*, pp. 5–19

'Beyond Belief', *The Guardian*, 'G2' (12 September 2001), p. 2

'Only Love and Then Oblivion. Love Was All They Had to Set Against Their Murderers', *The Guardian* (15 September 2001), p. 1

'Mother Tongue: A Memoir', in Zachary Leader, ed., *On Modern British Fiction* (Oxford University Press, 2002), pp. 34–44. (The piece was first published in *The Guardian*, 13 October 2001)
'Faith v Fact' (contribution), *The Guardian*, 'G2' (7 January 2005), p. 6
Saturday (London: Jonathan Cape, 2005)

Secondary material

Acheson, James and Sarah C. E. Ross, eds, *The Contemporary British Novel* (Edinburgh: Edinburgh University Press, 2005)
Adamson, Jane, 'Against Tidiness: Literature and/versus Moral Philosophy', in Adamson, Freadman and Parker, eds, *Renegotiating Ethics in Literature, Philosophy, and Theory*, pp. 84–110
—— Richard Freadman and David Parker, eds, *Renegotiating Ethics in Literature, Philosophy, and Theory* (Cambridge University Press, 1998)
Allen, Brooke, 'Illustrations of Inertia and Compromise', *New Criterion*, 17: 8 (April 1999), pp. 60–4, www.newcriterion.com/archive/17/apr99/brooke.htm (accessed 12 June 2005).
Andrews, Lucilla, *No Time For Romance: An Autobiographical Account of a Few Moments in British and Personal History* (London: Harrap, 1977)
Anonymous, 'An Interview with Ian McEwan', *boldtype* (Random House) (1998), www.randomhouse.com/boldtype/1298/mcewan/interview.html (accessed 7 November 2005)
Antonaccio, Maria, 'Form and Contingency in Iris Murdoch's Ethics', in Maria Antonaccio and William Schweiker, eds, *Iris Murdoch and the Search for Human Goodness* (Chicago: University of Chicago Press, 1996), pp. 110–37
Arnold, Matthew, *'Culture and Anarchy' and Other Writings*, ed. Stefan Collini (Cambridge University Press, 1993)
Baker, Phil, 'Comfy Conspiracies', *Times Literary Supplement*, 4979 (4 September 1998), p. 9
Banville, John, 'A Day in the Life' (review of *Saturday*), *New York Review of Books*, 52: 9 (26 May 2005), www.nybooks.com/articles/17993 (accessed 20 October 2005)
Bell, Michael, 'The Metaphysics of Modernism: Aesthetic Myth and the Myth of the Aesthetic', in Fuller and Waugh, eds, *The Arts and Sciences of Criticism*, pp. 238–56
Bentley, Nick, ed., *British Fiction of the 1990s* (London: Routledge, 2005)
Bergson, Henri, *Time and Free Will: An Essay on the Immediate Data of Consciousness*, trans. F. L. Pogson (1889; third edition, 1913, rep. New York: Dover, 2001)
Blaxland, Gregory, *Destination Dunkirk: The Story of Gort's Army* (London: William Kimber, 1973)
Bohm, David, *Wholeness and the Implicate Order* (London: Routledge, 1980)

—— 'A New Theory of the Relationship of Mind and Matter', *Philosophical Psychology*, 3: 2 (1990), pp. 271–86; http://members.aol.com/Mszlazak/ BOHM.html (12 January 2005)

Booth, Wayne C., *The Company We Keep: An Ethics of Fiction* (Berkeley: University of California Press, 1988)

de Botton, Alain, 'Another Study in Emotional Frigidity' (review of *Amsterdam*), *Independent on Sunday*, 'Culture' (13 September 1998), p. 12

Bradbury, Malcolm, *The Modern British Novel*, revised edition (London: Penguin, 2001)

Brandt, Joan, 'Julia Kristeva', in Julian Wolfreys, ed., *The Edinburgh Encyclopaedia of Modern Criticism and Theory* (Edinburgh: Edinburgh University Press, 2002), pp. 382–90

Brockman, John, ed., *The Third Culture: Beyond the Scientific Revolution* (New York: Simon and Schuster, 1995)

Brown, Richard, 'Postmodern Americas in the Fiction of Angela Carter, Martin Amis and Ian McEwan', in Anna Massa and Alistair Stead, eds, *Forked Tongues? Comparing Twentieth-Century British and American Literature* (London: Longman, 1994), pp. 92–110

Burrows, Stuart, review of *Amsterdam*, *New Statesman* (11 September 1998), 127: 4402, pp. 47–8

Byrnes, Christina, *The Work of Ian McEwan: A Psychodynamic Approach* (Nottingham: Paupers' Press, 2002)

Childs, Peter, *Contemporary Novelists: British Fiction Since 1970* (Basingstoke: Palgrave, 2005)

Clark, Roger and Andy Gordon, *Ian McEwan's 'Enduring Love'* (London: Continuum, 2003)

Coe, Jonathan, 'Introduction' to Rosamund Lehmann, *Dusty Answer* (1927; London: Virago, 2000), [no pagination]

Connolly, Cyril, *Enemies of Promise* (1938), Parts One and Two reprinted in *The Selected Works, Volume One: The Modern Movement*, ed. Matthew Connolly (London: Picador, 2002), pp. 18–141

Currie, Mark, *Postmodern Narrative Theory* (Basingstoke: Macmillan, 1998)

Damasio, Antonio, *Descartes' Error: Emotion, Reason, and the Human Brain* (1994; New York: Quill, 2000)

Darwin, Charles, *The Origin of Species* (1859; Oxford University Press, 1996)

Dyer, Geoff, 'Who's Afraid of Influence?' (review of *Atonement*), *The Guardian*, 'Saturday Review' (22 September 2001), p. 8

Eakin, Paul John, 'The Unseemly Profession: Privacy, Inviolate Personality, and the Ethics of Life Writing', in Adamson, Freadman and Parker, eds, *Renegotiating Ethics in Literature, Philosophy, and Theory*, pp. 161–80

Evans, Walter, 'The English Short Story in the Seventies', in Dennis Vannatta, ed., *The English Short Story 1945–1980: A Critical History* (Boston: Twayne Publishers, 1985), pp. 120–72

Finney, Brian, 'Briony's Stand Against Oblivion: The Making of Fiction in Ian McEwan's *Atonement*', *Journal of Modern Literature*, 27: 3 (2004), pp. 68–82

Fray, Peter, 'The Enduring Talent of Ian McEwan' (29 January 2005), www.theage.com.au/articles/2005/01/28/1106850082840.html?oneclick=true (accessed 15 November 2005)

Fuller, David, and Patricia Waugh, eds, *The Arts and Sciences of Criticism* (Oxford University Press, 1999)

Gąsiorek, Andrzej, *Post-War British Fiction: Realism and After* (London: Edward Arnold, 1995)

Genette, Gérard, *Narrative Discourse*, trans. Jane E. Lewin (Oxford: Blackwell, 1980)

Gerard, Jasper, 'The Conversion of Mr Macabre' (interview with McEwan), *Sunday Times*, 'News Review' (23 January 2005), p. 5

González, Rosa, 'The Pleasure of Prose Writing vs. Pornographic Violence', *The European English Messenger*, I: 3 (Autumn 1992), pp. 40–5

Gottshcall, Jonathan and David Sloan Wilson, eds, *The Literary Animal: Evolution and the Nature of Narrative* (Evanston: Northwestern University Press, 2005)

Haffenden, John, 'John Haffenden talks to Ian McEwan', *The Literary Review* (June 1983), pp. 29–35. Reprinted in John Haffenden, *Novelists in Interview* (London: Methuen, 1985), pp. 168–90

Halliday, Fred, *Two Hours That Shook the World, September II, 2001: Causes and Consequences* (London: Saqi Books, 2002)

Hamilton, Ian, 'Points of Departure' (interview), *New Review* 5: 2 (1978), pp. 9–21

Hanks, Robert, 'Flashes of Inspiration' (interview), *The Independent*, 'Weekend Review' (12 September 1998), p. 14

Hanson, Clare, *Short Stories and Short Fictions, 1880–1980* (London: Macmillan, 1985)

Hardyment, Christina, *Dream Babies: Three Centuries of Good Advice on Child Care* (New York: Harper and Row, 1983)

Harpham, Geoffrey Galt, 'Ethics and Literary Criticism', in Christa Knellwolf and Christopher Norris, eds, *The Cambridge History of Literary Criticism: Twentieth-Century Historical, Philosophical and Psychological Perspectives*, volume IX (Cambridge University Press, 2001), pp. 371–85

Harrison, M. John, 'Beating the Retreat' (review of *Black Dogs*), *Times Literary Supplement*, 4655 (19 June 1992), p. 20

Head, Dominic, *The Cambridge Introduction to Modern British Fiction, 1950–2000* (Cambridge University Press, 2002)

Hutcheon, Linda, *The Politics of Postmodernism* (London: Routledge, 1989)

Kavanagh, Dennis, *Thatcherism and British Politics: The End of Consensus?*, third edition (Oxford University Press, 1996)

Keepin, Will, 'Lifework of David Bohm: River of Truth', www.satyana.org/ html/bohm3.html (accessed 12 January 2005)

Kellaway, Kate, 'At Home With His Worries' (author profile), *The Observer* (16 September 2001), http://books.guardian.co.uk/print/0,3858,4257898– 99930,00.html (accessed 17 November 2005)

Kemp, Peter, 'Master of the Mind Game' (review of *Saturday*), *Sunday Times*, 'Culture' (30 January 2005), pp. 41–2

Kermode, Frank, 'Point of View' (review of *Atonement*), *London Review of Books*, 23: 19 (4 October 2001), pp. 8–9

Kitzinger, Sheila *The New Pregnancy and Childbirth* (London: Penguin, 1997)

Knights, Ben, *Writing Masculinities: Male Narratives in Twentieth-Century Fiction* (Basingstoke: Macmillan, 1999)

Kristeva, Julia, *Powers of Horror: An Essay on Abjection*, trans. Leon S. Roudiez (New York: Columbia University Press, 1982)

Laclau, Ernesto, 'Politics and the Limits of Modernity', in Thomas Docherty, ed., *Postmodernism: A Reader* (London: Harvester, 1993), pp. 329–43

Lawson, Mark, 'Against the Flow' (review of *Saturday*), *The Guardian*, 'Review' (22 January 2005), p. 9

Lee, Hermione, 'If Your Memories Serve You Well' (review of *Atonement*), *The Observer*, 'Review' (23 September 2001), p. 16

Leith, William. 'Form and Dysfunction' (author profile), *The Observer*, 'Life' (20 September 1998), pp. 4–5, 7–8

Lezard, Nicholas 'Morality Bites', *The Guardian*, 'Saturday Review' (24 April 1999), p. 11

editors of *Lingua Franca*, *The Sokal Hoax: The Sham That Shook the Academy* (Lincoln and London: University of Nebraska Press, 2000)

Lodge, David, *Consciousness and the Novel* (London: Secker and Warburg, 2002)

Lord, Walter, *The Miracle of Dunkirk* (1982; Ware: Wordsworth Editions, 1998)

Louvel, Liliane, Gilles Ménégaldo and Anne-Laure Fortin, 'An Interview with Ian McEwan' (conducted November 1994), *Études Britanniques Contemporaines*, 8 (1995), pp. 1–12

Lukács, Georg, *Studies in European Realism*, trans. Edith Bone (London: Merlin Press, 1989)

McCrum, Robert, 'The Story of His Life' (author profile), *The Observer*, 'Review' (23 January 2005), p. 5

Macfarlane, Robert, 'A Version of Events' (review of *Atonement*), *Times Literary Supplement*, 5139 (28 September 2001), p. 23

McHale, Brian, *Postmodernist Fiction* (1987; rep. London: Routledge, 1991)

Malcolm, David, *Understanding Ian McEwan* (Columbia: University of South Carolina Press, 2002)

Mars-Jones, Adam, *Blind Bitter Happiness* (London: Chatto and Windus, 1997)
—— 'Have a Heart' (review of *Amsterdam*), *The Observer*, 'Review' (6 September 1998), p. 16
Martin, David C., *Wilderness of Mirrors* (1980; Guilford, Connecticut: The Lyons Press, 2003)
Massa, Anna, and Alistair Stead, eds, *Forked Tongues? Comparing Twentieth-Century British and American Literature* (London: Longman, 1994)
Massie, Allan, *The Novel Today, 1970–89* (London: Longman, 1990)
Matthews, Sean, '*Enduring Love*: Seven Types of Unreliability', in Peter Childs, ed., *Ian McEwan's 'Enduring Love'* (London: Routledge, forthcoming)
May, Charles E., ed., *Short Story Theories* (Ohio University Press, 1976)
Mengham, Rod, ed., *An Introduction to Contemporary Fiction* (Cambridge: Polity, 1999)
Morrison, Jago, *Contemporary Fiction* (London: Routledge, 2003)
Mullan, John, 'Elements of Fiction', *The Guardian*, 'Review' (29 March 2003), p. 32
Murdoch, Iris. 'Against Dryness: A Polemical Sketch' (1961), in Malcolm Bradbury, ed., *The Novel Today: Contemporary Writers on Modern Fiction*, revised edition (London: Fontana, 1990), pp. 15–24
—— *Metaphysics as a Guide to Morals* (1992; Harmondsworth, Penguin, 1993)
Noakes, Jonathan, 'Interview with Ian McEwan' (2001), in Margaret Reynolds and Jonathan Noakes, eds, *Ian McEwan: The Essential Guide* (London: Vintage, 2002), pp. 10–23
Parker, David, 'Introduction; The Turn to Ethics in the 1990s', in Adamson, Freadman and Parker, eds, *Renegotiating Ethics in Literature, Philosophy, and Theory*, pp. 1–17
Pearce, Joseph Chilton, *Magical Child* (1977; London: Plume, 1992)
Poe, Edgar Allan, 'Review of *Twice-Told Tales*', *Graham's Magazine* (May 1842), reprinted in May, ed., *Short Story Theories*, pp. 45–51
Post, Jerrold M., 'Explaining Saddam', www.pbs.org/wgbh/pages/frontline/shows/unscom/readings/post.html (accessed 9 February 2005)
Reeves, Richard and Nicole Veash, 'A War of Words', *The Observer* (22 August 1999), p. 14
Reynolds, Margaret and Jonathan Noakes, eds, *Ian McEwan: The Essential Guide* (London: Vintage, 2002)
Rimmon-Kenan, Shlomith, *Narrative Fiction: Contemporary Poetics* (London: Methuen, 1983)
Robinson, Roger 'Hardy and Darwin', in Norman Page, ed., *Thomas Hardy: The Writer and His Background* (London: Bell and Hyman, 1980), pp. 128–50

Rorty, Richard, 'Solidarity or Objectivity?', in John Rajchman and Cornel West, eds, *Post-Analytic Philosophy* (New York: Columbia University Press, 1985), pp. 3–19

Ruskin, John, *The Stones of Venice, Volume 2: The Sea Stories* (London: George Allen, 1906)

Ryan, Kiernan, *Ian McEwan* (Plymouth: Northcote House/British Council, 1994)

—— 'Sex, Violence and Complicity: Martin Amis and Ian McEwan', in Rod Mengham, ed., *An Introduction to Contemporary Fiction* (Cambridge: Polity, 1999), pp. 203–18

Schemberg, Claudia, *Achieving 'At-one-ment': Storytelling and the Concept of the Self in Ian McEwan's 'The Child in Time', 'Black Dogs', 'Enduring Love', and 'Atonement'* (Frankfurt: Peter Lang, 2004)

Scurr, Ruth, 'Happiness on a Knife-edge' (review of *Saturday*), *The Times*, 'Weekend Review' (29 January 2005), p. 13

Seaboyer, Judith, 'Sadism Demands a Story: Ian McEwan's *The Comfort of Strangers*', *Modern Fiction Studies*, 45: 4 (1999), pp. 957–86

—— 'Ian McEwan: Contemporary Realism and the Novel of Ideas', in Acheson and Ross, eds, *The Contemporary British Novel*, pp. 23–34

Segerstråle, Ullica, *Defenders of the Truth: The Sociobiology Debate* (Oxford University Press, 2000)

Seligman, Craig, review of *Amsterdam*, Salon.com (9 December 1998), http://dir.salon.com/books/sneaks/1998/12/09sneaks.html (accessed 12 June 2005)

Slay, Jack, *Ian McEwan* (New York: Twayne, 1996)

Smith, Zadie, 'Zadie Smith Talks with Ian McEwan', in Vendela Vida, ed., *The Believer Book of Writers Talking to Writers* (San Francisco: Believer Books, 2005), pp. 207–39

Snow, C. P., *The Two Cultures*, ed. Stefan Collini (1959, 1964; Cambridge University Press, 1998)

Sokal, Alan, 'Transgressing the Boundaries: Toward a Transformative Hermeneutics of Quantum Gravity', *Social Text*, Spring–Summer 1996, reprinted in *Lingua Franca*, eds, *The Sokal Hoax: The Sham That Shook the Academy*, pp. 11–45

—— 'Revelation: A Physicist Experiments with Cultural Studies', *Lingua Franca*, May–June 1996, reprinted in *Lingua Franca*, eds, *The Sokal Hoax: The Sham That Shook the Academy*, pp. 49–53

Stevenson, Randall, *The Oxford English Literary History, Volume 12, 1960–2000: The Last of England?* (Oxford University Press, 2004)

Sutcliffe, William, review of *Atonement*, *Independent on Sunday*, 'LifeEtc.' (16 September 2001), p. 15

Sutherland, John, 'What's it All About?' (review of *Amsterdam*), *Sunday Times*, 'Books' (13 September 1998), p. 12

Tait, Theo, 'A Rational Diagnosis' (review of *Saturday*), *Times Literary Supplement*, 5315 (11 February 2005), pp. 21–2

Tayler, Christopher, 'A Knife at the Throat' (review of *Saturday*), *London Review of Books*, 27: 5 (3 March 2005), pp. 31–3

Taylor, Charles, *Sources of the Self: The Making of the Modern Identity* (1999; rep. Cambridge University Press, 2002)

Taylor, D. J., *A Vain Conceit: British Fiction in the 1980s* (London: Bloomsbury, 1989)

—— *After the War: The Novel and England Since 1945* (1993; London: Flamingo, 1994)

Vannatta, Dennis, ed., *The English Short Story 1945–1980: A Critical History* (Boston: Twayne Publishers, 1985)

Vertosick, Frank T., *When the Air Hits Your Brain: Tales of Neurosurgery* (New York: W. W. Norton, 1996)

von der Lippe, George B., 'Death in Venice in Literature and Film: Six Twentieth-Century Versions', *Mosaic*, 32: 1 (March 1999), pp. 35–54

Waters, Juliet, 'The Little Chill: Has the Booker Prize Chosen the Nouveau Beaujolais of Fiction?', www.montrealmirror.com/ARCHIVES/1998/120398/book.html (accessed 13 July 2005)

Waugh, Patricia, 'Science and Fiction in the 1990s', in Nick Bentley, ed., *British Fiction of the 1990s* (London: Routledge, 2005), pp. 57–77

Whitney, Helen, 'Faith and Doubt at Ground Zero' (interview), *Frontline* (April 2002), www.pbs.org/wgbh/pages/frontline/shows/faith/interviews/mcewan.html (accessed 19 October 2005)

Williams, Raymond, *Culture and Society, 1780–1950* (1958; Harmondsworth: Penguin, 1982)

Wilson, Edward O., *On Human Nature* (Harvard University Press, 1978)

—— *Consilience: The Unity of Knowledge* (1998; London: Abacus, 2003)

Wood, James, 'Why it All Adds Up' (review of *Enduring Love*), *The Guardian*, 'G2' (4 September 1997), pp. 9–10

Wood, Michael, 'When the Balloon Goes Up', *London Review of Books*, 19: 17 (4 September 1997), pp. 8–9

Wright, Robert, *The Moral Animal: Why We Are the Way We Are* (1994; London: Abacus, 2004)

Index

Allen, Brooke 152
Amis, Kingsley 8
Amis, Martin 1, 2, 4, 25–6, 33, 34, 75
   Dead Babies 34
Amsterdam 6, 7, 8, 15, 24, 144–54,
   207
Andrews, Lucilla 166, 167–8
Arnold, Matthew 182–5, 189–91
   Culture and Anarchy 182–5
   'Dover Beach' 189–91
Atonement 6, 12–13, 15, 24–5, 103,
   156–74, 207
attack on America (9/11) 161–2,
   179, 182
Austen, Jane 34, 156, 163
   Northanger Abbey 163

Baker, Phil 153
Ballard J. G. 34
Balzac, Honoré de 56
Banville, John 196
Barnes, Julian 4
Bell, Michael 204–5
Berkeley, Michael 6, 71, 150
Big Issue, The 86
Black Dogs 6, 8, 15, 22, 23, 91,
   102–17, 120, 144
Blake, William 72
Blaxland, Gregory 166
Bohm, David 78–82
Booker Prize 6, 144, 148
Booth, Wayne C. 115

Bowen, Elizabeth 156, 158
   The Hotel 158
Bradbury, Malcolm 4, 6, 7, 92
   The History Man 7
   Stepping Westward 7
Bragg, Melvyn 67
Brockman, John 201
Burrows, Stuart 153
Byrnes, Christina 151

Carter, Angela 34
Cement Garden, The 15, 21, 30,
   31, 33, 46–50, 53, 120
   film version 51n.27
Child in Time, The 5, 6, 7, 8,
   12, 15, 18, 20, 22, 37, 70–1,
   73–87, 91, 120, 131, 132,
   193, 201
   timeslip in 22, 37, 75, 77–8, 87
Churchill, Winston 106
Clark, Roger 138
class 3, 8–9, 10, 52–3
Coe, Jonathan 158
Coetzee, J. M. 192
Cold War 92–102, 173
Collini, Stefan 183
Comfort of Strangers, The 5, 6,
   11, 15, 21, 22, 30, 31, 33, 43,
   50, 52, 56–68, 70, 120, 144
   film version 67–8
Connolly, Cyril 157–60
Conrad, Joseph 1, 47

contemporary literature 1, 8
Currie, Mark 16–17

Damasio, Antonio 19–20, 133–4
Darwin, Charles 24, 136–7, 191, 200
  The Origin of Species 191
Daydreamer, The 205–6
de Botton, Alain 153
Deighton, Len 92
Dickens, Charles 164
  Great Expectations 164
du Maurier, Daphne 59
  'Don't Look Now' 59
Dunkirk 156, 165–7, 170
Dyer, Geoff 156, 157

Enduring Love 7, 8, 10, 12, 15,
    23–4, 103, 120–41, 144,
    201, 202
  film version 142n.20
Engels, Friedrich 56
Evans, Walter 30–1
evolutionary psychology 9, 10, 24,
    121–9, 136–7, 139–41

Falklands War 3
Farrell, J. G. 33
feminism 5, 7, 21–2, 52–61, 66, 68
Finney, Brian 158, 173
First Love, Last Rites 6, 21, 30, 31,
    33, 34–41
  'Butterflies' 37–8
  'First Love, Last Rites' 38–9
  'Homemade' 21, 34–6, 39–41
  'Solid Geometry' 36–7
Forster, E. M. 156
Fowles, John 33
Fuller, David 203

Gallaz, Christophe 205
Gąsiorek, Andrzej 20
Genette, Gérard 164
Golding, William 47
  Lord of the Flies 47
Gordon, Andy 138

Granta magazine 6
Greene, Graham 92, 153
Greer, Germaine 5
Gulf War 181

Haffenden, John 32, 57
Halliday, Fred 179, 185
Hanson, Clare 31–2
Hardy, Thomas 136–7
  A Pair of Blue Eyes 136–7
Hardyment, Christina 83–4
Harpham, Geoffrey Galt 14
Harrison, M. John 106
Hemingway, Ernest 158
  The Sun Also Rises 158
Holocaust 103, 106, 108–10, 173
Hussein, Saddam 181–2, 183–4
Hutcheon, Linda 15

Imitation Game, The 5, 21, 52–6,
    62
In Between the Sheets 21, 30, 31,
    41–6
  'Dead as They Come' 43
  'In Between the Sheets' 43–4
  'Pornography' 21, 41–2
  'Psychopolis' 44–6
  'Reflections of a Kept Ape' 42–3
Innocent, The 8, 15, 22–3, 30, 33,
    91, 92–102, 120
  film version 102
Iraq war 181–2, 183–4
Ishiguro, Kazuo 1, 2

James, Henry 47, 156, 194
  The Golden Bowl 194
Joyce, James 35
  Dubliners 35
  Ulysses 192

Kemp, Peter 178
Kermode, Frank 147, 156, 157, 171
Knights, Ben 86
Kristeva, Julia 95–6, 99
Kundera, Milan 70, 131–2

Lawrence, D. H. 156
Leavis, F. R. 156, 173
Le Carré, John 92
Lee, Hermione 156
Lehmann, Rosamund 156, 158
   Dusty Answer 158
life writing 111, 114–17, 171–2
Lodge, David 18–20, 139–40
Lord, Walter 166, 167

McCrum, Robert 178–9
Macfarlane, Robert 156
Major, John 145
Malcolm, David 7–8, 46, 49, 64,
   77, 120
Mann, Thomas 59
   Death in Venice 59
Mars–Jones, Adam 75–6, 83
Millennium Dome 147
modernism/modernity 5–6, 14, 77,
   201, 204–7
morality 9–10, 14, 24, 46–7, 54,
   121–3, 137, 160–74
Morrison, Jago 18
Move Abroad, A 65, 72
Murdoch, Iris 8, 9, 10, 11, 12, 13,
   14, 33, 159–60, 195

narrative ethics 13–14
Or Shall we Die? 5, 22, 68, 70,
   71–4, 131

peace movement 7
Pearce, Joseph Chilton 80–3
Pinter, Harold 67
Ploughman's Lunch, The 3, 6, 22,
   70, 73, 131
Poe, Edgar Allan 31–2
postmodernism/postmodernity 5–6,
   14, 15–16, 20, 31, 207
punk movement 21, 33, 177

Raine, Craig 4
Rorty, Richard 14
Rose Blanche 205
Ryan, Kiernan 7, 25–6, 46, 77,
   85, 93–4, 96

Sage, Vic 188
Saturday 15, 25, 74, 132, 177–96
science 19–20, 25, 37, 72–4,
   77–83, 84, 120–41, 185–96,
   200–7
Scurr, Ruth 178
Seaboyer, Judith 58–9, 61
Seligman, Craig 147–8
shock-lit 30–50
Sillitoe, Alan 8
Slay, Jack 33–4, 74, 77, 98
Snow, C. P. 201
Sokal, Alan 138
South Bank Show, The 67, 68
Stevenson, Randall 103
Storey, David 8, 33
Suez crisis 3
Swift, Graham 1, 2

Tait, Theo 178, 180–1
Taylor, Charles 13
Taylor D. J. 85
Thatcher, Margaret 5, 11, 22, 73,
   84–6, 145
Turing, Alan 54

University of East Anglia 4, 6, 7

Vertosick, Frank T. 185–7

Wain, John 8
Waugh, Evelyn 94
   The Loved One 94
Waugh, Patricia 203
Welfare State 2, 10, 11, 159
Williams, Raymond 184–5
Wilson, Angus, 4, 6, 7, 8
Wilson, Edward O. 124–9, 200,
   202, 203
Wood, James 131
Wood, Michael 131–2
Woolf, Virginia 156, 158
   Mrs Dalloway 192
World War Two 10, 15, 52–6,
   103–6, 116, 156, 165–70,
   205
Wright, Robert 121–2, 137